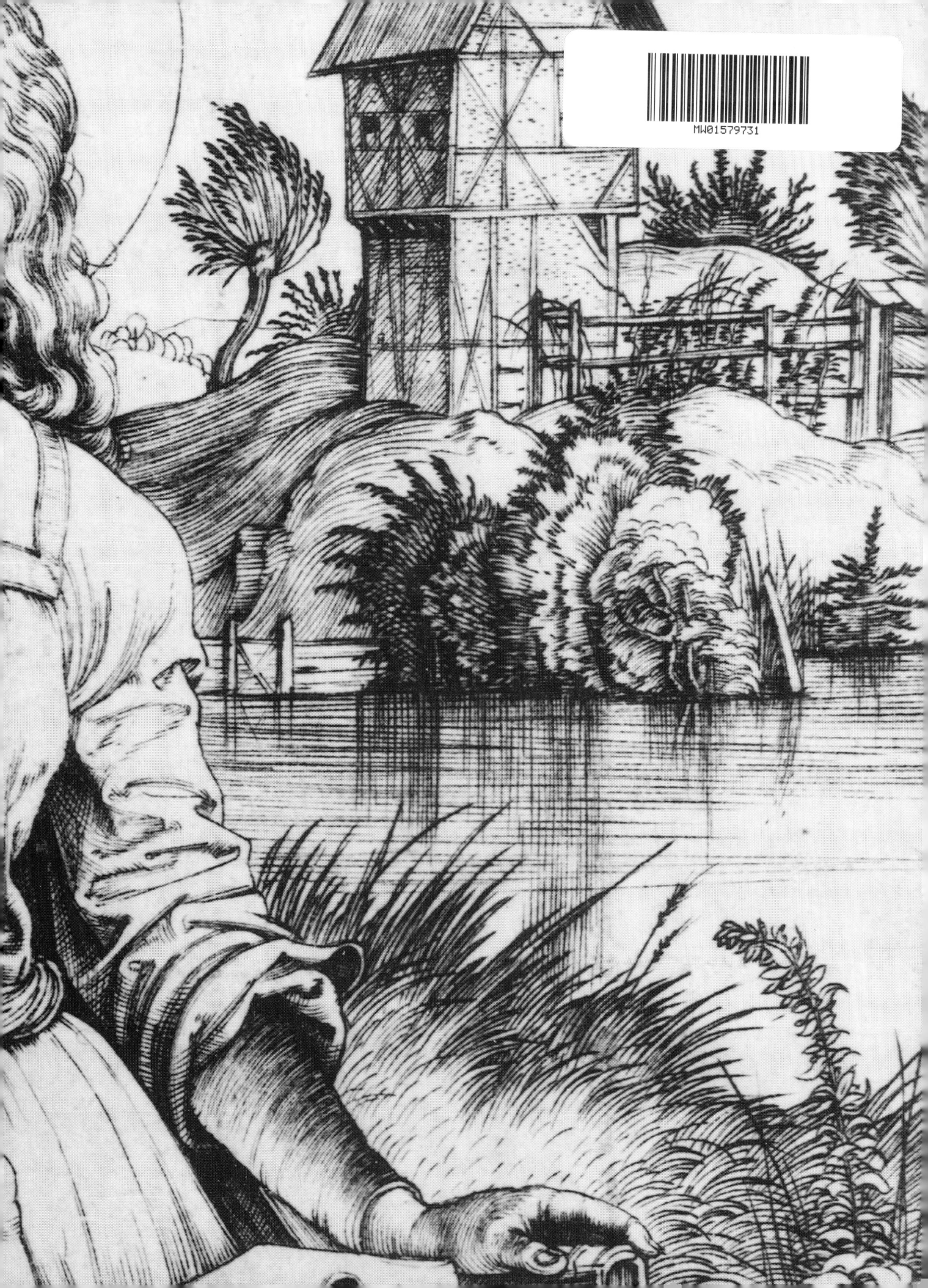

Faith and Humanism: Engravings and Woodcuts by Albrecht Dürer was published on the occasion of the exhibition of the same name originated by the Montgomery Museum of Fine Arts, Montgomery, Alabama, and on view there September 14 through October 20, 2002. The exhibition will travel to the Joslyn Art Museum, Omaha, Nebraska, January 18, 2003 through March 9, 2003.

Library of Congress Cataloging-in-Publication Data

Dürer, Albrecht, 1471-1528.
   Faith and humanism: engravings and woodcuts by Albrecht Dürer.
      p. cm.
Published on the occasion of the exhibition of the same name held by the Montgomery Museum of Fine Arts, Montgomery, Alabama, Sept. 14-Oct. 20, 2002.
Includes bibliographical references.
   ISBN 0-89280-038-0
   1. Dürer, Albrecht, 1471-1528–Exhibitions. I. Montgomery Museum of Fine Arts. II Title.
NE654.D9 A4 2002
769.92—dc21

2002010363

© 2002 Montgomery Museum of Fine Arts, Montgomery, Alabama.
All rights reserved.

ISBN Number 0-89280-0-38-0

Colophon

Terry Ann R. Neff, *t.a.neff associates, inc., Editor, Tuscon, Arizona*
Camille Leonard, *LWT Communications, Designer, Montgomery, Alabama*
Robert Fouts, *Fouts Commercial Photography, Montgomery, Alabama*
Skinner Printing Company, Montgomery, Alabama

Faith *and* Humanism

*Engravings and Woodcuts
by Albrecht Dürer*

Faith and Humanism

Engravings and Woodcuts
by Albrecht Dürer

Faith *and* Humanism

Engravings and Woodcuts by Albrecht Dürer

Montgomery Museum of Fine Arts

Acknowledgements

The board and staff of the Montgomery Museum of Fine Arts
express their most sincere appreciation to the following individuals who
participated in the organization and realization of this exhibition:

Mrs. Adolph Weil, Jr., Montgomery, Alabama

Brent R. Benjamin, director, the St. Louis Art Museum

Derrick R. Cartwright, director, and T. Barton Thurber, curator, Hood Museum of Art,
Dartmouth College, Hanover, New Hampshire

Earl A. Powell, III, director, National Gallery of Art and Sculpture Garden, Washington, D.C.

Barbara Butts, Ph.D. Toronto, Ontario, Canada

Gregory Jecmen, assistant curator of Old Master Prints, Department of Prints and Drawings,
National Gallery of Art, Washington, D.C.

Susan Dackerman, curator of Prints, Drawings and Photographs, Baltimore Museum of Art

Lenders to the Exhibition

Mrs. Adolph Weil, Jr., Montgomery, Alabama

National Gallery of Art and Sculpture Garden, Washington, D.C.

Hood Museum, Dartmouth College, Hanover, New Hampshire

The St. Louis Art Museum, St. Louis, Missouri

Exhibition Sponsors
The City of Montgomery

Montgomery County

Regions Bank

Mr. and Mrs. Fred Blackmon

Catalogue Sponsor
Mrs. Adolph Weil, Jr.

*The Montgomery Museum of Fine Arts is a department of the City of Montgomery
and receives further financial support from Montgomery County. Additional support is
made possible by grants from the Alabama State Council on the Arts.*

Table of Contents

Foreword
Mark M. Johnson

6

The Compass to Paradise: Albrecht Dürer and
His Search for Beauty and Salvation
Barbara Butts

8

Catalogue Entries
Margaret Lynne Ausfeld and Gregory Jecmen

24

Catalogue of the Exhibition
Susan Dackerman

106

Bibliographic Citations

116

Glossary

118

foreword

The art of Albrecht Dürer was forged in an age of volatility that in every sense transformed life in Western Europe. Equally, this art was created by a man who was, by most definitions, a genius—one who possessed a vital, creative imagination tempered by a dedication to rational order and a constant search for knowledge of the inherent physical laws that govern all of nature. Although the term "Renaissance man" is overused, if it has ever applied to anyone, it would most certainly apply to Albrecht Dürer.

Dürer was first and foremost a seeker after knowledge, scientific as well as artistic. At the dawn of the sixteenth century, in Germany, where he lived and worked in the city of Nuremberg, such men were respected, and their work nurtured by a network of wealthy patrons. These patrons included not just the ruling nobility, but also a flourishing community of merchants, businessmen, clergy, scholars, and patrician civil servants. The tide of humanism—an interest in the classical civilizations of Greek and Rome that fueled the Italian Renaissance in Italy—was flowing north, and the great minds of Germany embraced what they acknowledged as "the genius of the ancients." Simultaneously, the rigid grip of the Catholic Church in Rome on the minds and hearts of the populace was loosening, as a result of the Church's own complacency and the slow spread of education. The Protestant Reformation, which occurred near the end of Dürer's life, was the culmination of a century of change that would sound the death knell of the Middle Ages.

This was the world into which Albrecht Dürer was born in 1471. His youthful training in Nuremberg and his *Wanderjahr* of exploration visiting the cities of Colmar, Basel, and Strasbourg in search of artistic training and experience began his journey of art and learning, which was punctuated by visits to northern Italy with its burgeoning Renaissance culture. He was thoroughly engaged with the refinement of Italian society and the discovery of its treasury of classical culture—philosophy, literature, and Dürer's most cherished interest, the canons of ideal proportion.

Although Dürer trained and worked as a painter, a major part of his artistic legacy is the printed images that he produced steadily and with increasing skill. The exhibition *Faith and Humanism: Engravings and Woodcuts by Albrecht Dürer* and this accompanying catalogue present forty significant examples of Dürer's print oeuvre. The essay by Dürer scholar Barbara Butts considers the wider range of the artist's career, with a special emphasis on the spiritual issues that informed his character and his culture. Images such as *Melencolia I*, *Knight, Death and the Devil*, and *St. Jerome in His Study* are considered landmarks of printmaking and are a part of the foundation of this medium in Western art. Catalogue entries by Montgomery Museum of Fine Arts Curator Margaret Lynne Ausfeld and Dr. Greg Jecmen of the National Gallery's Department of Prints and Drawings examine individual works, the media Dürer utilized, and the history of these seminal images.

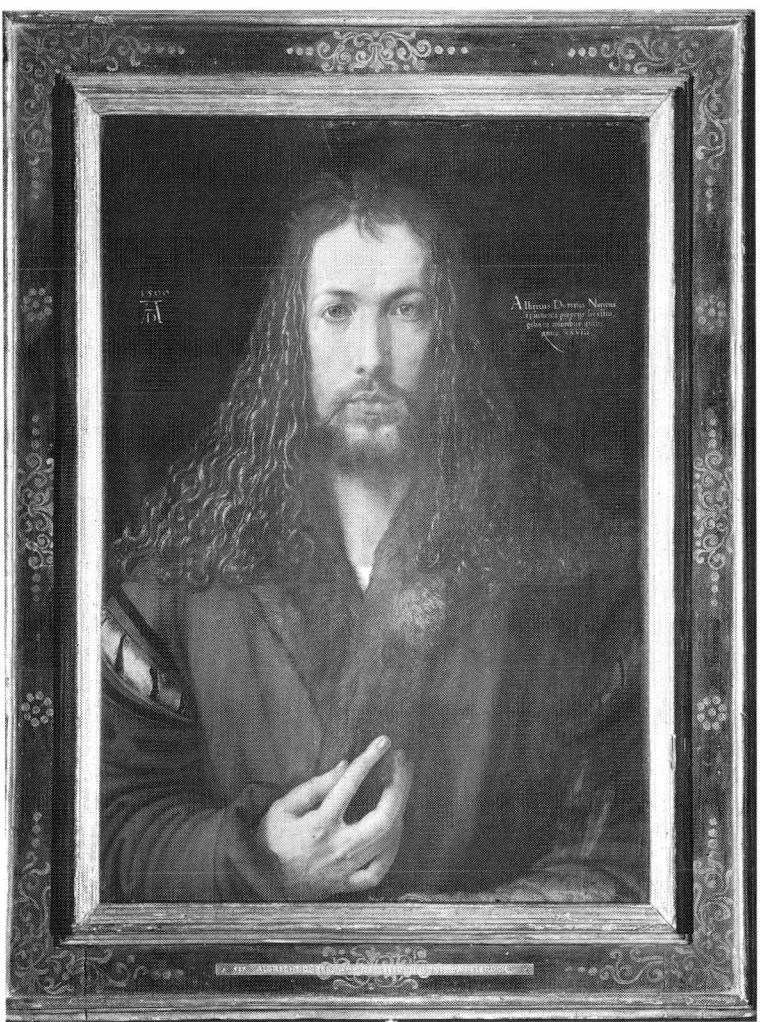

Figure 1 *Self-Portrait in Fur-trimmed Coat*, 1500, Oil on limewood, Munich, Alte Pinakothek.

This project had its genesis in 1999, when Mrs. Jean K. Weil gave the Montgomery Museum over thirty impressions by Dürer as a part of the legacy of her husband Adolph Weil, Jr.'s outstanding collection of Old Masters. Her gift in his memory has realized Mr. Weil's long-held vision for the museum: a print collection of quality, diversity, and lasting educational value. This exhibition is the second in a series of projects devoted to interpreting these prints and to honoring "Bucks" and Jean Weil for their generous spirit and dedication to the museum's permanent collection.

When he died in 1528, Albrecht Dürer was a highly respected artist, and his reputation has continued to flourish over the ensuing 400 years. This exhibition follows a long-standing tradition of honoring this great artist, but also recognizes with deep gratitude the individual who had the foresight to appreciate and collect his work for the benefit of the Montgomery community.

Mark M. Johnson
Director

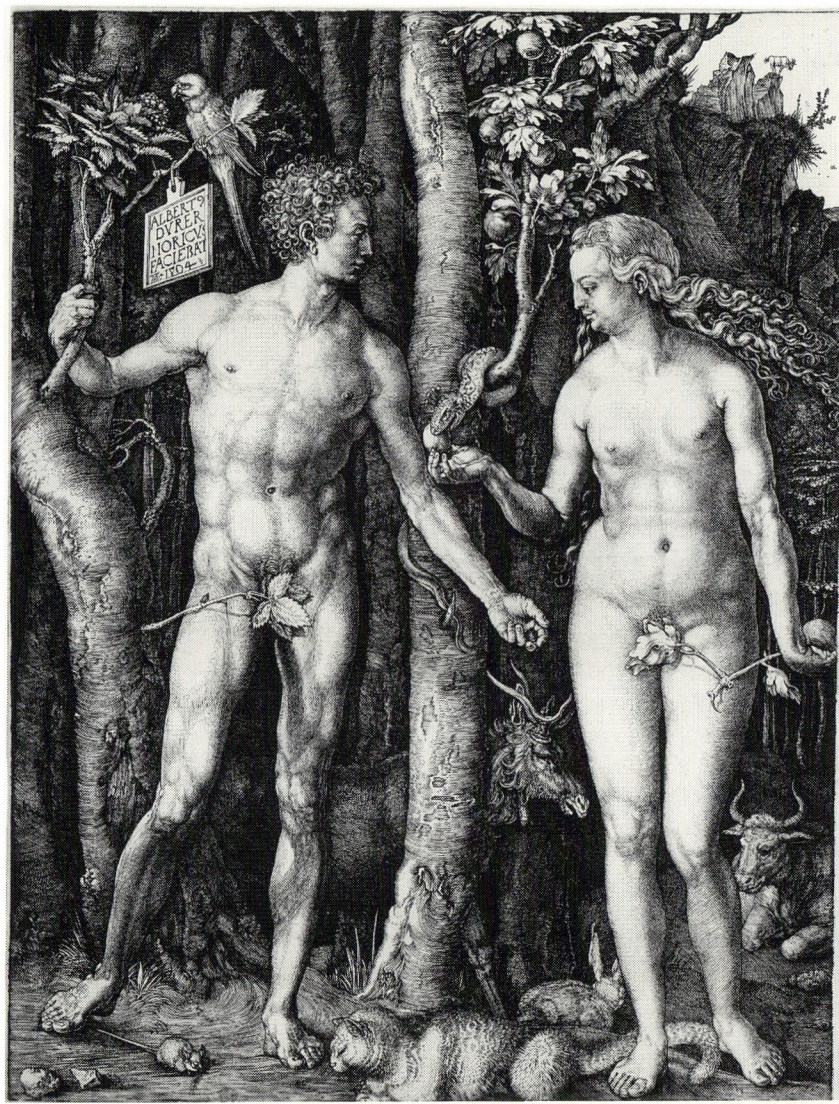

Figure 2 *Adam and Eve*, 1504, Engraving on laid paper, Washington, National Gallery of Art, Gift of R. Horace Gallatin, 1949.1.18

The compass to paradise
Albrecht Dürer and His Search for Beauty and Salvation

By Barabara Butts

Introduction

The leading figure of German Renaissance art, Albrecht Dürer (1471-1528), is celebrated for introducing the forms and ideas of the Italian Renaissance into Northern Europe. In art and in life, Dürer continually strived for perfection. Describing the artist in 1532, in the preface to his Latin translation of the artist's treatise on human proportion, Joachim Camerarius (1500-1574) praised his character as highly as his art and said that his only vice was being so self-critical that he could never cease researching a thing.[1]

A combination of prodigious artistic talent and a restless desire to learn made the goldsmith's son from Nuremberg one of the foremost chroniclers of his age. He traveled widely by the standards of his time—to Colmar, Basel, and Strasbourg, perhaps by way of Frankfurt am Main and Mainz (1490-94), to Italy (1494-95 and 1505-1507) and to the Netherlands (1520-21). In addition to a journal of his trip to the Netherlands, letters, and records of various kinds, Dürer left to posterity about 2,000 drawings and watercolors depicting the work of other artists, the countenances of both famous and anonymous contemporaries, local and foreign costumes, landscapes, plants, animals, his own artistic inventions, even one of his dreams and his own nude body. Not content with his remarkable ability to represent the world as it appeared to his eyes, Dürer delved beneath the surface for the mathematical order of God's universe. Thus from about 1500 until the end of his life, he studied perspective and human and animal proportions, eventually authoring *Manual of Measurement* (1525) and *Four Books on Human Proportion* (published posthumously in 1528 by his widow).

Although Dürer was not university-educated, his exceptional capacity for friendship gained him access to humanist circles ordinarily closed to a craftsman's son and to advanced learning that found visual expression in his art—an oeuvre of about seventy paintings and hundreds of prints that encompasses mythological and allegorical subjects in addition to portraits and traditional Christian themes. Respected for his ideas as much as for his manual skills, Dürer also designed diverse objects to be made by others, including stained-glass windows, large-scale bronze sculpture, armor, table fountains, goblets, jewelry, chandeliers, and ceremonial robes. He strived for knowledge in areas other than the visual arts, taking dancing lessons in Venice in 1506, trying his hand at poetry, and publishing a book on fortification in 1527.

No less important than his artistic, intellectual, and social aspirations was Dürer's engagement with the religious debates of his day. In 1520 he eagerly awaited new publications in German by Martin Luther.[2] Two years earlier he was included in a list of members of the Sodalitas Staupitziana, a humanist study group in Nuremberg that discussed religious issues and was instrumental in Nuremberg's embrace of Luther's cause in March 1525. In his poems, as in his art, Dürer grappled with the question of salvation.

The Early Years

Dürer initially trained as a goldsmith with his father, Albrecht Dürer the Elder (1427-1502), from 1485 to 1486. From 1486 to 1489 he was apprenticed to the painter Michael Wolgemut (1434/7-1519) in Nuremberg's largest workshop for altarpieces and woodcut illustrations. Dürer's most famous watercolors and drawings—*A Young Hare* (1502), *The Great Turf* (1503), and a study of praying hands for an altarpiece completed in 1509—exemplify the tradition of Netherlandish realism passed on by Wolgemut. But it was to the Greek artist Apelles (fourth century BC), not to Jan van Eyck (d. 1441), that Dürer was compared by learned contemporaries. Already in 1500, Dürer was likened to the classical painter whose deceptive realism blurred the distinction between nature and art.

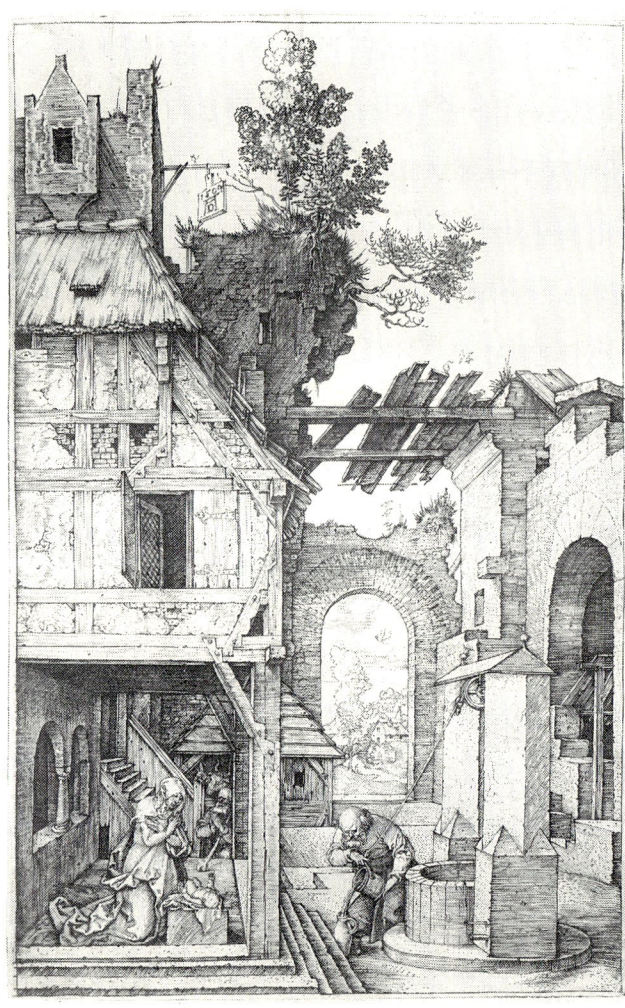

Figure 3 *The Nativity*, 1504, Engraving on laid paper, Washington, National Gallery of Art, Rosenwald Collection, 1943.3.3557.

Like the praying hands, many of Dürer's studies from nature were incorporated within his paintings, stained-glass windows, and prints, lending an unprecedented lifelike quality to depictions of saints and other religious subjects. Jerome's retreat in the engraving *St. Jerome Penitent in the Wilderness* (p. 37) is based on Dürer's studies of a quarry near Nuremberg. The plants and trees could have been observed in that quarry, while Jerome's lion was probably derived from a work by another artist, since Dürer's first extant studies of live lions were made in 1521 in the Netherlands. In an engraving depicting one of Christ's parables, *The Prodigal Son Amid the Swine* (p. 30), Dürer placed his protagonist in a farmyard that was typical of the outskirts of Nuremberg. The beautiful and serene engraving *Madonna with the Monkey* (p. 55), incorporates a Nuremberg *Weierhaus* (pond house) that Dürer had represented in watercolor. The monkey, a popular pet in the fifteenth century, may also have been based on a watercolor, while the Madonna and Child reflect Italian painting. Dürer's woodcuts likewise were dependent on careful studies from nature. The horrible torture of a bishop in *The Martyrdom of the Ten Thousand* (p. 35) employs a study of a man drilling a hole in a board.

A Spiritual Life

Dürer's artistic striving cannot be separated from his search for spiritual improvement. Like many of his contemporaries, he seems to have been an adherent of the *devotio moderna*, a popular form of piety that centered on the fifteenth-century devotional work *The Imitation of Christ*. Dürer's desire to place Christ at the center of his life is vividly expressed in his famous *Self-Portrait* in oils of 1500 (Munich, Alte Pinakothek, fig 1, p. 7). By idealizing his features to conform with depictions of Jesus and painting the reflection of a window cross in his eyes, he identified himself as one who has taken up the cross of Christ, his "compass to paradise."[3] In accordance with humanist belief inthe dignity of man, Dürer depicted himself not only as created in God's image (Genesis 1:27), but also with his right hand prominently displayed, as one who could use his God-given talents to create in a manner akin to the Almighty. Indeed, in striving for likeness to Christ, Dürer created himself, demonstrating the free will ascribed to mankind by Giovanni Pico della Mirandola (1463-1494) in *Oration on the Dignity of Man* (1498).[4]

Dürer singled out Christ's suffering and death on the cross as a subject to which an artist could fruitfully apply his talents.[5] He eventually published two series of woodcuts and one of engravings devoted to Christ's Passion. The first of these, the *Large Passion* in woodcut, was begun around 1497 and completed and published as a book in 1511 with a title page depicting *Christ, Man of Sorrows, Mocked by a Soldier* (p. 85). Verses by Benedictus Chelidonius (d. 1521) accompanying the image suggest that Christ still suffers for the sins of mankind: "I still take floggings for thy guilty acts…." In *The Flagellation* (p. 50), Dürer endeavored in the faces and postures of Christ's mockers to evoke mankind's cruelty and stupidity.

The work that best epitomizes the young Dürer's artistic ambitions and religious concerns in the late 1490s is the *Apocalypse* (1498), a book of woodcuts, including the famous *Four Horsemen* (p. 40), and biblical text from Revelation. Dürer, who was the godson of the most important publisher in Germany, Anton Koberger (c. 1445-1513), proudly identified himself as both artist and publisher of the book. Its fifteen 15-by-11-inch prints gave visual expression to contemporary fears of the arrival in 1500 of the millennium, the thousand years mentioned in Revelation during which Christ would reign on earth following a cosmic cataclysm destroying the forces of evil. Their scale was uncommon but not unprecedented: Wolgemut had contributed larger woodcut illustrations to the *World Chronicle*, published by Koberger in 1493. But Dürer, most likely with the aid of professional block cutters, wrested from the recalcitrant wood a degree of naturalism that undoubtedly was astonishing at the time.[6] Although created by numerous strokes of the knife rather than by the continuous movement of a pen or burin, the lines emulate the calligraphic beauty and subtle modulation of drawn and engraved lines. The fluent contours and hatchings convincingly model three-dimensional form, making palpable the terrible visions of St. John. As the art historian Erwin Panofsky aptly noted of Dürer's *Apocalypse*, because Dürer so compellingly depicted his scenes according to the "laws of ordinary physical life," he was able to suggest more forcefully the temporary suspension of those laws.[7] Dürer's experience in Italy in 1494-95, particularly his study of Andrea Mantegna (1431-1506), is apparent in the physical exertion and intent expressions of the figures.

Published simultaneously in Latin and German, Dürer's *Apocalypse* was aimed at the broadest possible public. The large engraving *Hercules at the Crossroads (Jealousy)* (p. 52), on the other hand, seems to address an educated audience. The print weds classical subject matter (a hero of antiquity) and classical form (an idealized nude figure indebted to the art of Mantegna and Antonio Pollaiuolo [1431/32-1498]). It was once thought to represent a simple moral choice made by Hercules, but in 1991 Peter-Klaus Schuster argued convincingly that rather than supporting Virtue (embodied by the clothed female) in her attack on Pleasure (represented by the nymph), Hercules mediates between the two.[8] Thus Schuster maintained that the engraving depicts the humanist ideal of moderation in the sense of *concordia discors* (discordant harmony). According to this reading, Hercules' winged helmet associates him with Mercury, god of eloquence and reason, and thus distinguishes him as an intellectual as well as a physical athlete: reason governs his instincts, while instinct empowers reason to earn fame, honor, and immortality.

The Search for Ideal Proportions

In Dürer's engraving *The Temptation of the Idler (The Dream of the Doctor)* (p. 58), a naked figure is associated with the deadly sin of sloth. In *Hercules*, by contrast, the idealized nude symbolizes the nobility of man, created in the image of God. Soon after, around 1500, Dürer embarked on an unflagging search for the ideal proportions for the human figure. In accordance with the Christian Platonist thinking of his humanist friends, he was convinced of the hidden mathematical order and harmony in God's creation. This order was thought to be manifest in Christ, the perfect embodiment of godly wisdom, and in the first man and woman, Adam and Eve, before they disobeyed God and ate from the tree of the knowledge of good and evil. In a draft for the introduction to a projected manual of painting, Dürer instructed that just as the artists of antiquity gave Apollo the most beautiful physique, so modern painters should give Christ the same ideal proportions.[9]

In 1504 Dürer chose Adam and Eve before the Fall as the subject of an ambitious artistic statement incorporating all he could learn about ideal proportions from the Roman architect and engineer Vitruvius (c. 88-26 BC), antique sculpture, and mathematical study. Dürer's engraving *Adam and Eve* (M. 1, B. 1) (fig. 2, p. 8) manifests textures and tonal gradations of a subtlety never before achieved in prints. But just as the multiplicity of nature was thought to clothe a geometrically harmonious universe, the sensuous surfaces of *Adam and Eve* cover the perfect proportions of human beings created in the image of God. In addition to the ideal proportions described by Vitruvius, Dürer clearly knew the antique *Apollo Belvedere*, found in Rome c. 1489/90, which he used as a prototype for Adam; for Eve he chose a classical Venus. Furthermore, Dürer's preliminary studies for *Adam and Eve* show that the figures were derived as far as possible from geometric forms, such as a compass-drawn circle. (The circle, without a beginning or an end, was the shape thought to best mirror God in his infinite simplicity.)

Dürer's pursuit of ideal human proportions paralleled his studies of one-point perspective and the ideal proportions of the horse. He demonstrated his newfound command of linear perspective in his engraving *The Nativity* (fig. 3, p. 10), and subsequently employed it in rich profusion in the woodcut series *Life of the Virgin*, for example, in *The Death of the Virgin* (p. 78). By 1510 Dürer was pushing woodcut to the limit of its potential in terms of the tonal range that could be achieved.

Royal Patronage

While Dürer's painted altarpieces and portraits brought him acclaim, it was primarily through his more lucrative work in engraving and woodcut that his influence became widespread in Europe. Starting in 1512 he increasingly turned his attention away from painting to concentrate on prints. It was also around this time that his humanist admirers introduced him into the circle of the Holy Roman Emperor Maximilian I (1459-1519). From that time until the emperor's death on January 12, 1519, Dürer participated in a number of imperial projects, even designing an imperial suit of armor. He made drawings for over-life-size bronze sculptures for Maximilian's tomb and presumably helped his former pupil Hans von Kulmbach to conceptualize the emperor's monumental stained-glass window in Nuremberg's Church of St. Sebald.[10] In collaboration with other artists, he created a gigantic *Triumphal Arch* for the emperor in woodcut. He shared in the design of Maximilian's immense *Triumphal Procession* in woodcut and was one of several artists to make marginal illustrations in pen and ink in a *Book of Hours* belonging to the emperor.

When not occupied with work for Maximilian, Dürer experimented with drypoint and etching. His three drypoints were made in 1512; his six etchings were made between 1515 and 1518. In one etching from 1515, Dürer returned to the theme of the *Agony in the Garden* (p. 92), now using stark contrasts of light and shadow and dynamic line to emphasize the charged emotion inherent in the subject.

Salvation and the Master Engravings

The years 1512 to 1519 were also years in which Dürer wrestled intensely with the question of salvation, a concern for him until his death in 1528. Salvation is the theme of the artist's so-called "master engravings," *Knight, Death and the Devil* (fig. 4, p. 14), *Melencolia I* (fig. 5, p. 15), and *St. Jerome in His*

Study (fig. 6, p. 16). Along with the *Adam and Eve* (fig. 2, p. 8) of a decade earlier, the three engravings are unmatched achievements of the engraver's art, compelling in the articulation of textured surfaces and in the nuanced play of light—the sheen of the Christian knight's steed in a shadowy forest, the brilliance of a comet in the night sky above Melancholy, and the reflection of light through the bottle-glass windows of St. Jerome's study.

One way to look at the "master engravings" is as an attempt to link humors with virtues. According to Schuster, Dürer's four ambitious prints form a unified group showing how individuals of choleric, melancholic, and phlegmatic temperaments can return to the blessed "sanguine" state of Adam and Eve before the Fall. Adam and Eve, whose "humors" were perfectly balanced before the Fall, making them sinless and immortal, are contrasted in the earlier print with the cat, rabbit, ox, and elk, which represent the choleric irascibility, sanguine sensuality, phlegmatic lethargy, and melancholic gloom to which mankind was thought to be subject afterwards, when one humor predominated.[11] The parrot symbolizes the Virgin Birth of Christ, who will save mankind from sin and death. Schuster built on Panofsky's observation that the equable sanguine temperament was considered more desirable than the others. Sometimes, Panofsky wrote, the sanguine temperament was identified with perfect equilibrium, in which case "it was assumed that man, originally sanguine pure and simple, had become more or less severely contaminated by the three other 'humors' when biting the apple."[12]

Intellectual Virtue: The Christian Melancholic

Dürer's journal of his trip to the Netherlands indicates that he sometimes gave away as a pair *St. Jerome in His Study* and *Melencolia I*. Panofsky asserted that the two engravings contrast "a life in the service of God" (*St. Jerome*) with "a life in competition with God" (*Melencolia I*).[13] He proposed that the latter depicts a type of melancholic genius described by Cornelius Agrippa of Nettesheim (1486-1535) in *De Occulta Philosophia* (circulated in manuscript 1509/10, published in 1531): the imaginative melancholic, a type that included artists and artisans. Because his "imagination" is stronger than his "mind" or "reason," the imaginative melancholic moves in the sphere of spatial quantities; the metaphysical world is beyond his reach. Panofsky characterized the figure in *Melencolia I* as a personification of Melancholy and Geometry and as a spiritual self-portrait of an artist (Dürer) who cannot arrive at an understanding of beauty based on mathematical theory since, "Nobody knows [what absolute beauty is] except God."[14] For Panofsky, *Melencolia I* depicts a secular genius' surrender to depression and inertia in the face of his inability to penetrate the secrets of God's creation.

Schuster's interpretation seems more compelling. For him, the figure in *Melencolia I* personifies Melancholy, Astronomy, and Philosophy. It is not Geometry, but Astronomy—the science of the celestial bodies—that is represented with wings, as is Philosophy. The Greek letters on the figure's belt, Theta and Pi, abbreviations for theory and practice, are among the attributes of Philosophy, based on a passage in *De Consolatione Philosophiae* by the late Roman moralist and scholar Boethius (c. 480-524). Astronomy offered the mathematically gifted melancholic, which Dürer considered himself to be, the surest means to ascend towards godly wisdom: through the study of the mathematical order of God's creation. The compass in Melancholy's hand and the scale touching her right wing represent measure, the key to perfection in art and morality. Unlike Panofsky, Schuster interpreted *Melencolia I* as an optimistic statement in the face of mankind's inability to fully comprehend God's creation. He connected the print with the concept of "learned ignorance" (or wise unknowing) expounded by the German churchman, mathematician, philosopher, and humanist Nicholas of Cusa (Cusanus, 1401-1464) in *De Docta Ignorantia* (1440) and taken up in

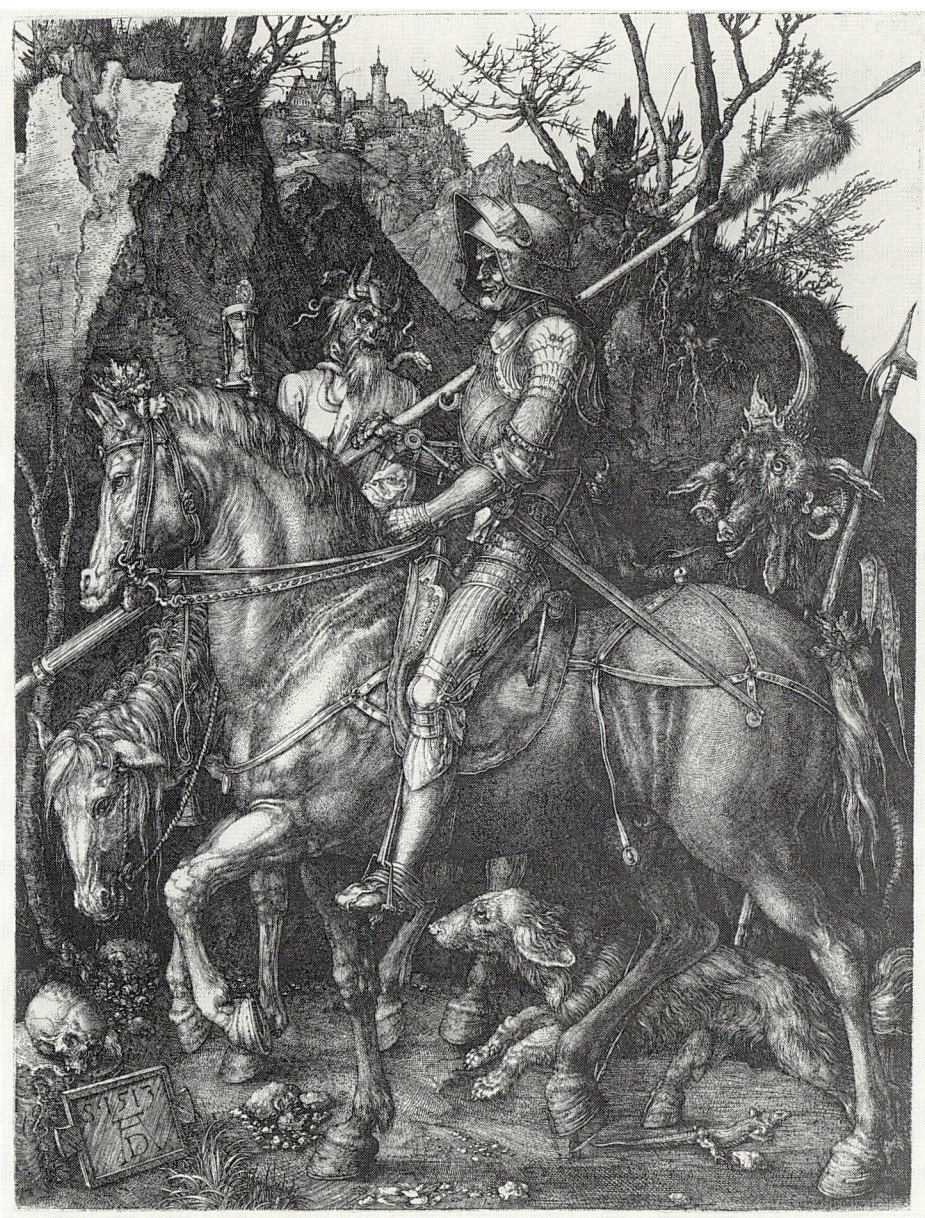

Figure 4 *Knight, Death and the Devil*, 1513, Engraving on laid paper, Washington, National Gallery of Art, Gift of W.G. Russell Allen, 1941.1.20.

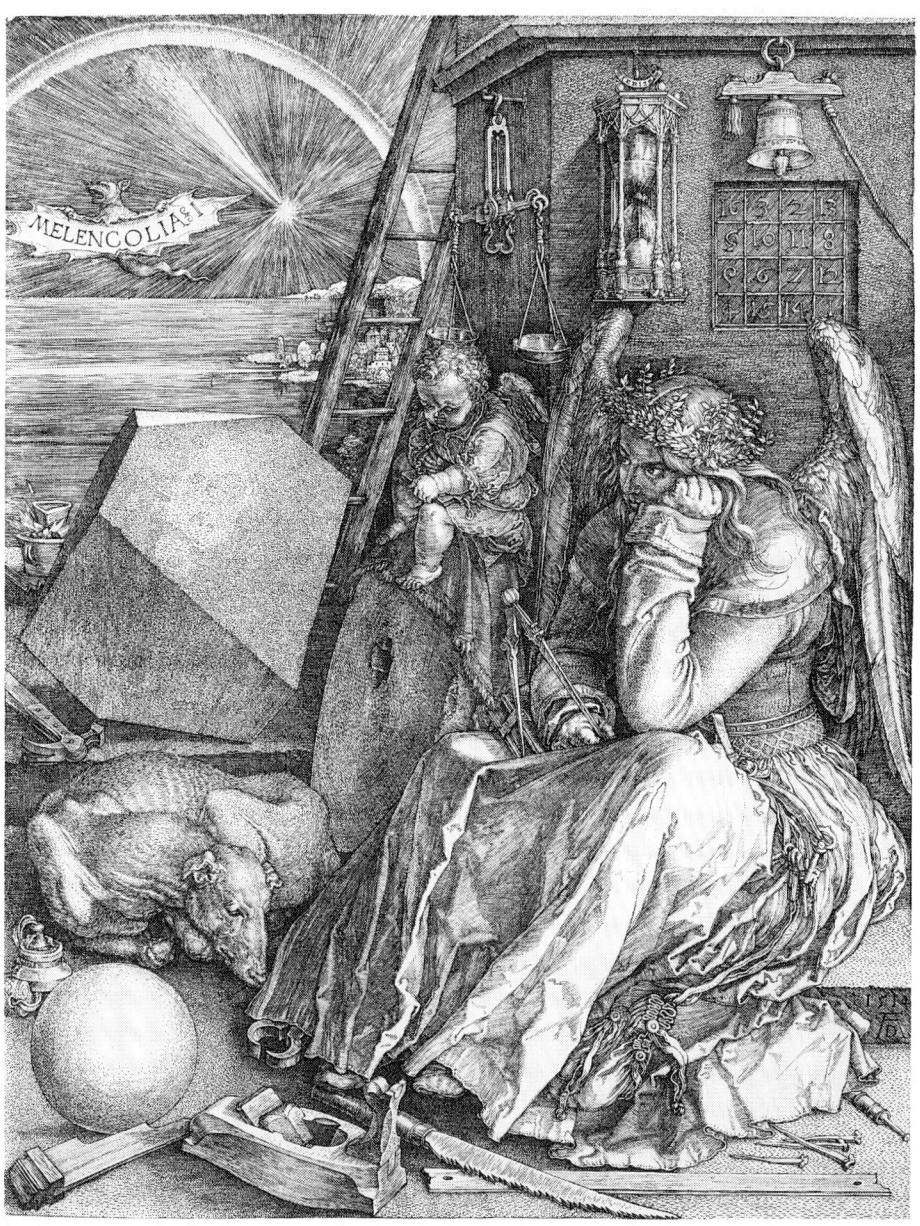

Figure 5 *Melencolia I*, 1514, Engraving on laid paper, Washington, National Gallery of Art, Rosenwald Collection, 1943.3.3523.

texts such as Pico's *Oration* and Charles de Bouelles's (Carolus Bovillus, after 1470-between 1553/1567) *Liber de Sapiente* (1510/11). Cusanus used the Aristotelian theme of an owl blinded by the sun to illustrate the limitations of human knowledge in relationship to godly wisdom. (In Dürer's *Melencolia I*, a bat is blinded by a comet.) But knowing that he does not know, the wise man gains faith that transcends reason. Thus, according to Schuster, Melancholy does not succumb to despair, but instead makes the ascent to God, symbolized, as in Pico's *Oration*, by the ladder. According to Cusanus, the learned man, aware of his own ignorance, is led to faith in Christ, the union between divine and human nature and the embodiment of godly wisdom. Hence, Schuster noted, the figure of Melancholy intentionally evokes Dürer's depictions of Christ as the Man of Sorrows, and the architect's and artisan's tools—ladder, nails, hammer, and tongs—are also the instruments of the Passion. Schuster explained the Roman numeral I in the title of the print in terms of the desired oneness of man with the hidden God. One represents God, who is conceived by Cusanus as the hidden, irreducible unity behind all multiplicity, the *coincidentia oppositorum* (coincidence of all contradictions) and, as such, the highest augmentation of *concordia discors*. Schuster summarized: "In its emphasis on knowledge as God-given, on ignorance as the highest form of knowledge, on the imitation of Christ as the perfection of faith, and on moderation as the absolute ethical position, Dürer's sheet illustrates a humanistic attitude to living that was universally disseminated among the intelligentsia."[15]

Theological Virtue: The Christian Phlegmatic

Melencolia I therefore represents intellectual virtue as displayed by a melancholic person, specifically a secular genius gifted in mathematics and art. *St. Jerome in His Study* embodies theological virtue as expressed by a Christian scholar at work. Jerome, who was learned in Hebrew, Greek, and Latin, was the saint most admired by humanists. In contrast to *St. Jerome Penitent in the Wilderness* (p. 37), here the saint inhabits a sunlit cell. Schuster asserted that the saint is depicted as a phlegmatic who, while being especially devout, must avoid sloth, represented by his comfortable surroundings.[16] Unlike his counterpart in Dürer's engraving *The Temptation of the Idler* (p. 58), Jerome does not give way to comfort and inactivity, but remains focused on his studies and on Christ, represented by the crucifix and by the window cross. Schuster also pointed out that the saint apparently avoids eating the gourd, a watery plant that promotes a phlegmatic person's inclination toward sloth. The gourd, Schuster proposed, has been hung up to dry and will become a suitable container for wine (that is, the Eucharistic blood that brings new life in Christ) and thus symbolizes the saint's training his body through mortification to be a vessel for God.

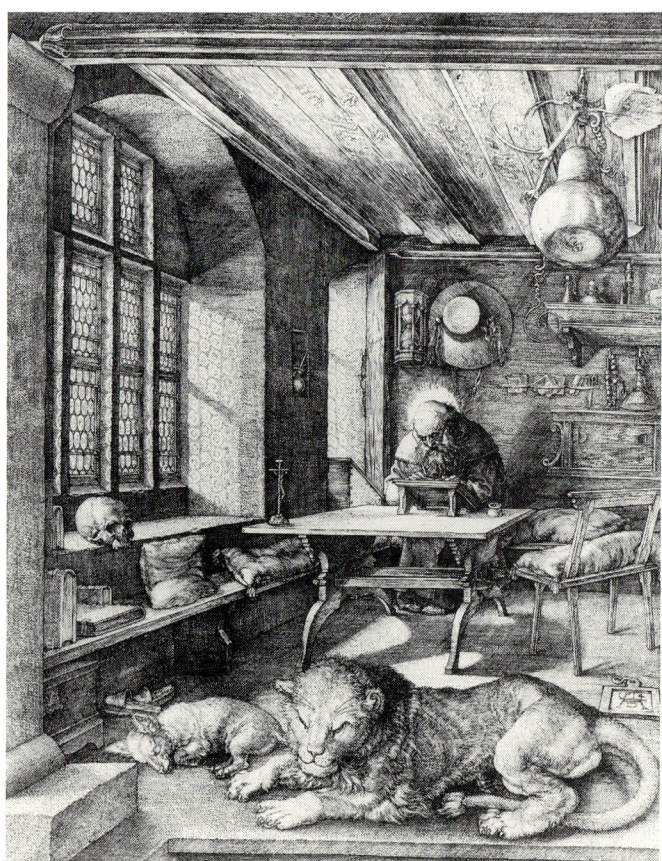

Figure 6 *St. Jerome in His Study,* 1514, Engraving on laid paper, Montgomery, Alabama, Collection of Jean K. Weil.

Moral Virtue: The Christian Choleric

The theological virtue of the phlegmatic St. Jerome is contrasted with the moral virtue of the choleric Christian knight in *Knight, Death, and the Devil*. While Jerome lives a contemplative life withdrawn from the world, the knight lives an active life in the world. His virtue is exemplified by his difficult ascent toward a fortress and by the idealized proportions of his horse, whose body length and height form a square, each side of which is equal to three head lengths. As Schuster noted, the horse is a symbol of mankind's carnal nature; but the bridle and the idealized proportions, accentuated by the placement of the animal parallel to the picture plane, represent instinct moderated by reason.[17] Schuster observed that the knight's overcoming the threat of his choleric nature is also represented by the salamander, a symbol of purity because, according to tradition, it withstands fire.

Dürer and Martin Luther

Dürer's expression of ideas on mankind's salvation was not confined to artistic statements such as the "master engravings." By January 7, 1518, at the latest, Dürer was debating religious issues as part of a humanist study group in Nuremberg named Sodalitas Staupitziana after its founder, Johann von Staupitz (c.1468-1524), vicar-general of the German Congregation of Augustinians. In 1519 the group changed its name to Sodalitas Martiniana, after Staupitz's famous protégé, Martin Luther. Luther credited Staupitz with saving him from the threat of despair or arrogant indifference in the face of his spiritual anguish about his salvation.[18] Dürer similarly credited Luther with helping him "out of great distress."[19]

It can be assumed that Dürer shared Luther's anger at the Church's sale of forgiveness of sins (of indulgences) and found comfort in the reformer's revolutionary formulations about the means to salvation: *sola fide, sola scriptura, sola gratia* (by faith alone, by the preaching of God's word alone, by trust in God's grace alone).[20] For Luther, whatever exceeded the perception of empirical reality was either grounded in God's word or was fantasy.[21] Upon hearing false reports of Luther's arrest and possible murder after Emperor Charles V (1500-1558) condemned him as a heretic at the Diet of Worms, a distraught Dürer wrote on May 17, 1521, that Luther suffered "for the sake of Christian truth and because he has fought with the un-Christlike papacy, which strives with its heavy load of human laws against the redemption of Christ."[22] Dürer went on to pray for "the holy pure gospel which is not darkened by human doctrine." *Sola scriptura* was Dürer's admonition to Nuremberg's leaders in 1526 when he gave the City Council his painting of *Four Apostles* (Munich, Alte Pinakothek), inscribed with a warning against taking "human delusion for the word of God." Verses written below the figures were taken from Luther's 1522 German translation of the New Testament.

Contrary to Dürer's fears in May 1521, Luther did not become a martyr to his cause. The reformation did, however, have martyrs. The first were two Augustinian monks, Johannes von Essen and Heinrich Vos, who were burned before the town hall of Brussels on July 1, 1523. The anxiety that Dürer shared with others who embraced Luther's cause is palpable in his correspondence. Antwerp's city clerk, Cornelius Grapheus (1482-1558), wrote guardedly to Dürer on February 23, 1524, "In these parts the persecution on account of the Gospel is increasing daily. Our brothers, the bearers of this letter, will tell you about it more clearly."[23] Later the same year, on December 5, Dürer wrote to Niclas Kratzer (1486/87-1550), a German mathematician and astronomer in the court of Henry VIII. He inquired about a German translation of Euclid that Kratzer had planned to publish, continuing, "We remain in danger and disgrace for our faith in Christianity. They call us heretics and heap abuse upon us. May God grant us grace and strength by his word. We must obey him rather than man. It is better to lose life and property than to be cast, body and soul, into the fire of hell by God. May he make us firm in goodness and may he enlighten our adversaries, those poor, blind miserable creatures, else they will perish by their errors."[24]

Luther and his followers must have thought often of the early Christian martyrs, whom Luther regarded as the beacon and standard for the church, along with Christ crucified, because they "spread the Gospel through belief and profession of faith and not by means of earthly power and armed force."[25] When Dürer depicted the martyr saints Bartholomew and Simon in two engravings dated 1523 (pp. 100 and 102), he gave them more breadth and bulk than their counterparts of 1514 (p. 90), using their blocky forms to evoke courage and fortitude. An additional factor in their massiveness was Dürer's theoretical interests, specifically his investigation of how figures could be constructed from geometric solids.[26]

Dürer's Technique: A New Austerity

Dürer's ability to suggest a variety of textures in his engravings was undoubtedly the reward of countless hours of experimentation with the burin. The highly organized hatching and cross-hatching systems, the result of the artist's extraordinary control of the engraver's tool and his emulation of the great Colmar engraver Martin Schongauer (c. 1450-1491), lend an awe-inspiring stillness even to early prints such as *Madonna with the Monkey*, c. 1498 (p. 55). The unadorned surfaces of his work after his return from the Netherlands—austere in texture, in contour, and, in the case of the paintings, in color—perhaps reflect reformation concerns that the faithful not be distracted by sensuous renderings of holy personages. As early as 1510, austere forms had served Dürer as a metaphor for the mortification of the flesh in imitation of Christ in the woodcut of a flagellant with long hair and a beard like his own (p. 76). Austerity is particularly apparent in *The Last Supper* woodcut of 1523 (fig 7, p. 19). The hatching systems and the resulting play of light and shadow are simple. Devoid of ornament, the setting emphasizes the humility of Christ. (The contrast of Christ's humility and the papacy's love of splendor was a major theme of a pamphlet by Luther's ally Philip Melanchthon [1497-1560]—*Passional Christi et Antichristi* [1521], illustrated with woodcuts by Lucas Cranach the Elder [1472-1553].) During his trip to the Netherlands, Dürer made drawings for what seems to have been a projected printed Passion series in horizontal format. Only *The Last Supper* was realized, reflecting perhaps the artist's strong interest in reformation debates about that sacrament. Luther rejected the doctrine of transubstantiation, which attributed to priests the miraculous power to change the Eucharistic elements of bread and wine into the real body and blood of Christ. While never going as far as others who denied the corporeal presence of Christ in the bread and wine, Luther maintained that it was the belief of the individual Christian that gave the sacrament its efficacy. Furthermore, he argued that the laity should receive both the bread and the wine and not just the bread, as was the practice in the Roman Catholic Church. In *The Last Supper*, Dürer placed the bread basket and wine jug, simple vessels associated with the laity, within the reach of all his viewers, thereby giving visual form to Luther's ideas.[27]

Dürer and his humanist friend Willibald Pirckheimer were still debating about the sacrament during one of Melanchthon's visits to Nuremberg to advise the City Council on the establishment of a free secondary school (either late in 1525 or in May 1526). Melanchthon recalled that Pirckheimer vehemently opposed an opinion put forth by Dürer, saying, "What you say cannot be painted," to which Dürer, "an excessively subtle disputant," replied, "Nay! But what you advance cannot be put into words or even figured in the mind."[28] Dürer's position is not clear from his statement. What is clear is his reference to learned ignorance: that which is not visible is inexpressible and unfathomable, and therefore the highest completion of the intellect is in faith.[29]

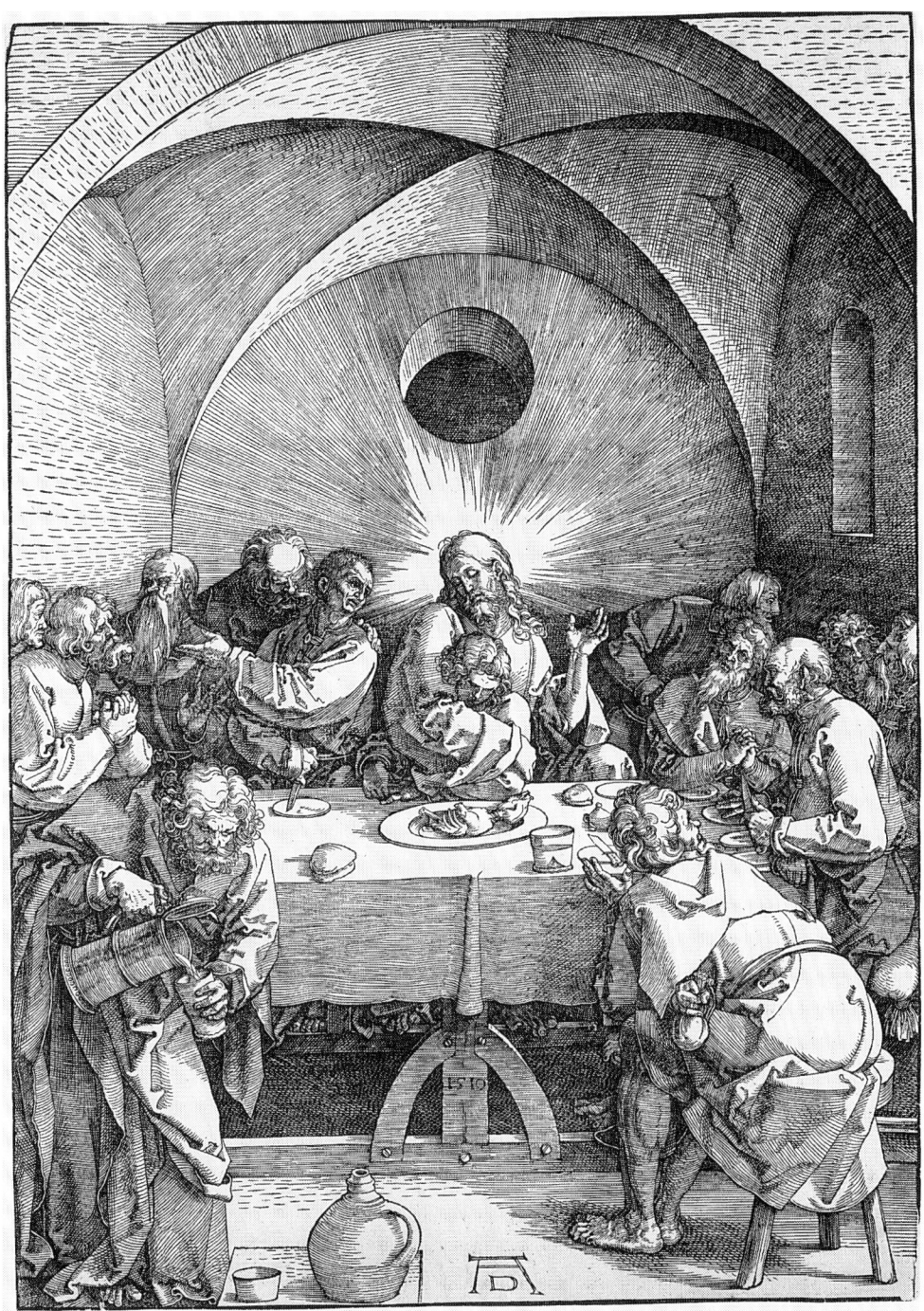

Figure 7 *The Last Supper*, 1510, Woodcut on laid paper, Washington, National Gallery of Art, Gift of W.G. Russell Allen, 1941.1.23.

The Limitations of Human Knowledge and the Search for God through Measurement

Dürer never abandoned his search for godly wisdom through measurement. It was one of the things that, in the words of Camerarius, he "could never cease researching." Dürer eventually made detailed measurements of hundreds of individuals, arriving at a flexible system of measurement to replace the single canon of beauty described by Vitruvius. In the context of his search for ideal proportions, Dürer said: "What beauty may be I do not know—one person may view or make a more beautiful picture than another, but never to the point of perfection so that a yet more beautiful one might not be made, for that is not within the scope of man; only God knows it, and to whomever he reveals it, he will know it too."[30] Dürer's thoughts on beauty conform closely to Nicholas of Cusa's understanding of human knowledge as an approximation: an idea conforms roughly to the reality it represents, and no matter how precisely an idea is formulated, there still exists the possibility of another idea that is more exact. Interestingly, given the polyhedron and sphere in *Melencolia I*, Cusanus said that understanding is to truth as a polygon is to a circle: The more angles the polygon has, the more it will resemble the circle without ever exactly matching the circle's shape.[31]

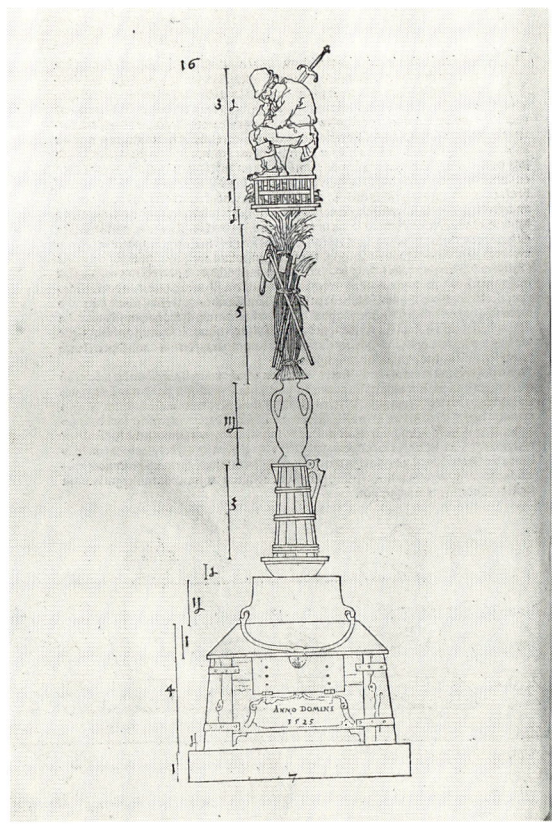

Figure 8 *Monument to Commemorate a Victory Over the Rebellious Peasants...*, 1525, (from The Manual of Measurement) Engraving on laid paper, St. Louis, The Saint Louis Art Museum, Museum Purchase, 175:1942.

Dürer, Humanism, and Luther

In 1525, in his *Manual of Measurement*, Dürer made an enigmatic visual statement about another topic that, like the Last Supper, was cause for heated debate. He included a woodcut titled *Monument to Commemorate a Victory over the Rebellious Peasants* (fig. 8, left). Was Dürer, as his title suggests, condemning the German peasants who rose up against their landlords in 1524-25?[32] The peasants had been encouraged by Luther's "revolt" against the papacy, but the reformer unequivocally condemned them in his tract *Against the Robbing and Murdering Hordes of Peasants* (May 1525). Although Dürer's peasant is stabbed, as Luther said he should be, he is seated atop the abundant fruits of his labor. One cannot help but compare him to the cattle bound for slaughter below, thus recalling the words of the Apostle Paul: "Just as it is written, 'For Thy sake we are being put to death all day long; We were considered as sheep to be slaughtered.' But in all these things we overwhelmingly conquer through Him who loved us" (Romans 8:36-37). Was Dürer taking the radical stance that the defeated peasants would have their spiritual reward in God's love for them? Schuster, who noted that the peasant's pose evokes both the figure of Melancholy and the Man of Sorrows in Dürer's prints, asserted that Dürer looked to the irony of Erasmus of Rotterdam (1466?-1536) and the humanist's abhorrence of war. Rather than backing either Luther in his call for retribution or the peasants, Dürer mocked the peasants as inept warriors in order to make the inhumanity of their "immoderate slaughterers" all the more apparent.³³ A plea for "measure" would be entirely appropriate to a *Manual of Measurement*.³⁴ Dürer, who met Erasmus in Brussels, depicted him in an engraving of 1526 (fig. 9, right).

Another humanist depicted by Dürer in an engraving of 1526 (p. 104) was Luther's more conciliatory associate Melanchthon, a professor at the University of Wittenberg from age twenty-one. Luther admired Melanchthon's methodical thinking, and indeed Melanchthon's *Loci Communes* (1521) presented the reformation's principles systematically for the first time. In October 1525, seven months after officially embracing Luther's cause, the Nuremberg City Council heeded Luther's call for governments to found schools by inviting Melanchthon to Nuremberg to advise on the establishment of Germany's first municipal secondary school. Melanchthon's visits to Nuremberg late in 1525 and in May 1526 allowed Dürer to study his features. Still, the artist modestly wrote in the portrait's inscription, "Dürer was able to depict Philipp's features as if living, but the skilled hand could not portray his soul." Dürer did depict a window with crosslike mullions reflected in Melanchthon's eye (the window to his soul) even though the setting is outdoors, thus showing that the imitation of Christ is the reformer's "compass to paradise."

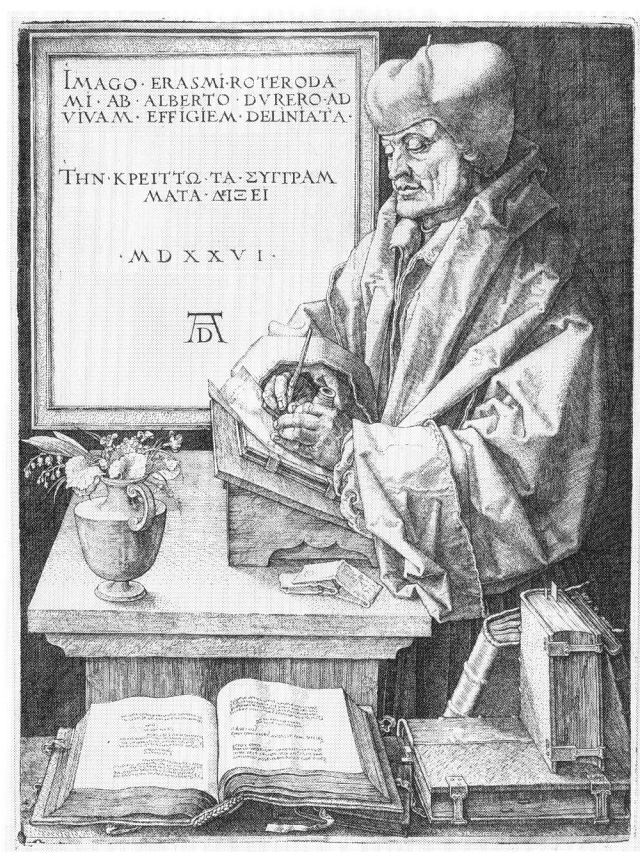

Figure 9 *Erasmus of Rotterdam*, 1526, Engraving on paper, Washington, National Gallery of Art, Rosenwald Collection, 1943.3.3554.

The enduring nature of Dürer's admiration for Melanchthon in particular and the Lutheran cause in general is demonstrated by an endowment made by Dürer's widow, who died in 1539. Melanchthon was pleased when he learned that Agnes Dürer (b. 1475) had stipulated that after the deaths of herself and her sister an annuity Dürer had purchased in 1524 should be used for a scholarship fund enabling a craftsman's son to study liberal arts and theology at the University of Wittenberg.³⁵ The endowment probably indicates the kind of education that the childless Albrecht and Agnes, the son of a goldsmith and the daughter of a brass worker, would have wanted for a son of their own.

The Death of Albrecht Dürer

Dürer died on April 6, 1528, ten years earlier than the woman who had been his wife for more than three decades. Erasmus, in a dialogue, *The Right Way of Speaking* (1528), praised his artistic achievements, particularly as a printmaker. He said that while Apelles was a "prince" of painting, Dürer, an excellent painter, could also

> *express absolutely anything…with black lines only—shadows, light, reflections, emerging and receding forms, and even the different aspects of a single thing as they strike the eye of the spectator. His harmony and proportions are always correct. Above all, he can draw the things that are impossible to draw: fire, beams of light, thunderbolts, flashes and sheets of lightning, and the so-called clouds on the wall, feelings, attitudes, the mind revealed by the carriage of the body, almost the voice itself.* [36]

Luther, hearing of Dürer's death, wrote about him as an excellent and wise Christian:
> *As to Dürer, it is natural and right to weep for so excellent [a] man; still you should rather think him blessed, as one whom Christ has taken in the fullness of his wisdom and by a happy death from these most troublous times, and perhaps from times even more troublous which are to come, lest one, who was worthy to look upon nothing but excellence, should be forced to behold things most vile. May he rest in peace. Amen.* [37]

At the age of fifty-six, Dürer's striving, both artistic and spiritual, was over.

Notes

Author's note: When Peter-Klaus Schuster published his two-volume *Melencolia I. Dürers Denkbild* (1991), he called it an attempt at a new monograph that would demonstrate the humanist thinking throughout Dürer's work (vol. 1, p. 105). Despite the seemingly narrow focus of his book—Dürer's engraving *Melencolia I*—Schuster succeeded. This essay is deeply indebted to Schuster's book, which by firmly establishing Dürer as a participant in the humanist thinking of his day laid the foundation for future assessments of the artist and his oeuvre.

1. Rupprich, vol. 1, pp. 307-11, esp. p. 310. Schuster, vol. 1, p. 369. Camerarius was headmaster of Nuremberg's secondary school after 1526.
2. See Dürer's letter to Georg Spalatin (1484-1545), court chaplain and secretary to Luther's protector, Friedrich the Wise (1463-1525), in Hutchison, pp. 124-25.
3. On the cross as a "compass to paradise," see Thomas à Kempis, *The Imitation of Christ*, trans. William C. Creasy (New York: Book-of-the-Month Club, 1989), p. 156. Even the AD monogram that Dürer combined with the dates on his paintings and prints can be seen as a pun on the words *anno Domini* (in the year of the Lord), as noted by A. Hyatt Mayor in *Prints and People: A Social History of Printed Pictures* (Princeton, NJ: Princeton University Press, 1971), text before discussion of illustration 265. The connection between Dürer's portrait and the imitation of Christ was made by Erwin Panofsky in his monograph *Albrecht Dürer*, 2 vols. (Princeton, New Jersey: Princeton University Press, 1943), which is quoted here (p. 43) and in the following notes from the more easily available 1971 printing, hereafter abbreviated as Panofsky. Panofsky noted the idealization of Dürer's features; the frontal, vertical arrangement of the figure and the placement of the right hand that evoke depictions of Christ as *Salvator Mundi*; and Dürer's belief that his creative power derived from the creative power of God. On the link between the window cross in the eye (the window of the soul) and the sitter's focus on Christ's Passion in this and other works by Dürer, see Schuster, vol. 1, pp. 238-40, and vol. 2, pp. 501-502, notes 533-45, who also summarizes earlier literature on the subject.
4. On Dürer's creating (or molding) himself and showing godly wisdom as the foundation and goal of all the arts in this self-portrait, and on the connection with Pico, see Schuster, vol. 1, p. 235, and vol. 2, pp. 499-500, notes 504-508. In his *Oration*, Pico has God, "the best of artisans," grant Adam free will so that "as though the maker and molder of thyself, thou mayest fashion thyself in whatever shape thou shalt prefer. . . . Thou shalt have the power, out of thy soul's judgment, to be reborn into the higher forms, which are divine." See Pico's *Oration* in English translation in Ernst Cassirer, Paul Oskar Kristeller and John Herman Randall, Jr., *The*

Renaissance Philosophy of Man (Chicago and London: The University of Chicago Press, 1948), pp. 223-54, esp. pp. 225-26. On Dürer's *Self-Portrait*, see also Joseph Leo Koerner, *The Moment of Self-Portraiture in German Renaissance Art* (Chicago and London: The University of Chicago Press, 1993).

5 He did so in an introduction to a book, *Nourishment for Painters' Apprentices*, that was never completed. See Strauss 1974, vol. 3, pp. 1300-1301.
6 For the arguments for and against Dürer's having cut some of his early woodblocks himself, see Landau and Parshall, pp. 172, 174.
7 Panofsky, pp. 55-56.
8 Contrast Schuster's interpretation, vol. 1, pp. 268-70, and vol. 2, pp. 514-16, notes 729-44, with Panofsky's, pp. 73-76.
9 Rupprich, vol. 2, p. 104.
10 On the former, see Jeffrey Chipps Smith, *German Sculpture of the Later Renaissance, c. 1520-1580, Art in the Age of Uncertainty* (Princeton, NJ: Princeton University Press, 1994), pp. 185-92. On the latter, see Los Angeles, The J. Paul Getty Museum, and Saint Louis, The Saint Louis Art Museum, *Painting on Light: Drawings and Stained Glass in the Age of Dürer and Holbein*, text by Barbara Butts and Lee Hendrix (with the assistance of Scott C. Wolf), and with contributions by Barbara Giesicke, Timothy B. Husband, Mylène Ruoss, Hartmut Scholz, and Peter van Treeck (Los Angeles, 2000), pp. 156-59, cat. no. 49.
11 On the temperaments and the symbolism of the animals in *Adam and Eve*, see Panofsky, pp. 84-85.
12 See Schuster, vol. 1, pp. 331-35, and Panofsky, p. 85.
13 Panofsky, pp. 151-71, esp. p. 156.
14 Ibid., p. 171: "But what absolute beauty is, I know not. Nobody knows it except God."
15 Schuster, vol. 1, p. 90: "In seiner Betonung des Wissens als gottgewollter Gabe, des Nichtwissens als höchster Form des Wissens, der Imitatio Christi als Vollendung des Glaubens und der Mässigkeit als der sittlichen Haltung schlechthin illustriert Dürers Blatt eine im Kreise Gebildeter allgemein verbreitete humanistische Lebenshaltung." It is difficult to cite specific pages in Schuster's study of *Melencolia I*, since he develops his arguments throughout his book. However, on the main figure as a personification of Astronomy and Philosophy, see vol. 1, pp. 85-86, 123-47. On measure in art and morality, including *concordia discors* and *coincidentia oppositorum*, see vol. 1, pp. 89-90, 246-96. On learned ignorance, see vol. 1, pp. 88-89, 222-31, 310-12. On Christ as godly wisdom, see vol. 1, pp. 88-89, 231-46.
16 For his discussion of *St. Jerome in His Study*, see especially Schuster, vol. 1, pp. 332, 343-47.
17 For his discussion of *Knight, Death, and the Devil*, see especially ibid., vol. 1, pp. 332, 338-42.
18 Heiko A. Oberman, *Luther: Man between God and the Devil*, trans. Eileen Walliser-Schwarzbart (New York, London, Toronto, Sydney, Auckland: Image Books, Doubleday, 1992), p. 182.
19 See Dürer's letter to Spalatin (note 2).
20 For an excellent discussion of Luther's beliefs, see Eugene F. Rice, Jr., *The Foundations of Early Modern Europe, 1460-1559* (New York and London: W.W. Norton & Company, 1970), pp. 125-34.
21 Oberman (note 18), p. 161.
22 Dürer's lament for Luther is found in English translation in Roger Fry, ed., *Dürer's Record of Journeys to Venice and the Low Countries* (New York: Dover Publications, Inc., 1995), pp. 83-88.
23 Rupprich, vol. 1, pp. 108-109. English translation from Strauss 1974, vol. 4, p. 2249.
24 Rupprich (note 1), vol. 1, p. 113. English translation from Strauss 1974, vol. 4, pp. 2250-51.
25 Oberman (note 18), pp. 253-54.
26 See Strauss 1974, vol. 3, pp. 1790-91, cat. no. 1519/18, for a drawing, dated 1519, that juxtaposes the figure of St. Peter with two heads composed from geometric solids. I do not accept Strauss' suggestion that the figure of Peter was drawn in 1514, five years earlier than the two heads. Instead it would seem that at a single moment Dürer was considering how the figure of St. Peter might be analyzed as a sculptural form.
27 Two years earlier, in 1521, Andreas Bodenstein von Karlstadt (1480-1541), professor of theology and jurisprudence in Wittenberg, dedicated a pamphlet on the symbolic interpretation of the Last Supper to Dürer. See Hutchison, p. 166, and n. 6 on p. 217. Panofsky, p. 222, argued that the empty charger (without the sacrificial lamb) showed Dürer's support for Luther's assertion that "Holy Mass was not a 'sacrifice,' but a mere 'testament and sacrament, wherein, under the seal of a symbol, a promise is made of the redemption of sin.'"
28 The discussion is recorded by Kaspar Peucer (1525-1602), son-in-law of Melanchthon, in his *Tractatus Historicus de Ph. Melanchthonis Sententia de Controversia Coenae Domini* (1596), p. 11. It is reprinted in Rupprich, vol. 1, pp. 306-307. Quoted here in English from Wendell Glen Mathews, "Albrecht Dürer as a Reformation Figure," PhD dissertation, The University of Iowa, 1968 (Ann Arbor, MI: University Microfilms, Inc.), p. 55.
29 Schuster, vol. 1, p. 310, and vol. 2, p. 529, notes 62, 64, discusses this aspect of Cusanus's concept of learned ignorance as reflected in Bovillus's *Liber de Sapiente*. He treats the argument between Pirckheimer and Dürer in the context of learned ignorance in vol. 1, pp. 232-33.
30 Rupprich, vol. 3, p. 293. English translation from Strieder, p. 35.
31 See the passage from Cusanus, *On Learned Ignorance*, in James Bruce Ross and Mary Martin McLaughlin, eds., *The Portable Medieval Reader* (Harmondsworth, Middlesex, England: Penguin Books Ltd, 1983), pp. 667-75, esp. p. 671.
32 On the monument as a "celebration of order," see Stephen Greenblatt, "Murdering Peasants: Status, Genre, and The Representation of Rebellion," *Representations* 1, 1 (February 1983), pp. 1-29.
33 Schuster, vol. 1, pp. 365-68, and vol. 2, pp. 560-62, n. 215-43.
34 I should like to thank Thomas E. Rassieur, who made this observation when I was writing about Dürer's woodcut for Saint Louis, The Saint Louis Art Museum, and Cambridge, Massachusetts, Arthur M. Sackler Museum, Harvard University, *The Printed World of Pieter Bruegel the Elder*, essays by Barbara Butts and Joseph Leo Koerner, with narrative commentary by Betha Whitlow (Saint Louis, 1995).
35 See Mathews (note 28), p. 62; Hutchison, p. 185; and Ernst Rebel, *Albrecht Dürer. Maler und Humanist* (Munich: C. Bertelsmann, 1996), p. 457.
36 *Collected Works of Erasmus*, vol. 26: *Literary and Educational Writings, 4: De Pueris Instituendis. De Recta Pronuntiatione* (Toronto, Buffalo, London: University of Toronto Press, 1985), p. 399. The "clouds on the wall" are discussed in Erasmus's *Adagia* and, as Panofsky, p. 44, noted, defined as "something most similar to nothing or a dream."
37 English translation from Mathews (note 28), p. 61.

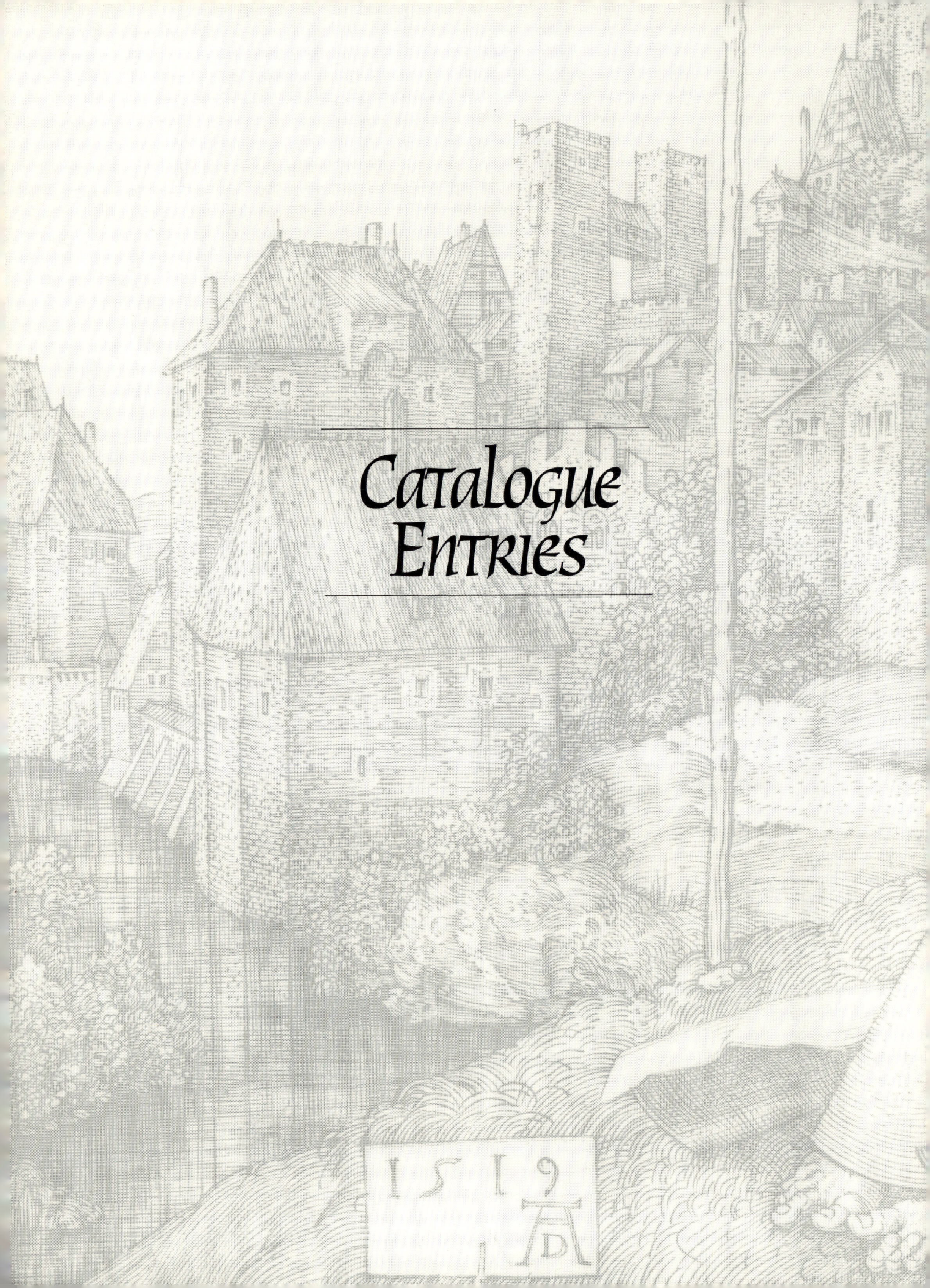

Catalogue Entries

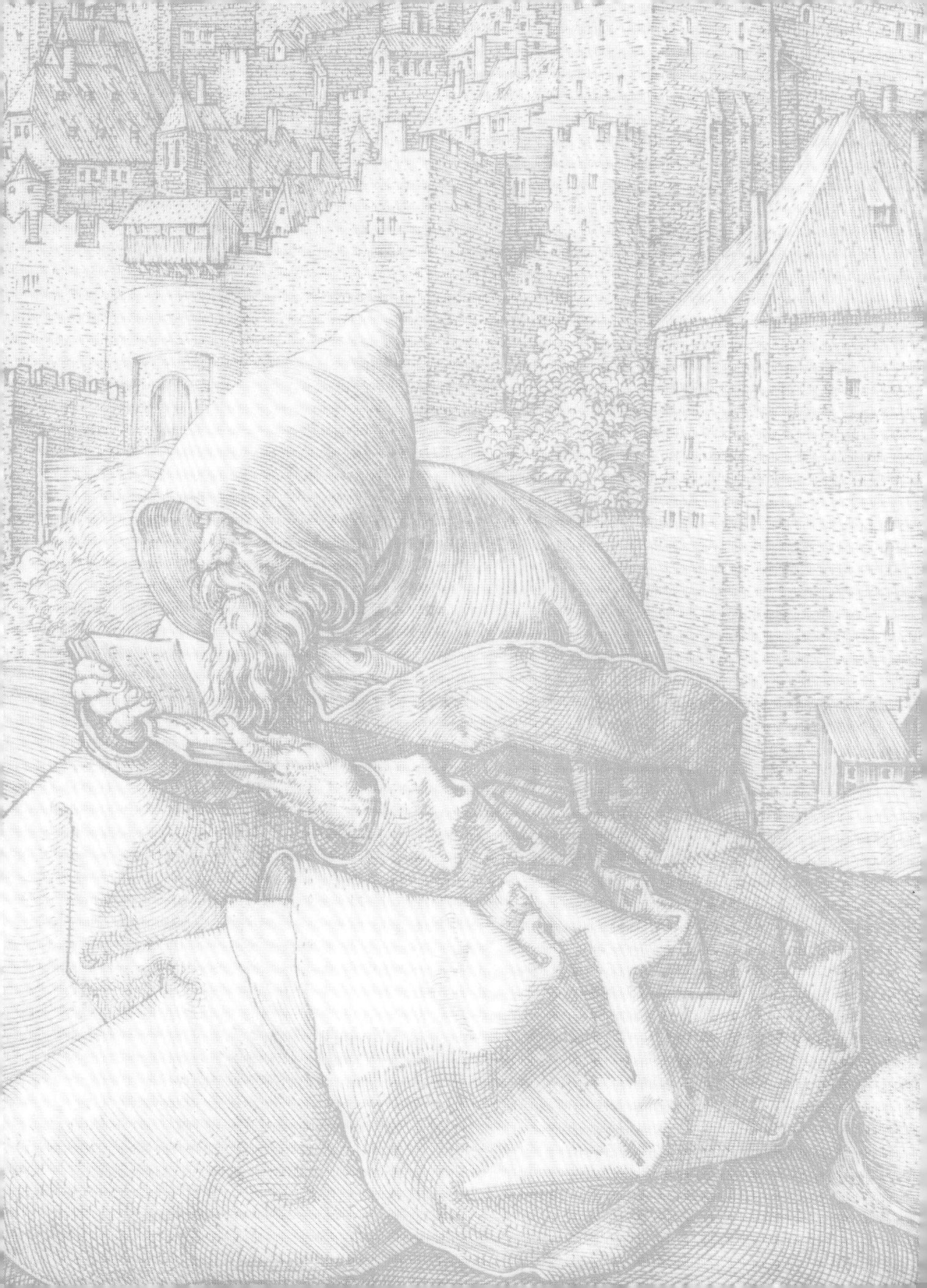

catalogue entry 1

Fortune (Das Kleine Gluck), 1495

Engraving
Laid paper
Meder 71 c; Hollstein 71; Bartsch 78
Watermark: Bull's Head (not described by Meder)
Sheet: 108 x 64 mm
Signed, recto: Monogram AD (bottom center)
1999.7.22
Catalogue number 1

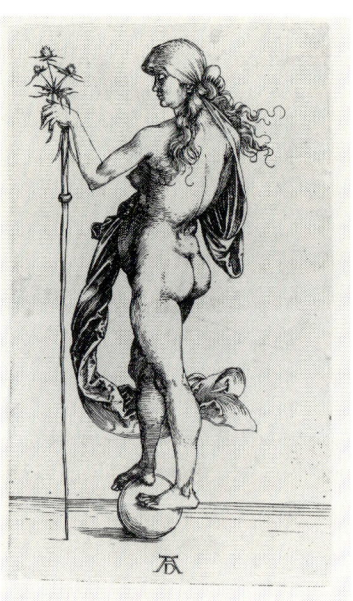

Fortune, as the title suggests, is one of Dürer's two engraved portrayals of the classical goddess Fortuna, who was thought to direct mankind's fate for good or ill.[1] One of his first engravings containing a female nude, it demonstrates Dürer's early and abiding interest in the subjects from classical art that formed the basis for art of the Italian Renaissance. Dürer's experiences and his exposure to classical motifs in Northern Italian Renaissance art on his first journey to Venice (1494-1495) may have prompted the creation of this work after his return to Nuremberg. Dürer's depictions of the nude were at least partially inspired by his fascination with the study of human proportion. It is likely that his friend Willibald Pirckheimer, one of the foremost humanists in Northern Germany at the time, introduced him to the writings of the Roman architect Vitruvius, who briefly treats the subject of human proportion.[2]

Conceived on a very small scale compared to Dürer's other engravings of the period, the figure of the goddess is the sole feature of the composition, which places all its visual emphasis on the dynamic, twisting pose and proportions of her body. Fortune is seen here in profile from the back, balancing on a sphere with the help of a staff in her left hand. Caught between her thumb and forefinger is a sprig of *Eryngium*, a plant said to have aphrodisiac qualities.[3] Drapery wraps around her head and descends over her right shoulder to cascade below her knees.

Closely related (in reverse) to this figure of Fortune is *Nude with Staff Seen from Behind* a drawing from the same year (W. 85, Paris, Musée du Louvre, fig. 10, right). Drawn primarily with a brush, it shows a female nude from the back, her weight on her right leg and supported by a staff in her right hand. Draperies float from the top of the staff across the front of her body and over her left shoulder. Dürer treated nude subjects similarly in several drawings from the second half of the 1490s, including *Nude Woman with a Herald's Wand* (W. 947, Sacramento, Crocker Art Museum), *Women's Bathhouse* (W. 152, formerly Bremen, Kunsthalle), and *Fortuna in a Niche* (W. 154, Robert Lehman Foundation). Each of these works, as well as the engraved *Fortune*, shows the influence of Dürer's Northern European tradition of depicting nude figures with high waists, protruding stomachs, and elongated proportions, combined with poses and postures that suggest his exposure to Italian paintings and sculpture.[4] In mythological subjects such as the *Fortune*, Dürer seemingly drew inspiration from classically inspired sources, thus melding the content of the work with its visual form.[5]

In Dürer's era, Nuremberg was prosperous and cultured, one of the great centers for the development of printing and book production, with a significant interest in the literary and visual arts accomplishments of the classical civilizations to the south. Indeed, the cities of Northern Italy were the focal points for international monetary exchange, and Nuremberg's merchants and bankers were fixtures in this world of business and commerce. By establishing his home and career in Nuremberg, Dürer ensured that he was surrounded by a society that valued both innovation and learning. The collection of pictorial subjects offered by the rediscovery of classical literature expanded as the Northern humanists, who were also Dürer's friends and acquaintances, began to acquire and disseminate classical texts.

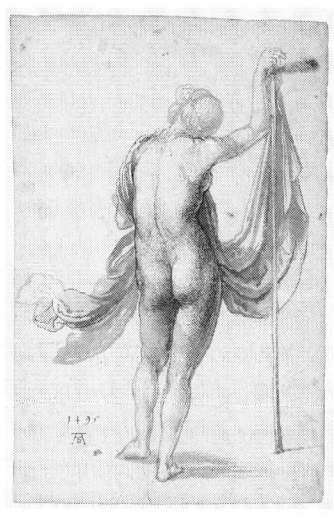

Figure 10 *Nude Woman Seen from the Back*, 1495, Brush and Pen on paper, Paris, Louvre.

As a pagan goddess, Fortuna was worshipped by various cults in ancient Rome. She was identified by multiple personifications described in classical literature—Fortuna Dux and Fortuna Redux—were associated with seafaring; Fortuna Virilis with love and marriage. She was consistently depicted in prints during and after the Renaissance, usually accompanied by attributes of the sphere, proclaiming her worldwide dominion, and the wheel, signifying her fickle nature. The fact that Fortune is depicted as a woman is often interpreted by scholars as a commentary on the perceived erratic behavior of females. In time, Fortune was conflated with other personifications, such as Love, Opportunity, and Death, to convey a melding of these factors in the life of mankind.[6]

In this engraving Fortune's pose atop the sphere contrasts with other Renaissance depictions, in which the sphere is placed at her feet. Most scholars believe Dürer's textual source for this depiction is the *Cebetis Tabula*, a Stoic dialogue of the first or second century A.D., which describes Fortune as a blind woman standing upon a round stone.[7] Her vacant eyes (she is typically shown as blind or blindfolded) are consistent with the concept that Fortune was impartial, delivering good or bad luck without discrimination. A particularly distinctive element of this composition is the presence of the *Eryngium*, in the goddess' fingers. By including this reference to romantic love, Dürer has effected the type of conflation described above; combining the elements of love and fate implies that love is a precarious, and unreliable, state.[8] **M.L.A.**

---

1 A second, later engraving was sometimes called *The Great Fortune*, but is more properly titled *Nemesis* (c. 1501-1502; B. 77, M. 72) based upon Dürer's reference to it in his diary of 1520. Nemesis refers to the Greek goddess of retribution, and Fortune to the Roman goddess Fortuna, who was associated with luck or chance. *Nemesis* shows a larger and winged female nude also balanced on a sphere. She is more specifically associated with the concepts of reward and punishment, signified by her attributes of a chalice and a bridle. Christopher White notes that *Das Kleine Gluck (The Small Fortune)* could also represent an allegory of the concept of chance that was popularized in the medieval period. See White, p. 36.

2 Strieder, p. 34. Vitruvius's treatise appeared in print for the first time in 1486, but had been circulated in manuscript versions since its discovery at Montecassino in 1414. Strieder notes that a translation (probably from about 1508 and in Dürer's hand) of Vitruvius's writings on human proportions still exists. Dürer eventually used Vitruvius' discussion of the subject as the basis for his own *Four Books of Human Proportion*, when he published Book I around 1523.

3 Also called Sea Holly, the plant was described by Pliny (Natural History, Book 22, ch. 9). See Washington 1971, p. 115. It appears in several other works by Dürer, including his *Self-Portrait with Sea Holly*, 1493 (Paris, Musée du Louvre).

4 Washington 1971, p. 38. Here it is noted that the original source for the pose of Fortune may have been the figure of a dancing muse in Andrea Mantegna's painting *Parnassus*, and perhaps a lost intermediate drawing made after that figure (also see p. 115).

5 Strieder, p. 10, notes that the engravings of Mantegna were making their way into Northern Europe at this time and were being used as sources in Northern workshops. Panofsky, p. 31, records that Dürer made several drawings after engravings by Mantegna in 1494.

6 For a detailed discussion of Fortune and her depiction in Renaissance art, see chapter VII of Russell, pp. 205-26.

7 Washington 1971, pp. 115-16. Strauss 1975, p. 34, notes that a copy of this dialogue was found in the library of Willibald Pirckheimer.

8 Panofsky, p. 70, says, "In transferring the attribute of the *Eryngium* to the goddess Fortuna, Durer found a humanistic way of saying that love is both omnipotent and fickle."

catalogue entry 2

The Ill-Assorted Couple, 1495

Engraving
Laid paper
Meder 77 c; Hollstein 77; Bartsch 93
Watermark: None
Sheet: 150 x 140 mm
Signed, recto: Monogram AD (bottom center)
1999.7.23
Catalogue number 2

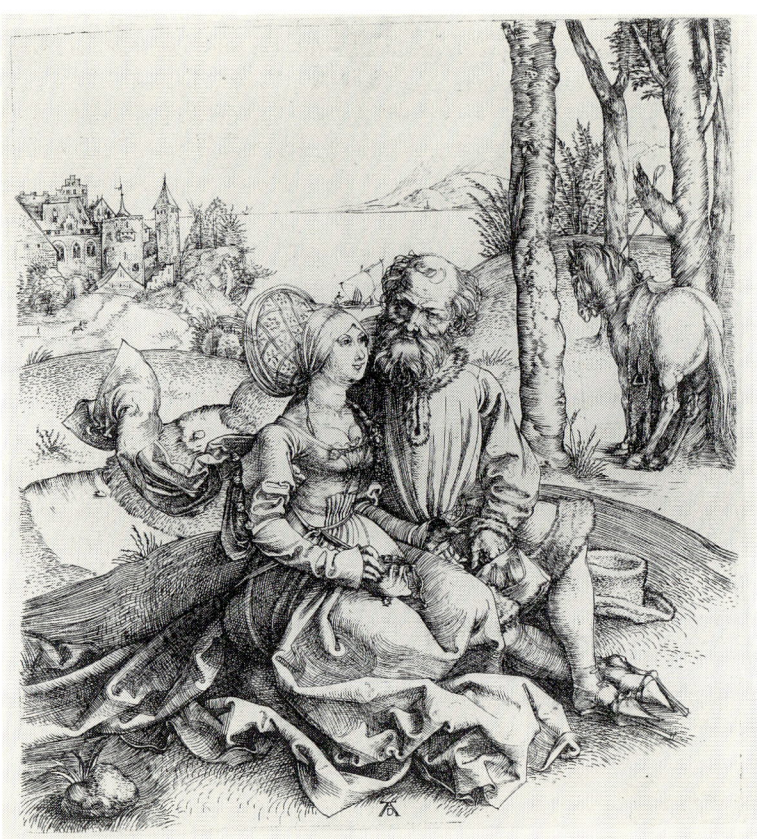

While religious subject matter predominated in prints produced in the fourteenth and early fifteenth centuries, scenes illustrating contemporary life and other secular subjects quickly gained popularity. The event depicted in this work, an encounter between an older man and a younger woman, falls within a group of themes that form one of the earliest sources for secular imagery. "The Power of Women" themes first emerged in the thirteenth century as a source of decoration for objects such as wedding chests, tapestries, and household furnishings. The subjects focused on the relationship between the sexes, specifically on the ways that women used cunning or sexual wiles to control men.

One of the primary subjects within this theme is that of the Unequal Couple (or Unequal Lovers). Focusing on sexual relationships between men and women mismatched in age, it appears in numerous satirical stories, poems, and plays beginning in antiquity. These literary sources were accompanied by illustrations or served as sources for visual expression. Most artists concentrated on showing the foolish, lascivious nature of the older person and the greed of the younger one. Visual puns or other references to the erotic nature of the encounter are also common, suggesting that such prints were intended to provide an intimate experience of a subject that was censored in art of a more public expression.[1]

As an early engraving by Dürer, *The Ill-Assorted Couple* shows the still significant influence of works by Martin Schongauer and the Housebook Master not only in its subject, but in its style, compositional structure, and execution as well. It has been noted that the landscape receding into the distance with the small town on a hill is similar to Schongauer's approach to distance views, particularly comparable to one in his *Crucifixion* (B.25; L.14). In addition, it has been noted that the head of the old man bears a resemblance to the same Schongauer's St. Anthony in *The Tribulations of St. Anthony* (B.47; L.54).[2]

Dürer's familiarity with the art of engravers such as Israhel van Meckenem, Martin Schongauer, and the Housebook Master undoubtedly included their works on this theme.[3] In the year before he executed *The Ill-Assorted Couple*, he had already produced a woodcut titled *Old Wife and Young Fool* as an illustration for Sebastian Brant's *Das Narrenschiff* (or *The Ship of Fools*), published in 1494. In a similar vein as *The Ill-Assorted Couple*, it shows a young man in the center of the composition flanked on one side by an older woman with a bag of money; on the other side a donkey turns his hindquarters toward the viewer. As the young man accepts the bag of money from the woman, he grasps the tail of the donkey, thereby alluding to the baseness of his own behavior.[4]

A similar monetary exchange constitutes the primary activity depicted in *The Ill-Assorted Couple*. The older man clasps the woman around her shoulders and reaches into his purse to find money to place in her waiting palm. With her other hand, she opens her own purse to deposit the payment she so obviously solicits. In the background a horse, tethered to a broken tree branch, pulls against its restraint. The horse, a traditional symbol of violent and unrestrained passion, alludes to the nature of the bargain being struck in the foreground.

Unlike the illustration for Brant's *Narrenschiff*, this depiction of an Unequal Couple is not overtly moralizing. Their business transaction aside, the figures are presented as dignified and elegantly dressed. This sophisticated treatment of the subject has led to speculation that Dürer may have intended to depict a specific narrative or event, but there is no direct evidence that this is the case.[5] Furthermore, the subtlety of the image may be attributable to the differing audiences for woodcuts and for engravings. The labor intensive and thus more expensive engravings were directed toward a wealthier segment of society. In Dürer's case the humanist audience was important, and this group would have been more likely to appreciate the delicacy of the image as well as the rather refined demeanor of the participants. **M.L.A.**

1 Russell, p. 21.
2 Washington, 1971, p. 113.
3 A primary source for information on this theme and its importance in literature and art, as well as the major artists who interpreted it between the fourteenth and sixteenth centuries, is Alison G. Stewart, *Unequal Lovers: A Study of Unequal Couples in Northern Art* (New York: Abaris Books), 1977.
4 Strieder, p. 94. The author of *The Ship of Fools* was from Basel, where Dürer resided briefly (1491-93) during his *Wanderjahre*. The book was published there by Johann Bergmann von Olpe in 1494. Its various chapters describe examples of mankind's folly, and Dürer translated the text rather literally into pictorial images. See also Stewart, p. 59, for further discussion of this work and its text.
5 Suggestions that this print may illustrate the biblical story of Judah and Tamar (Genesis 38: 12-19) have been largely dismissed by scholars (see Washington 1971, p. 113). Another suggestion has a popular poem as a source: "Oh, the cunning of woman, how diverse/Are your surprises and your power/To the one who experiences your spiteful trick!/The wild youths want to tame you/The old fools want to lame you, with their purses." See Stewart, p. 24 and n. 54. An even earlier suggestion was that the couple was the prominent Nuremberg residents Berthold Tucher and Anna Pfinzing (see Strauss 1975, p. 31).

catalogue entry 3

The Prodigal Son Amid the Swine, c.1496

Engraving
Laid paper
Meder 28 c; Hollstein 28; Bartsch 28
Watermark: Gothic P with Flower (Meder 321)
Sheet: 250 x 192 mm (trimmed along the plate mark)
Signed, recto: Monogram AD (bottom center)
1999.7.10
Catalogue number 3

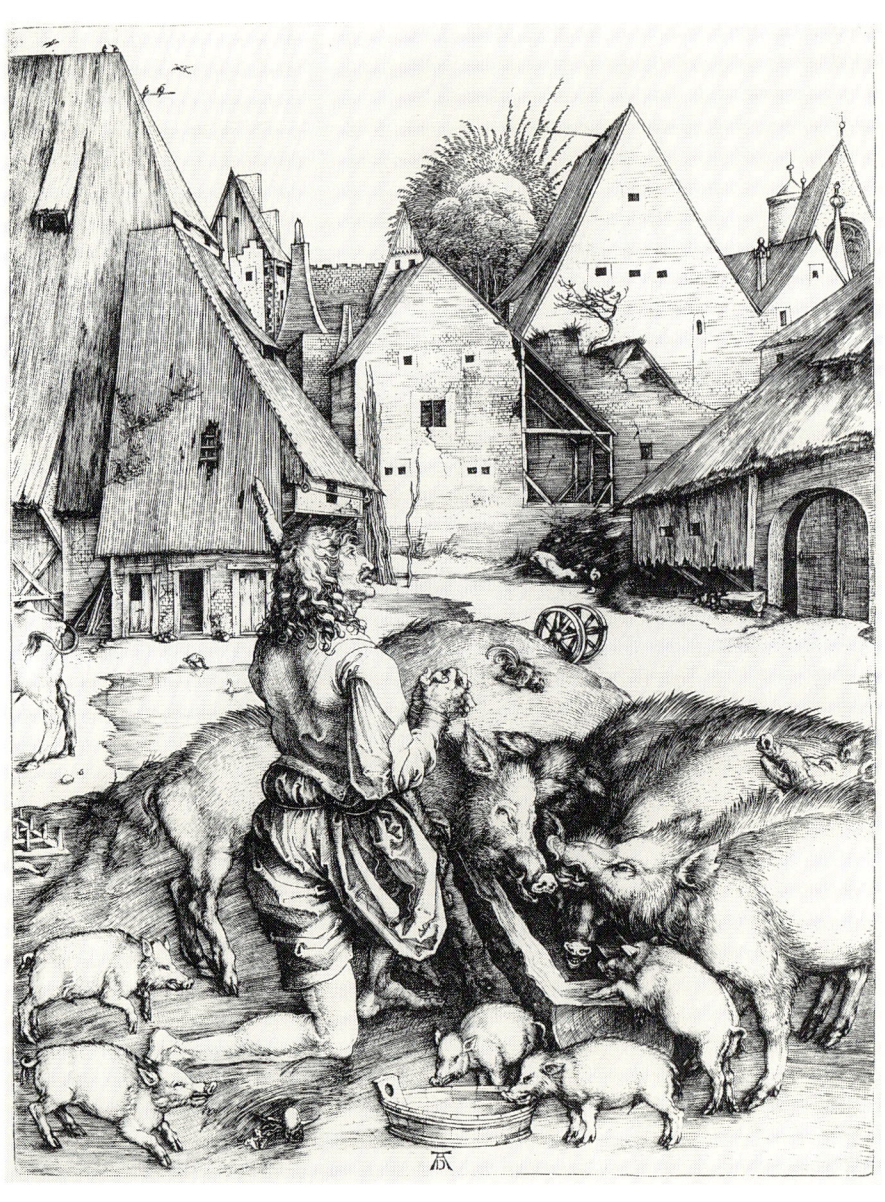

Christ's parable of the Prodigal Son (Luke 15:11-32) relates the story of a father and his two sons. The younger son demanded his share of the family estate, converted the property into cash, and left home. Quickly squandering his fortune on reckless living, he was reduced to tending swine. Reconsidering his wasted life, he decided to return home to his father. While he was still a distance away, the father recognized his son and ran to meet and embrace him. The son replied, "Father, I have sinned, against God and against you; I am no longer fit to be called your son." The father, however, called for a feast in celebration of his son's safe return. Angered at his father's generosity, the elder son refused to attend the festivities, arguing that he had stayed and worked for his father for years and never disobeyed an order. "'My boy,' said the father, 'you are always with me, and everything I have is yours. How could we help celebrating this happy day? Your brother here was dead and has come back to life, was lost and is found.'"

The originality of Dürer's engraving is found in his choice of the moment to depict. Instead of showing the prodigal son in a brothel or tavern, or discontentedly tending to the swine—both popular subjects in the early fifteenth century[1]—Dürer portrayed him in penance, kneeling with hands clasped and gazing upward, in the middle of a barnyard setting rather than the field mentioned in the original text. The buildings have been identified as existing in Dürer's day on a farm known as the "Himpelshof," near Nuremburg.[2] In addition to this novel focus, Dürer also brilliantly began to master the techniques of engraving, taking them to levels not previously seen. Through varying the shape, length, and depth of the engraved lines, together with adding quick flecks of the burin tool, Dürer successfully captured different textures, such as the pigs' bristles, and the wood, brick, and thatching of the buildings. His achievement in producing a rich vocabulary with engraving tools no doubt began with Dürer's early training as a goldsmith under his father. Though the print demonstrates some problems with anatomy and composition, particularly in the sharp transition between the central figural group and the background, it is nevertheless ambitious in technique and unique in iconography.

The Prodigal Son Amid the Swine evolved from several separate studies and one preliminary compositional drawing. Dürer probably first executed a study in pen and brown ink of only the kneeling figure (W. 146, Boston, Museum of Fine Arts, fig. 11, left).[3] The pose recalls the kneeling apostle from Martin Schongauer's engraving *The Death of the Virgin* (see fig. 20, p. 80). He then worked out the pen-and-black-ink compositional study (W. 145, London, British Museum), which is in fact the only extant preliminary drawing for a print from Dürer's early years.[4] Made in reverse, the drawing indicates that Dürer already knew how he wanted the print to appear. The differences between the drawing and the resulting engraving impart Dürer's gradual resolution of the composition. The

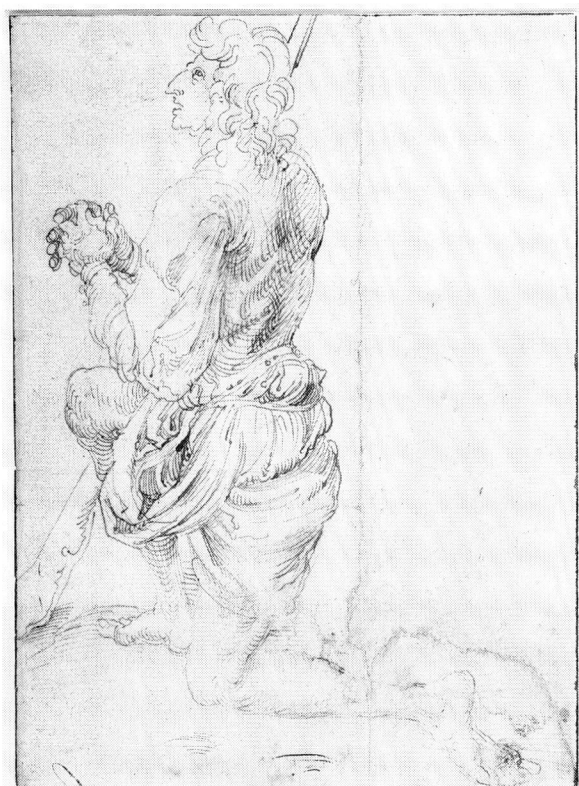

Figure 11 *The Prodigal Son*, c. 1496, Pen and brown Ink on laid paper, Boston, Museum of Fine Arts, 1931 Purchase Fund and Anna Mitchell Richards Fund.

background buildings are placed closer together in the engraving, giving a greater cohesion to the composition. The pigs feeding at the trough are also in closer proximity and five added piglets fill in the foreground.[5] The figure's upright head in the Boston sheet has been replaced with one slightly more tilted and with eyes raised as in the British Museum study. Though the figure of the Prodigal Son is more detailed in the compositional study than in the single figure study, especially in delineating the complicated folds of the drapery, both works reveal Dürer's difficulty in rendering the left foot. He partially resolved this in the final print by hiding the end of the foot behind one of the pigs. The hindquarters of a bull at the left side of the print might have been based on an earlier pen-and-ink study of the animal (W. 239, Chicago, The Art Institute of Chicago).[6]

The Prodigal Son heralded the young Dürer's renown as an engraver throughout Europe, particularly in Italy. It was copied not only by other printmakers, but also by painters of ceramics.[7] Giorgio Vasari, in his monumental *The Lives of the Most Excellent Painters, Sculptors, and Architects* (1568 edition), particularly praised the print. He aptly emphasizes its juxtaposition of emotional content with a rustic setting: "In another [print] he depicted the Prodigal Son, in the guise of a peasant, kneeling with his hands clasped and gazing up to Heaven, while some swine are eating from a trough; and in this work are some most beautiful huts after the manner of German cottages."[8]

Montgomery's superb impression has a distinguished provenance. It was once owned by the eminent French dealer, collector, and connoisseur Pierre Mariette (1634-1716), and by A.P.F. Robert-Dumesnil (1778-1864), one of the leading print scholars and cataloguers of his day. **G.D.J.**

1 Panofsky, p.76, cites two prints, both showing the Prodigal Son attending swine eating from a trough, which were probably sources for Dürer's inspiration. They are found in Bernhard Richel's *Speculum Humanae Salvationes*, published in Basel in 1476, and in *Spiegel menschlicher behaltnis*, published in Speyer in 1478 by Peter Drach.
2 Fritz Zink, "Albrecht Dürer in Nürnberg-Himpfelshof," *Jahrbuch für Landesforschung* 24 (1969), pp. 289-93. The farm later appeared in a panoramic view of Nuremberg published by Glockendon in c. 1570.
3 Strauss 1974, vol. 1, p. 412 (1496/10). See also Washington 1971, p. 30.
4 Strauss 1974, vol. 1, p. 414 (1496/11). See also London, p. 25.
5 Dürer no doubt would have known Martin Schongauer's amusing engraving *Pig Family* (Lehrs, vol. 5, p. 335, no. 91). Also dating from 1496 is Dürer's engraving entitled *The Monstrous Sow of Landseer* (M. 82, B. 95) depicting an eight-footed pig reportedly born March 1, 1496. A pen-and-ink study of a boar, similar to one in the British Museum sheet, is in the Sächsische Landesbibliothek, Dresden (Strauss 1974, vol. 1, p. 408 [1496/8]).
6 Strauss 1974, vol. 1, p. 410 (1496/9). See also Washington 1971, p. 28.
7 George Szábo, "Dürer and Italian Majolica: Four Plates with the Prodigal Son and the Swine," *American Ceramic Circle Bulletin*, 1972-73, pp. 5ff.
8 Vasari, vol. 6, p. 92.

catalogue entry 4

The Cook and His Wife, 1496

Engraving
Laid paper
Meder 85 a; Hollstein 85; Bartsch 84
Watermark: None
Sheet: 108 x 77 mm
Signed, recto: Monogram AD (bottom center)
1999.7.24
Catalogue number 4

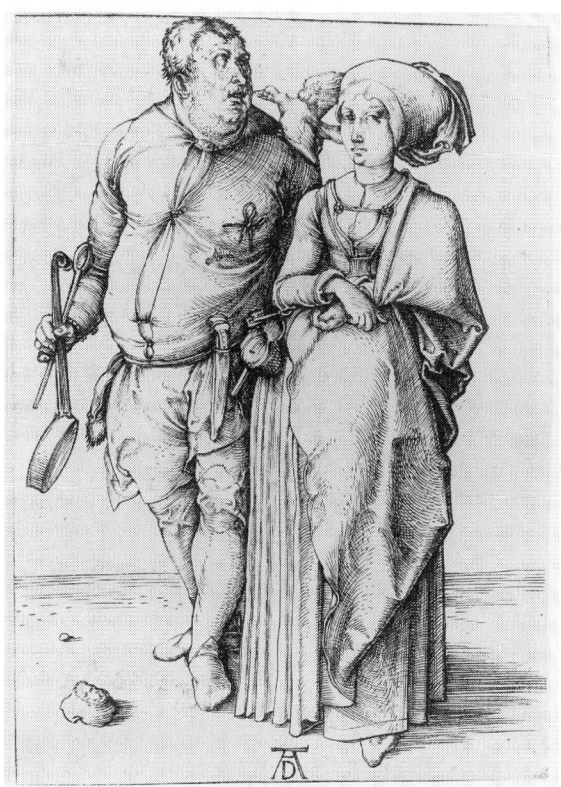

The Cook and His Wife is based upon a popular tale that dates to the fourteenth century. Apparently the story was so well known that the situation described by the print would have been sufficient for an audience in Dürer's time to recognize the reference to this humorous account of a cook, his wife, and their pet magpie. One of Dürer's earliest engravings, this work still displays the significant influence of prints by Martin Schongauer and the Housebook Master. A comparison of this print with earlier single figure engravings by Martin Schongauer shows a relationship in the ways that the figures are composed as silhouettes against vacant backgrounds, while anchored to a clearly delineated ground plane.[1]

The story of the cook and his wife is contained in a manual of comportment titled in German *Ritter von Turn*, with which Dürer was highly familiar, since he had provided forty-five woodcuts for a 1493 edition published by Michael Furter in Basel. Although Dürer did not illustrate this particular story while in Basel, the text was clearly known to him.[2] The tale involves a cook who kept an eel in his fish tank to serve to unexpected guests. His wife and a friend ate the eel, later telling the cook that it had been taken by an otter. However, the couple's talking magpie revealed the truth, and the wife, angered by the betrayal, plucked the bird's head bald. Thereafter, whenever the magpie saw a bald man, he would say, "So, you have been telling about the eel."[3] In his engraving Dürer depicted the bird on the cook's shoulder, whispering into his ear, while the wife shifts her gaze as if to avoid the argument that is certain to follow. The postures of the two figures clearly convey the cook's surprise and the wife's guilty discomfiture.

The purchaser of this work was necessarily a person of greater means than the characters depicted in the print. The engraving process was labor intensive and costly, which precluded most of the working class as a potential market. This engraving of a popular tale indicates that these secular stories had broad appeal, even within the monied classes, and that the humor of the story was widely appreciated. Although Dürer was raised in a lower middle-class family environment, his native intelligence and subsequent success ensured his acceptance into the more sophisticated milieu of the wealthy Nuremberg merchants who, along with the intelligentsia, formed a significant audience for his work.

Engravings such as *The Cook and His Wife* reveal both Dürer's appreciation for the foibles of human behavior and his interest in the dress and customs of the time. The wife, for example, wears the costume of a contemporary German *Hausfrau,* and a number of watercolor drawings by Dürer of similar costumes still exist.[4] The cook's refined *contrapposto* stance, with his left foot delicately pointed, contrasts with his tremendous girth and the shirt straining against his large belly. He rather incongruously mimics the courtly demeanor and refined delicacy of Schongauer's essentially medieval figures.[5] Like many of Dürer's prints depicting members of lower social classes, this engraving gently mocks the lack of polish and sophistication of the figures, most likely in order to address the tastes and prejudices of the print's potential audience among the urban elite.[6] **M.L.A.**

1 See, for example, Schongauer's *A Bishop* (B.61, L.55) and *St. Stephen* (B.49, L.66), illustrated in Alan Shestack, ed., *The Complete Engravings of Martin Schongauer* (New York: Dover Publications, 1969).
2 Stewart, p. 20. The original manual was written by the Chevalier de la Tour Landry in 1371 and was available in England, France, and Germany in various editions. Intended to be instructional, it used tales from various sources to promote virtuous behavior.
3 The story is summarized in Washington 1971, p. 117. This source notes that the subject was identified by Konrad Lange, "Die Atzel, die von dem Aal schwatzt." *ZfbK* 18 (1907), pp. 94-99.
4 Washington 1971, p. 117.
5 Washington 1971, p. 117, also notes the relationship of the woman's dress to a specific costume drawing by Dürer (W.226, Albertina, Vienna) and the cook's resemblance to a kneeling man receiving a painted cross on his forehead at the right of the composition in a Dürer' woodcut from the *Apocalyspe* series, *The Four Angels Holding the Winds* (M. 169, B. 66).
6 Strieder, p. 152.

catalogue entry 5

The Martyrdom of the Ten Thousand, c. 1496

Woodcut
Laid paper
Meder 218 b; Hollstein 218; Bartsch 117
Watermark: None
Sheet: 389 x 287 mm (trimmed at block mark)
Signed, recto: Monogram AD (bottom center)
1999.7.29
Catalogue number 5

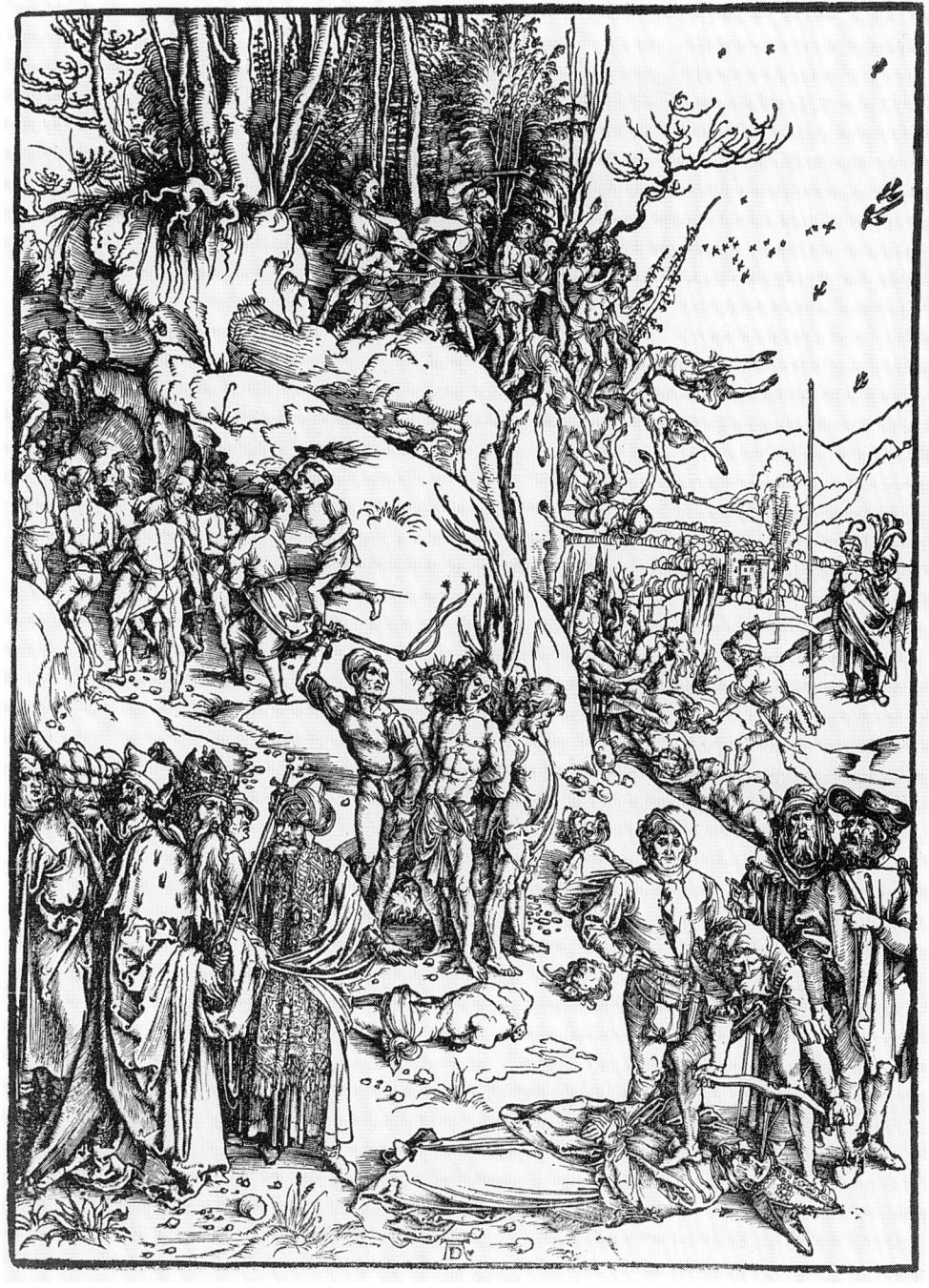

The precise subject of this print is rather unclear, and is perhaps a conflation of two different legends. First appearing in literature during the twelfth century in Germany and Switzerland, the story of the Martyrdom of Ten Thousand Christians was included as a supplement to Jacobus de Voragine's *The Golden Legend.* It is also found in Günther Zainer's *Passional oder der Heiligen Leben,* published in Augsburg in 1472.[1]

The more famous of these stories involves a troop of soldiers, under the command of St. Achatius, who were summoned to stop a rebellion in a region of the Euphrates. The troops were converted to Christianity by an angel who miraculously appeared to them just before the battle in which they proved victorious. However, when the Emperor Hadrian (117-138) learned of his soldiers' adopting a new religion, he reacted with fury and decided to torture the new converts, eventually having them crucified on Mt. Ararat. Dürer's woodcut might also refer to a massacre in Nicodemia of a large number of Christians during the reign of Diocletian (254-313). One of the tortured was Bishop Anthimos, who had his eye drilled out.[2] The figures at the lower left can be identified as Hadrian with several oriental rulers, including King Sapor of Persia. The figure being tortured in the lower right is either Saint Achatius or Bishop Anthimos.

Dürer possibly knew two paintings of this subject. The first, done by the so-called Master of the Saint Augustine Altarpeice, was in the Augustine church in Nuremberg. The other is by the Cologne Master of c. 1420.[3] The grisly detail of the bishop's eye being bored out appears in the Cologne painting. Dürer's multifigured composition is very similar to that of Geertgen tot Sint Jans's painting *Burning of the Relics of St. John the Baptist,* now in Vienna but in Haarlem in the fifteenth century.[4] Typical of Dürer's early woodcuts, *The Martyrdom of Ten the Thousand* is very linear and does not exhibit his later sophistication in the handling of shadows and texture.

The subject of Dürer's woodcut may have been suggested to him by one of his most important patrons, Frederick the Wise, Elector of Saxony.[5] He visited Nuremberg in April 1496 when Dürer painted his portrait. Later, Frederick, who is said to have possessed relics of the ten thousand martyred Christians, commissioned Dürer to do a painting of the theme, the *Martyrdom of Ten Thousand Christians* (1508; Vienna, Kunsthistorisches Museum).[6] The painting is markedly different from the woodcut of a dozen years earlier. The gruesome detail of tortured Saint Achatius (or Bishop Anthimos) disappears and is replaced by a scene recalling Christ's crucifixion on Mt. Calvary. Panofsky notes Dürer's analogy between the Martyrdom of Ten Thousand Christians and the Passion of Christ, perhaps appealing to Frederick's religious sentiments.[7] Appearing almost in the center of the painting are the full-length portraits of the recently deceased Konrad Celtis and of Dürer himself.[8]

A pen-and-ink study for the woodcut's figure with the drill is in Bayonne (W. 167).[9] The original wood block from which the print was made, one of around twenty-five Dürer blocks that still survive, is in the British Museum.[10] **G.D.J.**

1 Anzelewsky, p. 75.
2 Ibid. See also Washington 1971, p. 160.
3 Anzelewsky 1971, pp. 75-76.
4 Panofsky, p. 24. The possibility that Dürer went to the Netherlands in 1490 or 1491 is open to considerable debate. A year and a half of Dürer's life, from the time he left Nuremberg in April 1490 to early 1492 when he arrived in Colmar, is unaccounted for. Though several sixteenth- and seventeenth-century sources state he went to the Netherlands, most recently Hutchison points out that this is not at all certain (Hutchison, pp. 31, 36).
5 Frederick of Saxony (1463-1525), a leading patron of the arts during his day, also founded the University of Wittenberg in 1502 and was a supporter of Martin Luther. In addition to the painted portrait, Dürer engraved Frederick's likeness in 1524 (M.102, B. 102).
6 Anzelewsky, cat no. 105. A copy after Dürer's preliminary drawing of 1507 for the painting is now in the Albertina, Vienna (Strauss 1974, vol. 2, p. 1000 [1507/3]).
7 Panofsky, p.122.
8 Anzelewsky, p. 215.
9 Strauss 1974, vol. 1, p. 422 (1496/15).
10 Strauss 1979, Appendix B, pl. 10.

catalogue entry 6

St. Jerome Penitent in the Wilderness, c. 1496

Engraving
Laid paper
Meder 57 c; Hollstein 57; Bartsch 61
Watermark: City Crest with Three Towers, Meder 46 (top center)
Sheet: 315 x 222 mm (trimmed within plate mark)
Signed, recto: Monogram AD (bottom center)
1999.7.16
Catalogue number 6

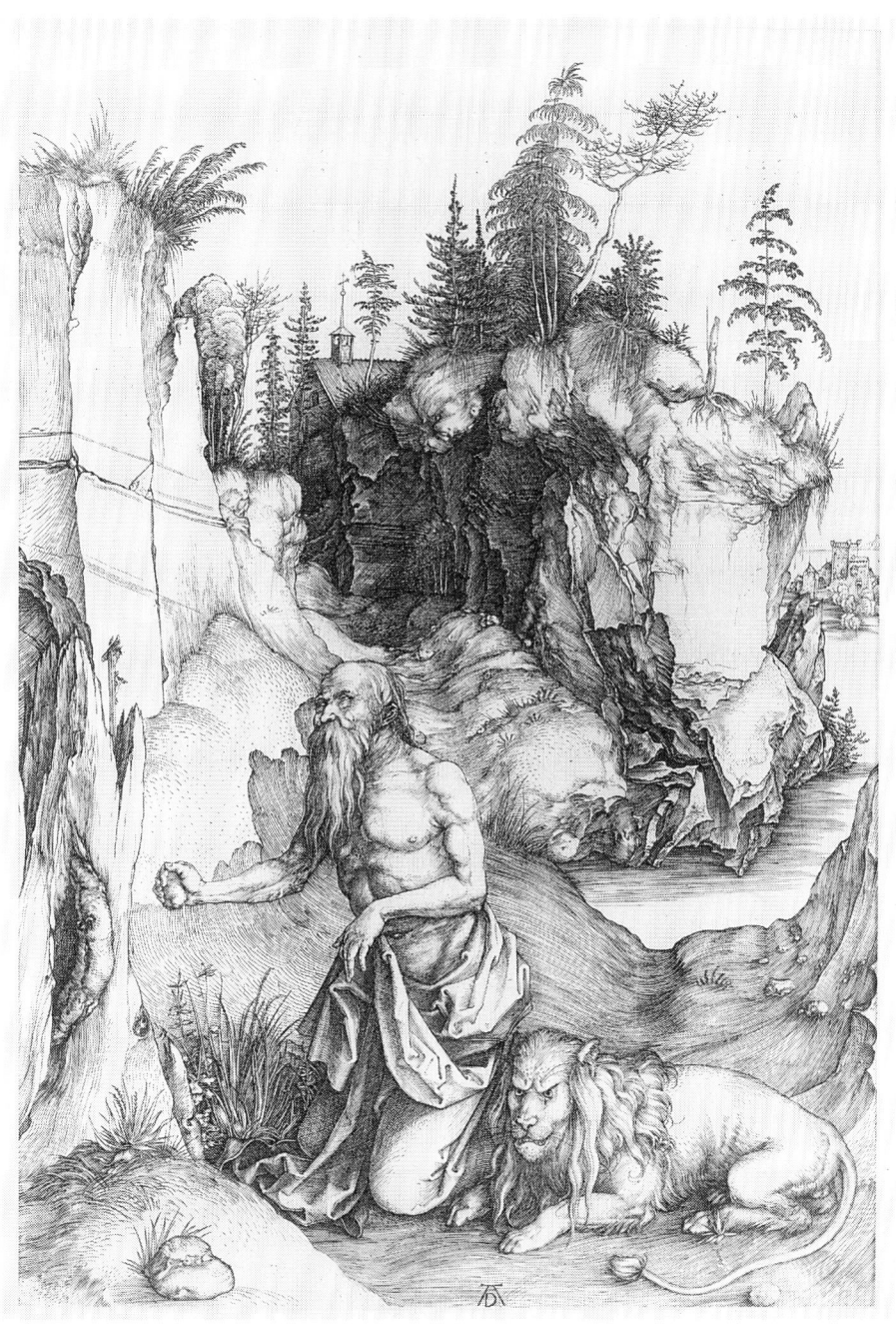

During the Renaissance, St. Jerome, one of the four Latin Church fathers, was also one of the most venerated saints, especially for humanists, and a particularly favored subject for Dürer. In addition to this early engraving, done shortly after the artist returned from Italy in 1495, he also executed the famous engraving of 1514 (fig.6, p. 16), a drypoint dated 1512, and three woodcuts, the first dating from very early in his career in 1492, and the last two done in 1511 (p. 88) and 1512.[1]

Jerome's story is told in Jacobus de Voragine's *The Golden Legend*, a compilation of saints' lives written in the thirteenth century and published in many languages by 1470. He was born to Christian parents around 340 in Dalmatia. Sent to Rome in 363 for a secular education, including instruction in Greek, Hebrew, and Latin, he then traveled to the Holy Lands. Jerome lived as a penitent hermit in the wilderness—the episode depicted in this print. He wrote of this experience, "Often I joined the days with the nights, not stayed from beating my breast until the Lord restored my peace of spirit. I dreaded to enter my cell, as if it were aware of my thoughts, and angered and stern with myself I sought the desert wastes alone; and as Lord is my witness, after all my weeping I sometimes seemed to be among the choir of angels."[2] Afterwards he was called to Rome by Pope Damasus to translate the Bible into Latin (known as the Vulgate because of its being written in the common, or vulgar, language of the people). The saint died in 420 in Bethlehem where he had founded a monastery.

St. Jerome is frequently depicted with a lion after a story that related how he pulled a thorn from the animal's paw and thereby gained a constant companion.[3] As in this print, the penitent Jerome is customarily shown kneeling at the foot of a crucifix and striking himself in reproach with a rock. Dürer undoubtedly was familiar with fifteenth-century book illustrations of the saint, especially from a German edition of *The Golden Legend* published in Nuremberg in 1488 by the artist's godfather, Anton Koberger.[4] While Northern iconography usually shows Jerome either at work in his study or removing the thorn from the lion's paw, Panofsky notes that depictions of the penitent saint originated and became popular in Italy.[5] In addition to the Southern iconography, Dürer's print also recalls in style and compositional elements Italian paintings by artists such as Andrea Mantegna (1431-1506), Giovanni Bellini (c.1427-1516), and Cima da Conegliano (1459/60-1517/18).[6] The works by these artists would still have been fresh in Dürer's mind after returning from Italy in the spring of 1495.

One of the most striking aspects of this fairly large engraving is the rugged landscape setting. Hidden in large rocky outcrops from which lush vegetation grows is a small church complete with steeple and cross. A castle on the banks of a body of water is seen on the horizon at the far right. Dürer, as was his custom, looked to his store of nature drawings for this detailed background. Two stunning watercolors that probably served as references (W. 108 and 109, formerly Bremen Kunsthalle) are inscribed in the artist's hand "steinpruch" or quarry.[7] The site in these drawings has been identified as the Schmausenbuck quarry, located outside Nuremberg.[8] Rainer Schoch has written that these rock formations provide a theological metaphor as they symbolize the foundation of the Christian Church, which is underscored by Durer's inclusion of the small church built on the rocky gorge in the center.[9] The various trees growing on the cliff above Jerome's head might also be symbolic. As related in *The Golden Legend*, the Latin version of the saint's name, Hieronymous, was derived from *gerar* (holy) and *nemus* (wood).[10] The stump of the dead tree might also refer to the Tree of Life from the Garden of Eden, which became the Tree of Death after the fall of man. Supposedly Christ's cross was hewn from the wood of this tree.[11] Panofsky aptly likens this print to *The Prodigal Son* (p. 30). Both show the main figure kneeling in penitence before what might be considered independent landscape studies and in both works the emotional aspect of the figures prevails.[12] Hutchison draws a possible parallel between these "penitential" prints and of the upcoming Holy Year of the Papal Jubilee in 1500. Special indulgences were given for those who visited pilgrimage shrines in a spirit of repentance.[13]

Like so many of Dürer's prints, *St. Jerome in the Wilderness* became extremely popular both in the North and in Italy soon after it was completed. Held in high esteem as a devotional image, the engraving was copied by other printmakers.[14] Dürer himself used the print as a basis for a painting done in 1496/98.[15] There is a unique first state of the print (Melbourne, Australia, National Gallery of Victoria) before Dürer added several dots and horizontal lines in the white space to the right of the stone in the left corner.[16] **G.D.J.**

1. The other St. Jerome prints are *St. Jerome in His Study* (1492), woodcut (M. 227), the earliest print that can be attributed to Dürer; *St. Jerome in His Cell* (1511), woodcut (M. 228, B. 114, cat. no. 27); *St. Jerome in a Cave* (1512), woodcut (M. 229, B.113); *St. Jerome by a Pollard Willow* (1512), drypoint (M. 58, B. 59); and *St. Jerome in His Study* (1514), engraving (M. 59, B. 98, cat. no. 30).
2. The Golden Legend, vol. 2, p. 589.
3. Dürer portrayed Jerome extracting the thorn from the lion's paw in his first woodcut of the saint, done in 1492 as a title page for the book *Epistolare Beati Hieronymi*, published by Nicholas Kessler in Basel (M. 227). See also Washington 1971, pp. 348-49.
4. Schoch et al. 2001, p. 39.
5. Panofsky, p. 77.
6. Isolde Lübbeke in Venice, Palazzo Grassi, *Renaissance Venice and the North: Crosscurrents in the Time of Bellini, Dürer, and Titian* (Milan: Bompiani, 1999), p. 270, cat. no. 40. For examples of Venetian paintings of St. Jerome, see cat. nos. 121 (Giovanni Bellini) and 39 (Conegliano).
7. Walter Strauss 1974, vol. 1, pp. 362-365, (1495/51 and 1495/52). Related to these two studies is the pen-and-ink drawing of a quarry entrance (W. 106, Bayonne, Musée Bonnat) (1495/53).
8. Friedrich Winkler, ed., *Zeichnungen von Albrecht Dürer in Nachbildungen*, vol. 7 (Berlin, 1929), no. 661.
9. Schoch et al., p. 30. For an interesting study on the anthropomorphic qualities of Dürer's art, including the quarry studies and the rock forms in *St. Jerome Penitent in the Wilderness*, see Karl Möseneder, "Blickende Dinger: Anthropomorphes bei Albrecht Dürer," *Pantheon* 44 (1986), pp. 15-23.
10. The Golden Legend, vol. 2, p. 587.
11. Amsterdam, Rijksmuseum, and London, British Museum, *Rembrandt the Printmaker*, text by Erik Hinterding et al. (Amsterdam: Waanders Publishers, 2000), p. 249.
12. Panofsky, p. 77.
13. Hutchison, p. 64.
14. Copies include one in reverse by Zoan Andrea (Hind, vol. 5, p. 68, no. 20); and one in the same direction by Hieronymus Hopfer (Hollstein, vol. 15, p. 198, no. 22).
15. Anzelewsky 1971, p. 122, no. 14.
16. Hollstein, vol. 7, p. 48, no. 57.

The Four Horsemen of the Apocalypse, 1498

From the Latin edition (1511) of the *Apocalypse*
Woodcut
Heavy laid paper
Meder 167; Hollstein 167; Bartsch 64
Watermark: Castle, Meder 259 (center)
Sheet: 397 x 280 mm (trimmed at block mark)
Signed, recto: Monogram AD (bottom center)
1991.3.1
Catalogue number 7

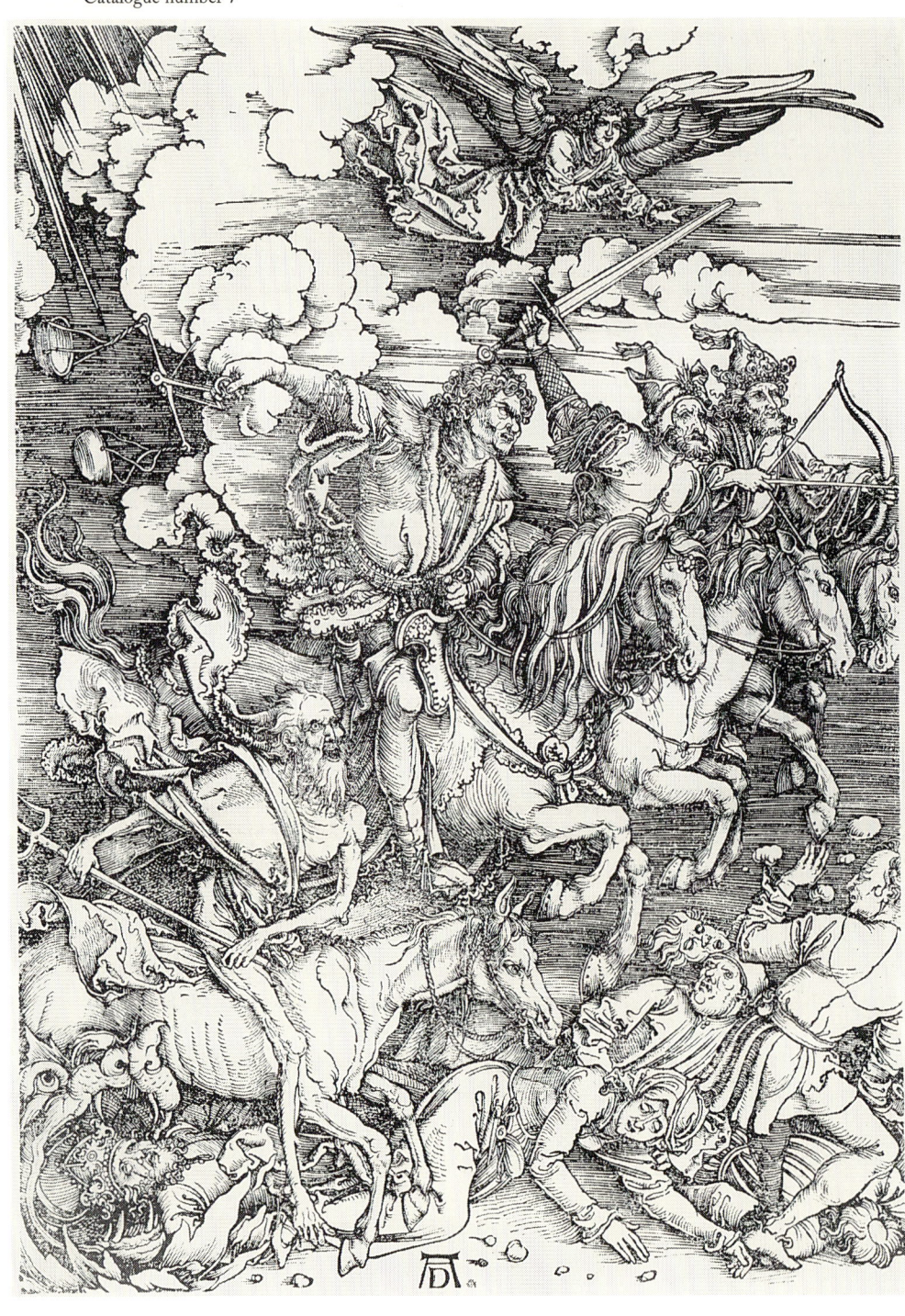

And I saw when the Lamb opened one of the seals, and I heard, as it were the noise of thunder, one of the four beasts saying, Come and see. And I saw, and behold a white horse: and he that sat on him had a bow; and a crown was given unto him: and he went forth conquering, and to conquer. And when he opened the second seal, I heard the second beast say, Come and see. And there went out another horse that was red: and power was given to him that sat thereon to take peace from the earth, and that they should kill one another: and there was given unto him a great sword. And when he had opened the third seal, I heard the third beast say, Come and see. And I beheld, and lo a black horse; and he that sat on him has a pair of balances in his hand. And I heard a voice in the midst of four beasts say, A measure of wheat for a penny, and three measures of barley for a penny and see thou hurt not the oil and wine. And when he had opened the fourth seal, I heard the voice of the forth beast say, Come and see. And I looked, and behold a pale horse: and his name that sat on him was Death and Hell followed with him. And power was given unto them over the fourth part of the earth, to kill with sword, and with hunger, and with death, and with the beasts of the earth (Revelation 6: 1-8).

Perhaps the best-known woodcut from Dürer's *Apocalypse* series, *The Four Horsemen of the Apocalypse* illustrates the third vision in the book of Revelation. Four horsemen of destruction are released from their seals and unleashed upon the world. The first rider, wearing a crown and holding a bow and arrow, is the Conqueror; the second rider, brandishing a sword, symbolizes War; followed by Famine, who carries the scales of justice; and lastly, the fourth horseman, Death, riding a "pale horse." In the lower left corner, the Mouth of Hell opens to devour a crowned ruler. The horsemen trample a cross section of society, including members of the middle class and the peasantry. In earlier representations of this vision, the horsemen are usually depicted separately.[1] However, by uniting the four figures in one formation as they ferociously gallop across the earth, Dürer has created a frighteningly memorable image fitting the awe-inspiring apocalyptic story.

One of the last prints executed in the series, done just prior to its initial publication in 1498, *The Four Horsemen* shows Dürer's mature woodcut technique. By skillfully varying the degree and shape of the lines, he achieved a great range of tonal values. While earlier practitioners of the woodcut primarily thought of the medium as a way to provide an outline drawing to be hand-colored, Dürer demonstrated that "color" can be achieved by the line and design alone. This virtuosity in printmaking was praised by Erasmus of Rotterdam, who compared Dürer to the famed ancient painter Apelles, even rating Dürer above the classical master because he could accomplish in black and white what Apelles did in color.[2]

The format of the *Apocalypse* prints, large, full-page illustrations with text on the reverse, is as unprecedented as the technique.[3] Because Dürer did not conceive of the woodcuts as literal illustrations but as a self-contained series, the prints and the text soon fall out of synchronization. Such full-page prints were not even attempted in the most ambitious publication project prior to Dürer, the so-called *Nuremberg Chronicle*.[4] Also noteworthy is the fact that the *Apocalypse* is the first illustrated book to be planned, executed, and published solely by the artist.

The Montgomery impression comes from a printing after the third edition (in Latin) published in 1511. **G.D.J.**

---

1 Noted in Strauss 1979, p. 186.
2 Erasmus's passage is cited in Panofsky, p. 44.
3 For the nature of book illustration prior to Durer's *Apocalypse*, see Cynthia A. Hall, "Before the *Apocalypse*: German Prints and Illustrated Books, 1450 – 1500," Harvard University Art Museums Bulletin 4, 2 (Spring 1996), pp. 9-25.
4 Appearing in 1493, this work was published by Dürer's godfather, Anton Koberger, and it is thought that the young artist might have designed some of the prints. See Panofsky, p. 20.

catalogue entry 8

The Beast with Two Horns Like a Lamb, 1496-97

From the Latin edition (1511) of the *Apocalypse*
Woodcut
Heavy laid paper
Meder 175; Hollstein 175; Bartsch 74
Watermark: Flower with Triangle, Meder 127 (center right)
Sheet: 389 x 277 mm (trimmed to the block mark)
Signed, recto: Monogram AD (bottom center)
1970.15
Catalogue number 8

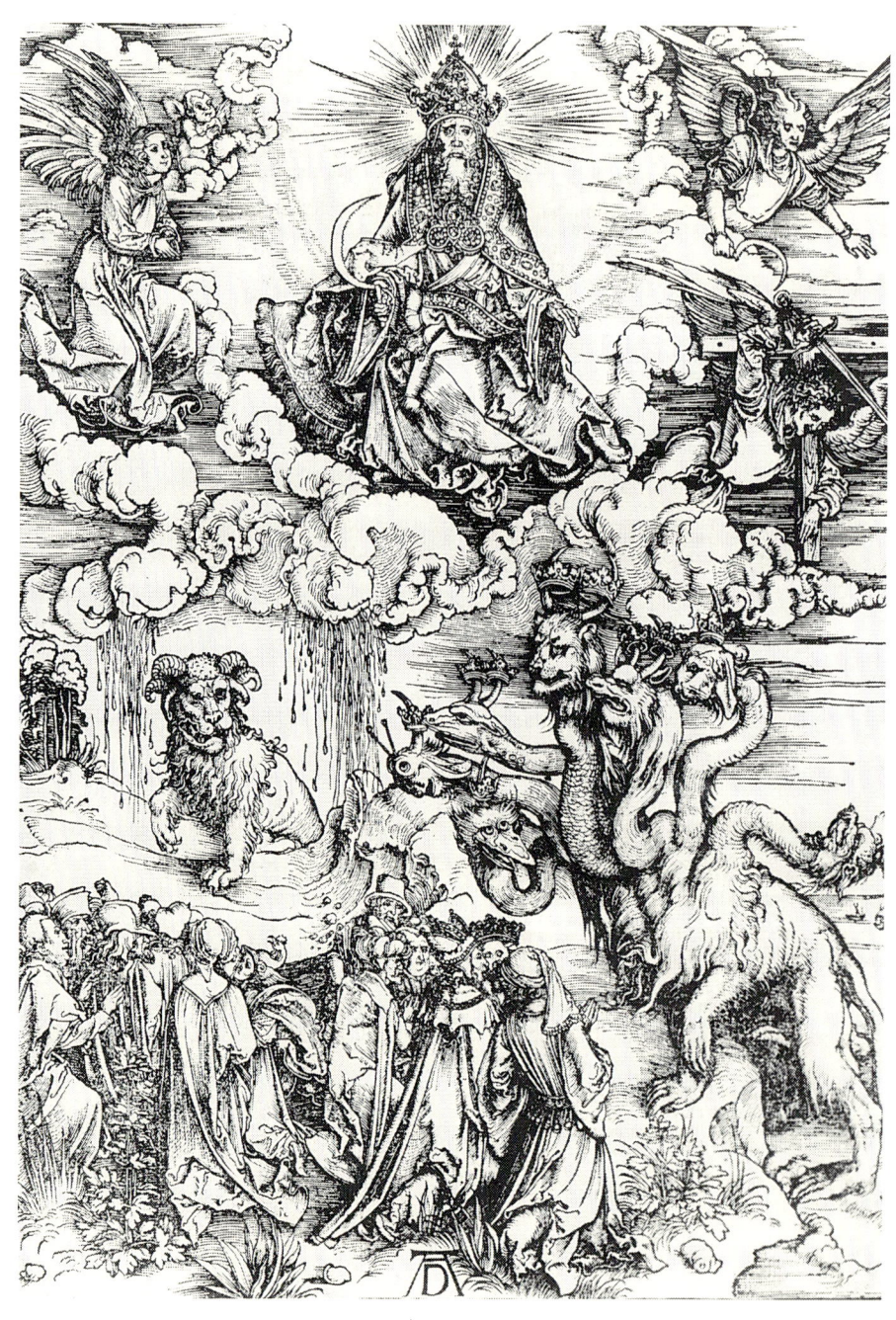

Then out of the sea I saw a beast rising. It had ten horns and seven heads. On its horns were ten diadems, and on each head a blasphemous name. The beast I saw was like a leopard, but its feet were like a bear's and its mouth like a lion's mouth. . . . One of its heads appeared to have received a death blow; but the mortal wound was healed. The whole world went after the beast in wondering admiration. . . . Then I saw another beast, which came up out of the earth; it had two horns like a lamb's, but spoke like a dragon. It wielded all the authority of the first beast in its presence, and made the earth and its inhabitants worship this first beast, whose mortal wound had been healed (Revelation 13:1-13; 14:14-18).

The Beast with Two Horns Like a Lamb is one of fifteen woodcuts that Dürer designed and published in a printed volume known as the *Apocalypse* that illustrates the *Revelation of St. John*. The book was first published in German and Latin editions in 1498; this specific impression was printed in 1511 when Dürer published a third edition, in Latin only. He was twenty-four years old and recently returned from his first trip to Italy, when he embarked on this venture—one of the most influential publishing projects undertaken up to that time. By signing the woodcuts in the block and publishing them under his own name, he became the first artist to act independently as the publisher of a book on this scale. The importance of the illustrations for *Apocalypse* cannot be overstated: for the artist, they represented a tremendous evolution in both originality and quality of design, forming the basis of his international reputation of as a master of printmaking.

The impetus and inspiration for this groundbreaking achievement likely lay in Dürer's experiences as an apprentice in the workshop of painter Michael Wolgemut, as well as his relationship with one of Nuremberg's premier printers, Anton Koberger. It was in Wolgemut's workshop (1486-1489) that Dürer participated in a key transition in art-making of the era in which panel painters began to exploit the potential of the woodcut to capture and disseminate their compositions to a broader audience.[1] Painters such as Wolgemut sought to transfer the subtle variations of light, shadow, and texture in painting to a print medium that had been considered crude. They began to employ more sophisticated cutting techniques to achieve more intricate arrangements of line and shape, as well as more elaborate patterns of hatching to suggest variations in tone. Dürer would have become familiar with the cutting technique that produced these more sophisticated images.

In addition to his skill as an artist, Dürer had the good fortune to be the godson of one of Germany's most important printers. Anton Koberger began his career in Nuremberg as a goldsmith like Dürer's father. In 1471 Koberger gave up his original profession to pursue printing, and quickly became so successful that he opened branch offices in Paris, Lyon, and Budapest, as well as in Leipzig, Regensburg, Breslau, and Frankfurt. When Dürer elected to self-publish his *Apocalypse*, Koberger placed his typefaces and printing equipment at his godson's disposal.[2]

The text of Revelation is a series of independent visions of the end of the world. Dürer's compositions capture this visionary imagery with extraordinarily powerful forms that match the prophetic language of the gospel. This plate, the eleventh in the series of fourteen visions, illustrates the seven-headed monster rising from the sea and the lion-like beast with lamb's horns coming up from the earth. A cross-section of mankind—princes with crowns as well as common folk—drop to their knees in fear at the appearance of these harbingers of disaster. A second register of figures appears in the sky with God the Father holding a scythe, accompanied by angels, two of whom also carry instruments of retribution.

Although no evidence exists to prove that Dürer cut the woodblocks for *Apocalypse* himself, many scholars believe that the tremendous expressive power of the images is owed not only to his innate imagination, but also to his ability to translate this vision to the block.[3] Social and political changes that were occurring in 1498 were heightened by the sense of foreboding that accompanied the approaching millennium year of 1500. Dürer added to the glory of the biblical text a sense of anticipation engendered by a world and culture being transformed. **M.L.A.**

1 Panofsky, p. 18. While Dürer was in the workshop, Wolgemut published *Schatzbehalter* (1491), a collection of sermons by Stephan Fridolin, and *The Nuremberg Chronicle* (1493) by the humanist author Hartmann Schedel. Each was illustrated with numerous woodcuts provided by the workshop, some perhaps by Dürer himself.
2 Hutchison, p. 17.
3 Washington 1971, p. 165. The usual procedure in Germany for the printing of woodcuts entailed an artist's designing the composition, which was then transferred to a prepared block and cut by a *Formschneider*, or professional woodblock cutter. For further description of the established process, see Landau and Parshall, p. 22, who largely disagree with the assessment that Dürer carved his own blocks. See pp. 172-174.

catalogue entry 9

The Angel with the Key to the Bottomless Pit, 1496-97

From the German edition (1498) of the *Apocalypse*
Woodcut
Heavy laid paper
Meder 178; Hollstein 178; Bartsch 75
Watermark: None
Sheet: 394 x 283 mm (trimmed at block mark)
Signed, recto: Monogram AD (bottom center)
1972.81
Catalogue number 9

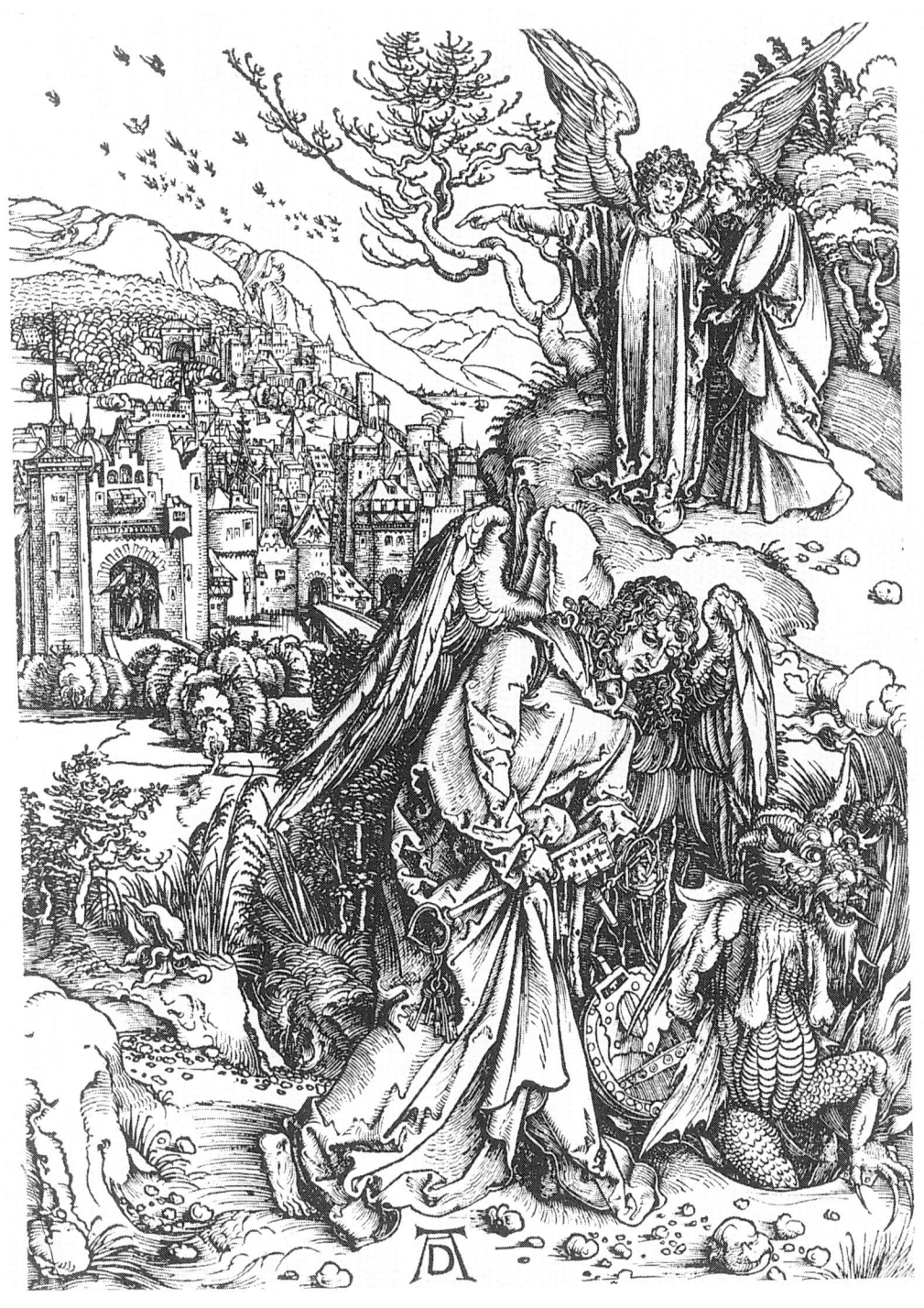

Then I saw an angel coming down from heaven with the key of the abyss and a great chain in his hand. He seized the dragon, that serpent of old, the Devil or Satan, and chained him up for a thousand years; he threw him into the abyss, shutting and sealing it over him…(Revelation 20:1-3).

Then one of the seven angels that held the seven bowls full of the seven last plagues came and spoke to me and said, "Come, and I will show you the bride, the wife of the Lamb." So in the Spirit he carried me away to a great high mountain, and showed me the holy city of Jerusalem coming down out of heaven from God. … It had a great high wall, with twelve gates, at which were twelve angels. … The city was built as a square, and was a wide as it was long. … The wall was built of jasper; while the city itself was of pure gold, bright as clear glass…(Revelation 21: 9-21).

The Angel with the Key to the Bottomless Pit illustrates the culminating vision of the author of the biblical text Revelation. Montgomery's impression is from the German-language edition of 1498. The two editions of 1498 (in Latin and in German) were the first to be published by an artist, featuring his own work and under his authority.[1] The scope and complexity of Dürer's images for this project far surpassed that of any previously published book illustrations, and established his reputation internationally as one of the most important printmakers of his era.

As a native of Nuremberg, Dürer lived in the birthplace of the printing tradition. The technology of printing with cast, movable type rapidly developed in the city, which also had flourishing industries in metalwork and papermaking.[2] Book publishing, combined with the presence of an important group of humanist thinkers, created an atmosphere that encouraged intellectual and educational innovation. Thus the elements favorable to the creation and printing of original illustrated books were in place by the time that Dürer, a young man of twenty-four, elected to publish this series of works. His experience as an apprentice in the workshop of painter Michael Wolgemut (1486-1489), and his relationship as his godchild with the prominent Nuremberg printer Anton Koberger virtually assured that Dürer would be successful in his first major project as a publisher.[3]

The artist's designs for *Apocalypse* were highly original, though inspired by a series of printed works that begin with manuscripts dating back hundreds of years. Dürer was familiar with earlier woodcut illustrations of the bible, and may have been directly influenced by those of the Cologne Bible (ca. 1479), which was reprinted by Koberger in 1483. He also seems to have been aware of some variants of the Cologne illustrations published in 1485 by Johann Grüninger in Strasbourg.[4]

Scholars have consistently noted that Dürer's motivation for creating the series is unknown, but the period in which the images were created seems to imbue them with particular contemporary relevance.[5] The book of Revelation comprises a series of visions and symbols that reveals the high level of anxiety current when it was written—at a time of persecutions of Jews and Christians by the Roman Empire.[6] In 1498 when Dürer began to create his *Apocalypse* images, the millennial year of 1500 was approaching and the political stresses within the Catholic Church that eventually led to the Reformation were growing, particularly in Northern Europe. Dürer succeeded in translating the feverish intensity of the text into visual imagery that forsakes the logical progression of narrative to capture the passionate and prophetic imaginings of a religious zealot. These intense descriptions of the destruction of mankind, the banishing of evil, and the ultimate victory of God Almighty reflected the anxiety of a society evolving from the spiritual orthodoxy of the medieval world to the science and humanism of the Renaissance.

The Angel with the Key to the Bottomless Pit, the final print in the series, depicts the triumph of good over evil in the bottom register, and the founding of the New Jerusalem, as shown to St. John by an angel, in the upper zone. Satan, in the form of a dragon in chains, is literally cast into a pit beneath the earth by an angel who holds a key with which he will imprison the Devil in darkness. A sense of the momentous finality of this action, which is mirrored in surrounding nature, is conveyed through the curving contours of drapery, rocks, flora, and even the locks of the angel's flowing hair.

The simultaneous victorious ascendancy of God is reinforced by the grand expanse of the New Jerusalem in the top left, depicted as a walled German city crowned with a flock of birds that sail overhead. These birds, as well as the spread wings of the angel and the tree that extends beyond his right hand, suggest the powerful wind of change that sweeps away the past and ushers in the earthly reign of God. **M.L.A.**

1 Dürer reprinted *Apocalypse* in 1511, but only with the Latin text.
2 Strieder, p. 52.
3 See cat. entry 8 and Landau and Parshall, p. 174.
4 Washington 1971, p. 165.
5 Various scholars' interpretations are summarized in Jan Bialostocki, *Dürer and His Critics, 1500-1971* (Baden-Baden: Verlag Valentin Koerner, 1986), pp. 265-88. The series has been extensively analyzed as a veiled commentary by Dürer on the corruption in the Roman Catholic Church, and particularly the political conflicts between the Church hierarchy and the secular rulers of Northern Europe.
6 The Roman persecution of the Jews and Christians at the time of Nero was of legendary proportions, and led to an uprising in Jewish Palestine that resulted in the death of Romans and Roman sympathizers there. In revenge for this killing, the Romans massacred 20,000 people in Caesarea in one day. In addition, earthquakes, famine, and pestilence all combined to create an atmosphere of great despair and the fear of Armageddon.

The Agony in the Garden, 1496-97

From the edition of the *Large Passion* after 1511 (without text)
Woodcut
Heavy laid paper
Meder 115; Hollstein 115; Bartsch 6
Watermark: None
Sheet: 389 x 283 mm (trimmed at block mark)
Signed, recto: Monogram AD (bottom center)
1986.1
Catalogue number 10

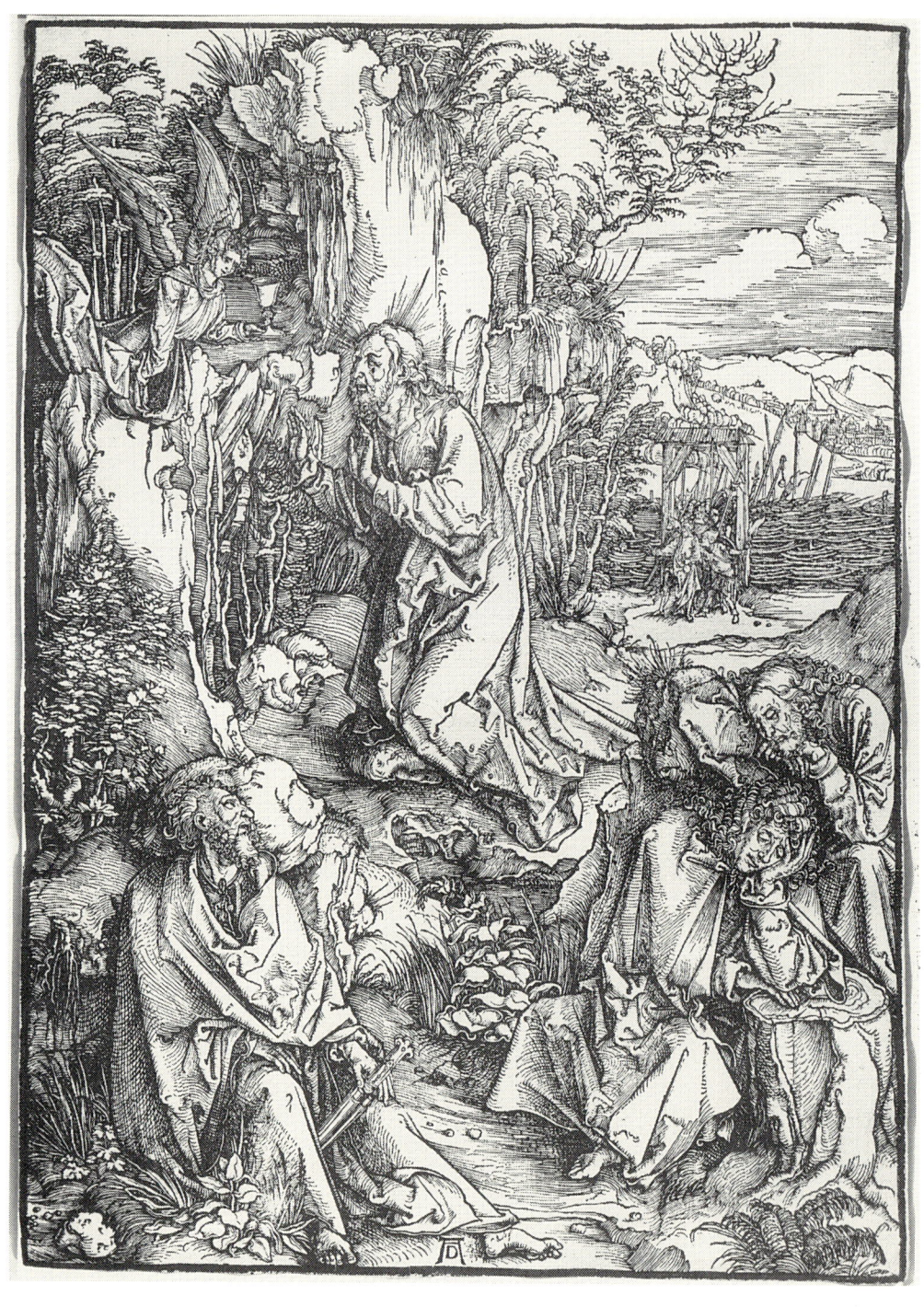

Dürer expressed a life-long interest in the Passion of Christ, executing six series on the subject in all. In addition to the *Large Passion*, from which this print comes, the others are the *Albertina Passion* (c. 1494), the *Green Passion* (1504), the *Engraved Passion* (1507-1513), the *Small Woodcut Passion* (1509-1511), and the *Oblong Passion* (1520-24).[1] The first seven prints from the *Large Passion* were done in the years 1496-99 and issued as single sheets. Dürer completed the series in 1510, when he depicted four remaining scenes. In 1511 he added a title page (p. 85) and published the series with a text in Latin by Benedictus Chelidonius. Dürer also published at this time the completed *Life of the Virgin* and reissued the *Apocalypse* of 1498. The three series, known collectively as "die grossen Bücher" (the large books), were often bound together.

The story of Christ's Agony in the Garden is recorded in the gospels of Matthew (26: 36-46), Mark (14: 32-42), and Luke (22: 39-46). After the Last Supper, Christ, together with Peter, John, and James, went to the Garden of Gethsemane on the Mount of Olives, outside Jerusalem. Luke writes that Christ,

> *withdrew from them about a stone's throw, knelt down, and began to pray: "Father, if it be thy will, take this cup away from me. Yet not my will but thine be done." And now there appeared to him an angel from heaven bringing him strength, and in anguish of spirit he prayed the more urgently; and his sweat was like clots of blood falling to the ground. When he rose from prayer and came to the disciples he found them asleep, worn out by grief. "Why are you sleeping?" he said. "Rise and pray that you may be spared the test"* (22: 41-46).

Panofsky rightly states that *The Agony in the Garden*, together with *The Flagellation* (p. 50) and the *Deposition* (M. 123, B. 12), are the earliest of the woodcuts from the *Large Passion*.[2] The composition of the first is crowded with a wealth of details, especially in the profusion of vegetation. In fact, the plants and rock formations are very similar to those in the 1496 *St. Jerome Penitent in the Wilderness* (p. 37). For Dürer, nature's details not only revealed the glory of God, but they also provided a basis for art. He writes, "Depart not from Nature … for Art is rooted in Nature, and whoever can pull it out, has it."[3] The later prints from the *Large Passion* display a greater unity with fewer details. In *The Agony in the Garden*, Dürer's woodcutting technique has yet to be refined. The thick, dark lines scarcely vary in width. Dürer has not quite discovered how to create the gray half-tones that are seen in his woodcuts after 1510, such as in the *Death of the Virgin* (p. 78). The expressive, linear style of the *Agony* is similar instead to the woodcuts from the *Apocalypse* series executed at this same time (see pp. 40, 42 and 45). Finally, there is an awkward shift between the foreground figures, Christ in the center, Peter at the left, and John and James at the right, and the background where Judas and the soldiers enter through the garden gate.

As Larry Silver has recently shown, *The Agony in the Garden* was a favorite subject in art at this time,[4] appearing not only in paintings and prints, but in sculpture. Silver connects the subject's popularity in Nuremberg with local devotions related to this event on the Mount of Olives.[5] All were associated with the worshipper's imitation of Christ's anguish and suffering. **G.D.J.**

---

1 Dürer's personal interest and evolving exploration in depicting Christ's Passion was a subject of a recent exhibition: Cambridge, Massachusetts, Harvard University Art Museums, *Dürer's Passions*, text by Jordan Kantor (Cambridge, 2000). See also Angela Hass, "Two Devotional Manuals by Albrecht Dürer: The Small Passion and the Engraved Passion." *Iconography, Context and Spirituality, Zeitschrift für Kunstgeschichte* 2 (2000), pp. 169-230.
2 Panofsky, p. 60.
3 Cited in Hutchison, p. 69.
4 Larry Silver, "The Influence of Anxiety: The Agony in the Garden as Artistic Theme in the Era of Dürer," *Umění. Bimonthly of the Institute for Art History of the Academy of Sciences of the Czech Republic* 45 (1997), pp. 420-29.
5 Ibid., pp. 421-22.

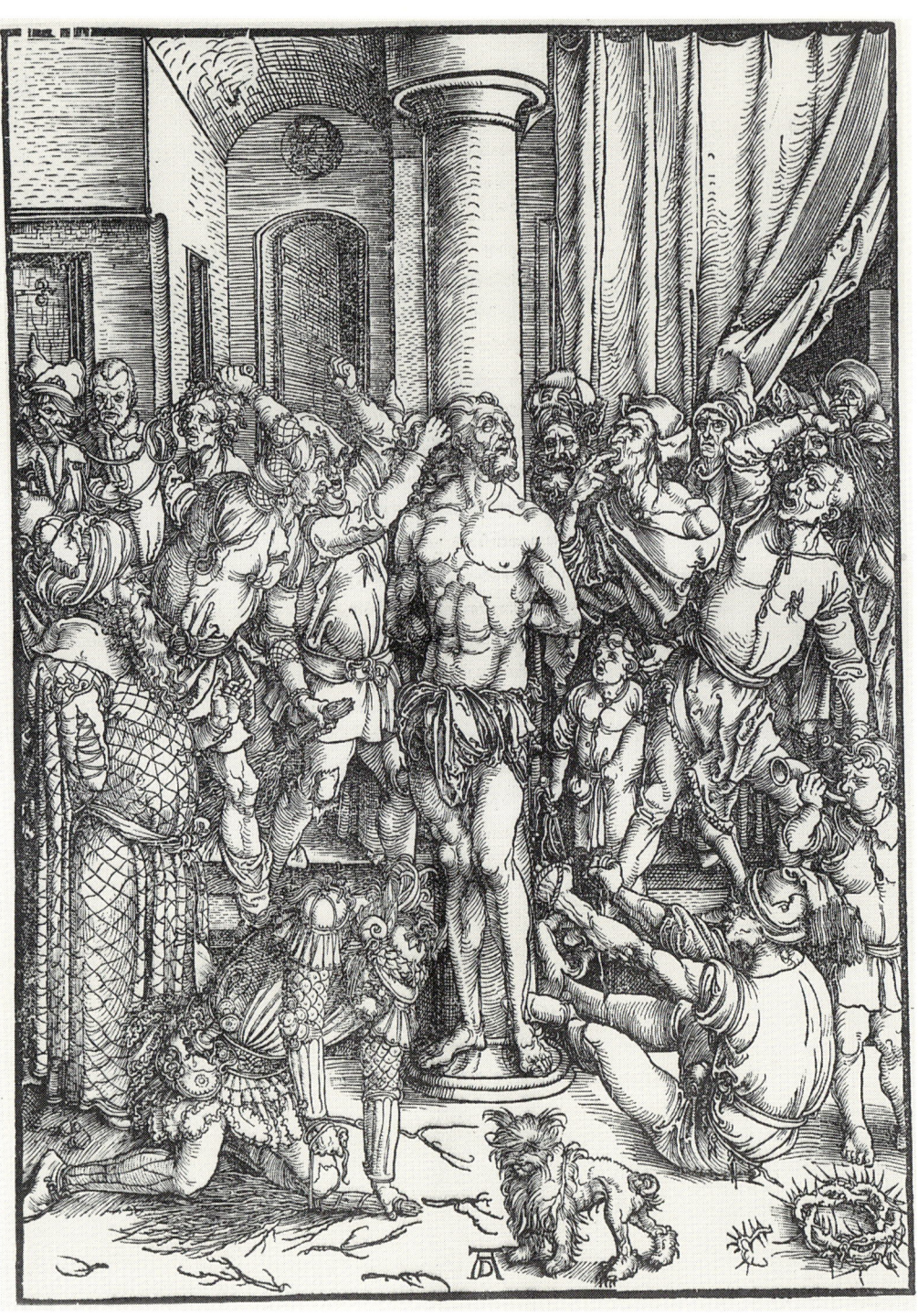

catalogue entry 11

The Flagellation, 1496-97

From the edition of the *Large Passion* after 1511
Woodcut
Heavy laid paper
Watermark: None
Meder 117; Hollstein 117; Bartsch 8
Sheet: 403 x 292 mm (trimmed at block mark)
Signed, recto: Monogram AD (bottom center)
1981.20.2
Catalogue number 11

In his unpublished treatise on painting, Dürer boldly states that illustrating Christ's Passion was one of the main purposes of art: "For the art of painting is employed in the service of the church and by it the sufferings of Christ are set forth."[1] Dürer was affirming the central belief of the Christian Church: Through his suffering of the Passion and his death, Christ redeemed mankind from the original sin brought about by the fall of Adam and Eve.[2]

Christ's flagellation is recorded in the gospels of Matthew (27: 26), Mark (15: 15), and John (19: 1-3), who writes:

"Pilate now took Jesus and had him flogged; and the soldiers plaited a crown of thorns and placed it on his head, and robed him in a purple cloak. Then time after time they came up to him, crying, "Hail, King of the Jews!" and struck him on the face." As in *The Agony in the Garden* (p. 48), *The Flagellation* is one of the earliest prints Dürer executed for the *Large Passion*. He encountered some difficulty in depicting the crowd of people, which is divided into two levels. Some proportions are awkward: Pilate, crowned with a turban and standing in the front at left, is dwarfed by the monumental figure of Christ, who is tied to a column. The spectators on the upper level appear to be a head shorter than Christ. However, Dürer's attention to the details helps to emphasize the emotional impact of the scene. There are a wide variety of facial types and dress. Dürer did not generalize the facial features and his depictions of the figures approach portraiture. A dog, staring directly out at the viewer, adjacent to the artist's monogram, adds an element of humor to the grim narrative. The boy blowing a horn at the far right is based on Dürer's drawing after Mantegna's *Battle of the Sea Gods* (W. 60 Vienna, Albertina).[3]

Dürer's woodblocks for the *Large Passion* enjoyed a long life after the 1511 edition, to which the Montgomery impression belongs. There were frequent reprintings during the course of the sixteenth century and in 1675 they came into the possession of the Augsburg publisher Jacob Koppmayer. He made more reprints, which further deteriorated the blocks. While the block for *The Flagellation* was damaged early on, its reuse caused additional problems, such as breaks in the border and lost areas in the shading.[4] **G.D.J.**

1 Cited in William Martin Conway, trans., *The Literary Remains of Albrecht Dürer* (Cambridge: Cambridge University Press, 1889), p. 196. See also Cambridge, p. 17
2 Cambridge, p. 16
3 Strauss 1979, p. 144. For Dürer's drawings, see Strauss 1974, vol. 1, p. 244 (1494/13).
4 Boston 1971, p. 66.

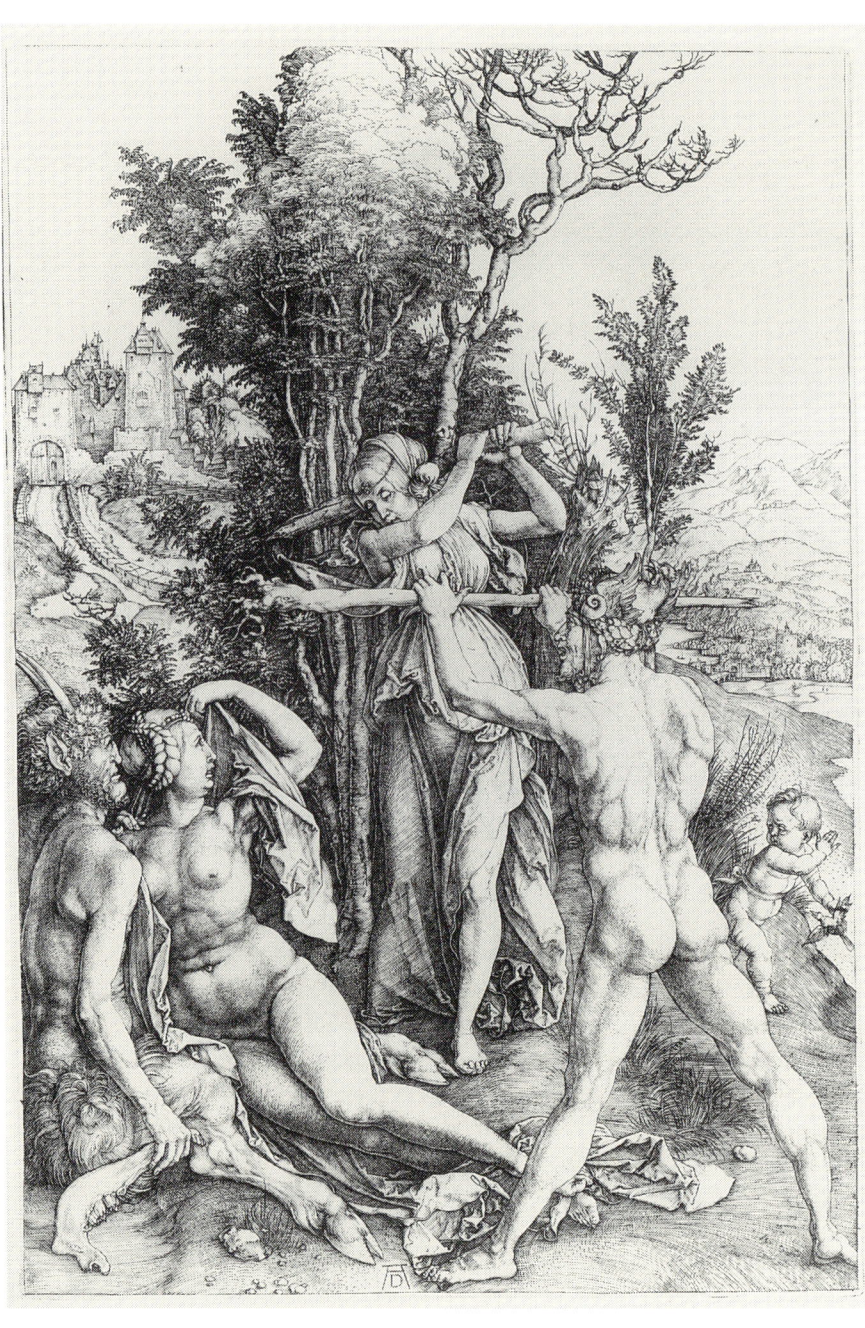

catalogue entry 12

Hercules at the Crossroads (Jealousy), 1498

Engraving
Laid paper
Meder 63 second state, a-b; Hollstein 63; Bartsch 73
Watermark: Small Jug, Meder 158 (top center)
Sheet: 323 x 225 mm (trimmed at plate mark)
Signed, recto: Monogram AD (bottom center)
1999.7.18
Catalogue number 12

Hercules at the Crossroads reflects Dürer's interest in two important manifestations of European culture in the Renaissance period: the literature of classical antiquity and the art of northern Italy. While Dürer's art was grounded stylistically in the work of his Northern predecessors such as Schongauer and the Housebook Master, he also was inspired by the art of Andrea Mantegna and other Italians, as well as by his relationship with his humanist circle in Nuremberg. In mythological subjects such as this one and *Fortune* (p. 26), he focused specifically on depicting the nude and exploring the problem of ideal proportion. Dürer's copy of Mantegna's *Battle of the Sea Gods* (W. 60, Vienna, Albertina) around 1494 proved preliminary to his creation of this and several other engravings featuring nudes that he made after his return from Venice in 1495.[1]

The humanist scholars of Northern Europe, many of whom studied at Italian universities, encouraged interest in classical literature.[2] These writings in turn provided source material for works containing secular imagery instead of the religious themes that were the primary focus during the medieval period.

In Hercules at the Crossroads, Dürer illustrated a scene from the life of the mythical hero Hercules, as recounted by the author Xenophon.[3] This episode takes place prior to the better-known "labors," as the young Hercules considers his choice of a path in life. Setting out to contemplate his future, Hercules is first approached by Voluptas (Pleasure) and then by Virtue, each describing the type of life she might offer a young man. Although Virtue's path is more difficult, Hercules chooses the certain rewards that are her promised gift.

Dürer's interpretation of the subject is radically different from earlier precedents, which centered on the philosophical debate between Virtue and Voluptas. In this more worldy and violent encounter, the dramatic twisting of Virtue's body as she swings her stick, and the recoil of Voluptas as she tries to ward off the blow, recall the medieval psychomachia—the more traditional, physical "battle" between virtue and vice. Hercules's role is ambiguous: it is not clear if he is attempting to join the fray or to act as a referee.[4] The relationship of the figures to one another and to the surrounding environment is equally ambiguous and has prompted various scholarly interpretations regarding the print's specific meaning.

Dürer's exploration of the alliance of classical themes and the nude figure in a number of engravings made in the late 1490s was a logical extension of his interest in human proportion. Panofsky notes that the figures in this print derive from various preexisting works by Dürer that are based on Italian antecedents. In addition to the *Battle of the Sea Gods* (which is the source for the figure of Voluptus), he used a *Rape of the Sabines* by Antonio Pollaiuolo as the source for a drawing (W. 82, Bayonne, Musée Bonnat), from which he derived his Hercules.[5] A larger portion of the composition—Virtue, the putto with a bird in his hand on the right, and the copse of trees in the center—are excerpted from his *Death of Orpheus* (1494; W. 58, Hamburg, Kunsthalle), a work also indirectly copied from Mantegna.[6] Since the time of Giorgio Vasari in the sixteenth century, scholars have contended that this work is grounded not in Dürer's desire to relate a particular story, but in the need to demonstrate his ability to depict the nude figure and underscore its importance as an element of art.[7]

Despite this basic premise, elements of Dürer's composition have led scholars to further speculation as to its meaning. Hercules's elaborate, winged helmet, for example, has suggested to some that this is the so-called Hercules Gallicus, a non-classical version of the traditional hero related more specifically to Northern European history.[8] Others have indicated that the work may be deliberately satirical, and that Dürer may have intended to make fun of Hercules who physically, verbally (note the open mouths of both Voluptas and Hercules), but especially foolishly is stepping into a dispute between two angry women.⁹ More contemporary opinion has proposed that Dürer's use of his *Death of Orpheus* as the centerpiece of *Hercules at the Crossroads* is meaningful because of its content and depiction of violence. Dürer essentially copied this drawing from a print that preserves a composition by Mantegna showing Orpheus being bludgeoned to death by two Thracian women outraged over his introduction of homosexuality into Thracian society. In this context, the source drawing and the print might be seen as a commentary on the persecution of homosexuality during the period.¹⁰

Regardless of its specific interpretation, this engraving remains one of Dürer's most visually arresting prints, combining elements of landscape, architecture, contrasting textures in foliage and drapery, as well as classically-inspired nude figures. His burin work describing these elements demonstrates the supreme confidence of absolute mastery of this difficult technique. **M.L.A.**

1. *Fighting Sea Gods (after Mantegna)* (1494; W.60,Vienna, Albertina); illustrated in White, p. 54. Dürer also copied Mantegna's engraving *A Bacchanal with Silenus* around the same time (Vienna, Albertina). *Fortune* (p. 26); *The Temptation of the Idler (The Dream of the Doctor)* (p. 58), and *The Sea Monster* (1498; M. 66, B. 71) are other engravings made after Dürer's return from his first Venice trip that feature nude figures.
2. For example, Dürer's great friend Willibald Pirckheimer, the son of a patrician family of Nuremberg merchants, studied at the university at Pavia.
3. Xenophon, *Memorabilia*, trans. E.C. Marchant (London: William Heinemann, 1923), book 2, pp. 21-34. The tale is credited to Prodicus.
4. Panofsky, p. 74.
5. Ibid., p. 73. This is reiterated in Washington 1971, p. 123.
6. Dürer's source is believed to be a Northern Italian print made after Mantegna's original composition.
7. See Strauss 1975, pp. 77-80, for summaries of these scholarly opinions.
8. Hutchison, p. 55. "Tacitus alleges, in Chapter III of the *Germania*, that Hercules had visited Germany personally, and in Chapter IX that the ancient German tribes worshiped him. Some Bavarians claimed descent from Hercules Alemannus, one of the offspring of Noah's son Tuyscon (born after the flood), who supposedly gave his name "teutsch" to the German people. Dürer's Hercules, a hero with the exaggerated musculature suggestive of the influence of Pollaiuolo, has been identified as Hercules Gallicus by virtue of the cock on his helmet." This interpretation was largely discredited by Panofsky. See Panofsky, p. 75.
9. See the article by Edgar Wind, "Hercules and Orpheus: Two Mock-Heroic Designs by Dürer," *Journal of the Warburg and Courtauld Institutes* 2 (1938-39), pp. 206-13.
10. See works by Peter-Klaus Schuster, "Zu Dürers Zeichnung 'Der Tod des Orpheus' und verwandten Darstellungen ," *Jahrbuch der Hamburger Kunstsammlungen* 23 (1978), pp. 7-24; and Betsy Rosasco, "Albrecht Dürer's 'Death of Orpheus': Its Critical Fortunes and a New Interpretation of its Meaning," *Jahrbuch der Hamberger Kunsthalle* 3 (1984), pp. 19-41.

catalogue entry 13

Madonna with the Monkey, 1498

Engraving
Laid paper
Meder 30 a; Hollstein 30; Bartsch 42
Watermark: High Crown, Meder 20
Sheet: 193 x 125 mm
Signed, recto: Monogram AD (bottom center)
2001.10
Catalogue number 13

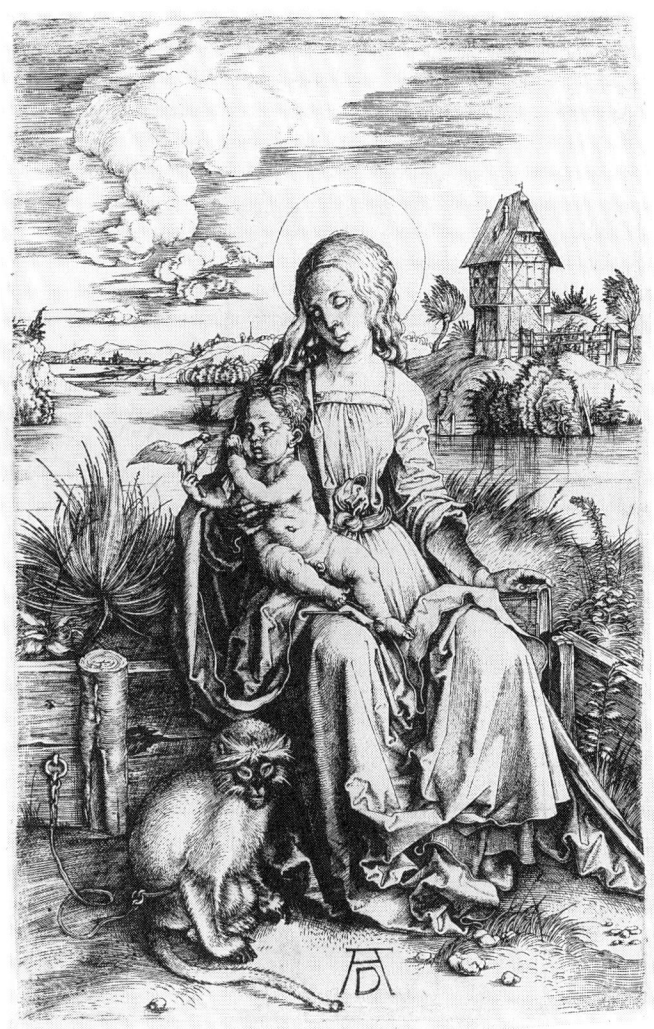

Devotion to Mary as the Mother of God originated in the fifth century and over succeeding generations became a primary tenet of the Catholic faith.[1] It prompted the creation of numerous images of the Virgin, particularly in art of the Middle Ages and Renaissance. In 1475 Jakob Spengler, a Dominican brother, founded the first Brotherhood of the Rosary at Cologne—one of the confraternities that quickly spread the devotion to Mary at the end of the fifteenth century. The approval of indulgences for the recitation of the rosary granted by Pope Sixtus IV in 1478 further increased the popularity of images of the Virgin. These images usually fall within two categories: those depicting the life of Mary (pp. 78 and 82) and those that are devotional, hence largely symbolic in type, such as the representation of the Madonna and Child. The devotional object sought to focus on Mary's role as an intercessor for divine favor, as the personification of mercy, and the embodiment of God's grace and purity.

One of the earliest of Dürer's fourteen engravings on the subject of the Virgin and Child is *The Holy Family with a Dragonfly* (ca. 1495-96, M. 42, B. 44), in which he placed the Virgin in an outdoor setting with long, panoramic vistas in the background, following the tradition of earlier artists such as the Housebook Master and Martin Schongauer.[2] This natural setting probably derives from a reference in *The Song of Solomon* (4: 12): "The garden enclosed is my sister, my spouse," which is an allusion to Mary's virginity.[3] But while earlier artists emphasized the enclosed garden as shielding the Virgin from the larger world and setting her apart, Dürer followed a tradition that began to flourish in the Renaissance, showing Mary within a vast and burgeoning landscape filled with worldly activity.

Madonna with the Monkey, created about three years later, is considered to be a significant advancement over *The Holy Family with a Dragonfly*, both in terms of Dürer's engraving technique and the clarity of the composition. Panofsky noted that the work, "marks a great advance in the realization of space, volume and texture."[4] Because of similarities in the posture of the Virgin and the sculptural solidity of the Christ Child, Wölfflin believed that Dürer went beyond Northern sources, and was influenced by his exposure to Italian versions of the Mother and Child, probably from the circle of Leonardo da Vinci.[5] Dürer's technique evolved so that he used the engraved line to define the contours of the objects and to integrate them in a rational fashion, rather than treating each section of the composition as an independent element. Consequently, the composition appears more unified; the background seems to encompass the group of foreground figures and serves as a jewel-like setting filled with intensely observed detail. Each rock, blade of grass, and fold of the Virgin's garment reflect an even, all-encompassing light.

Much of the success of the composition may be attributed to Dürer's extensive preparation; he created a number of drawings of the Virgin and Child, as well as *The Holy Family with a Dragonfly*.[6] He virtually copied the background from a watercolor titled *The "Weirhaus"* (W. 115; London, British Museum), a small landscape study he made in 1495 after his return from Venice. It appears to be a spontaneous observation of the countryside around Nuremberg: *Weirhäuser* were small cottagelike buildings, surrounded by water, used to house troops in times of unrest. Christopher White notes that Dürer was sensitive to the compositional variations necessary in the transfer to the engraved work— unlike those in the watercolor, the background trees in the engraving sway with the wind, since the bright light and billowing clouds of the print suggest a brilliant, breezy day.[7]

This engraving has always held a special appeal, both because of the delicate charm of Mary's demeanor, and because of the exotic character of the monkey chained at her feet.[8] In works of art of this period, monkeys signified attributes of human behavior such as lust or greed, and were also seen as representing evil or the devil.[9] It has been suggested that here the monkey is shown as a contrast to the Virgin, signifying the victory of spiritual purity over mankind's baser instincts. The chained monkey may also be an allusion to Eve, again in contrast to the Virgin and her role in vanquishing original sin. The serene and somber expression of the monkey contrasts markedly with the agitation of the bird, which flaps its wings in distress as the Infant firmly grasps its legs. The bird is commonly interpreted as an allusion to the human soul, in this situation probably captive and subject to the will of God.

Each of Dürer's subsequent compositions featuring the Virgin and Child is distinctive: from the sweet, domestic character of a mother holding a restless child, to the very formal, hieratic depiction of the pair as spiritual icons. Despite his commitment to the tenets of the Protestant Reformation (which discouraged the use of works of art as objects of devotion), he continued to make these images of great beauty and traditional piety, clearly finding their profound combination of spirituality and human tenderness to be of enduring appeal. **M.L.A.**

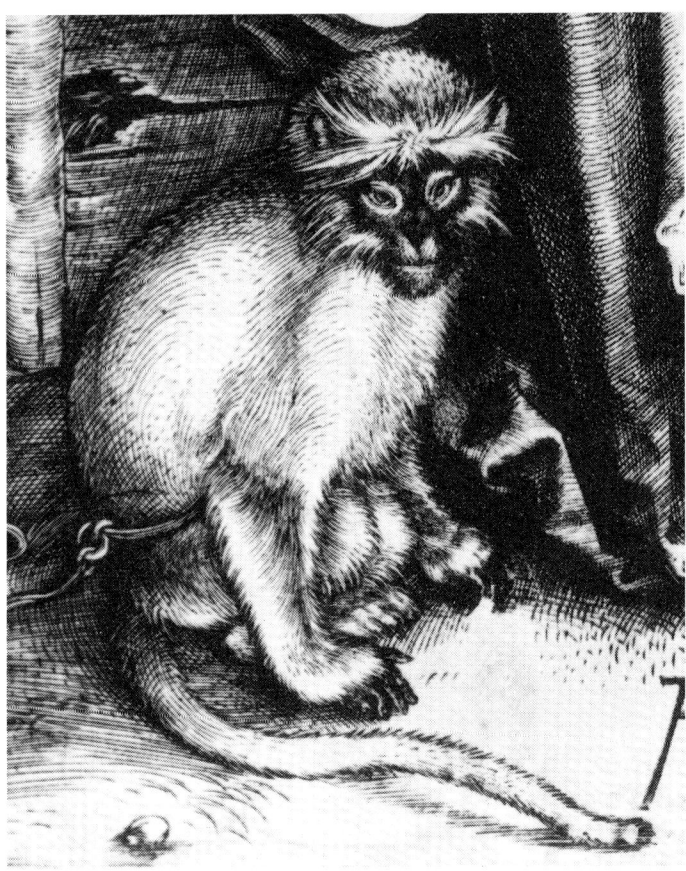

Figure 12 *Madonna with the Monkey* (detail), 1498 Engraving on laid paper.

1 The Council at Ephesus in 431 designated Mary as "Mother of God" for purposes of Church dogma. See Gertrude Schiller, *Iconography of Christian Art*, trans. Janet Seligman (Greenwich, CT: New York Graphic Society, Ltd., 1971), vol. 1, p. 28.
2 See Schongauer's *The Madonna and Child on a Grassy Bench* (1475-80; B. 30, L. 36), for a work that epitomizes the source for this subject in Northern European art. Dürer may have used it specifically for *The Holy Family with a Dragonfly*. See Washington 1971, p. 113.
3 Hanover, New Hampshire, The Art Gallery, University of New Hampshire, *Realism and Invention in the Prints of Albrecht Dürer* (Hanover, 1995), p. 16.
4 Panofsky, p. 67. See also Washington 1971, p. 121, and Landau and Parshall, p. 310.
5 Wölfflin, p. 100.
6 Washington 1971, p. 113. These are drawings of the Holy Family in Erlangen (W. 25) and in Berlin (W. 30). See Wölfflin, p. 100.
7 White, p. 60.
8 Tietze indicates that this species of monkey was a popular pet in the fifteenth century. In 1827 Heller noted that this engraving had been copied by at least fifteen engravers. The print was popular in Italy, where the novel architecture of the *Weirhaus* was particularly appealing. See Strauss 1975, p. 69.
9 For a general discussion, see H.W. Janson, *Apes and Ape Lore in the Middle Ages and the Renaissance*, London: Warburg Institute and the University of London, 1952.

The Temptation of the Idler (The Dream of the Doctor), 1498

Engraving
Laid paper
Meder 70 b; Hollstein 70; Bartsch 76
Watermark: None
Sheet: 190 x 123 mm
Signed, recto: AD (bottom center)
1999.7.21
Catalogue number 14

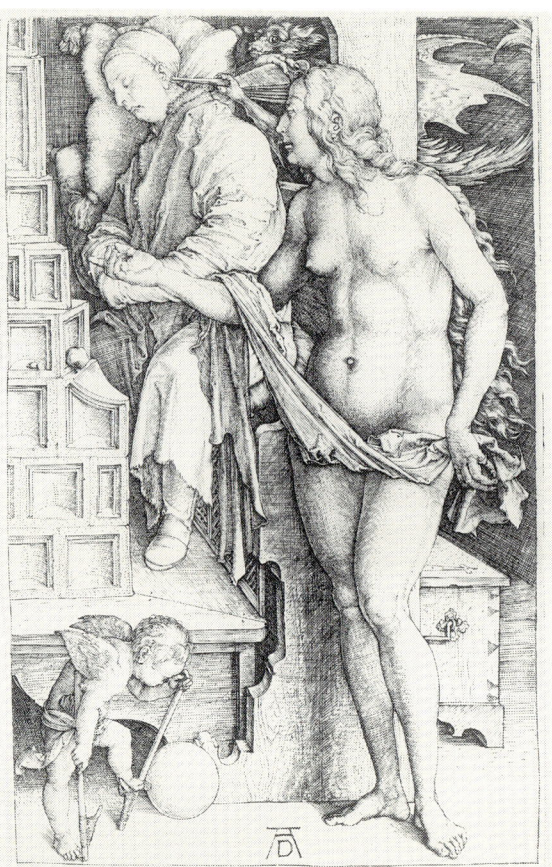

Dürer's intentions in producing *The Temptation of the Idler (The Dream of the Doctor)* were most likely two-fold: to reiterate his mastery of the classical nude female form, and to offer a visual equivalent of the moralizing narratives common in medieval literature. One of several prints made by Dürer in the late fifteenth century that prominently feature the nude female figure, the work possesses a combination of iconographic elements that immediately suggest the theme of "Acedia" or Sloth.[1] Panofsky identified the most likely source for the imagery in this print as a passage from Sebastian Brant's *Das Narrenschiff* (*The Ship of Fools*), a book of verses satirizing the weaknesses of human nature. Published in Basel in 1494, it became one of the most widely distributed books of its time. Dürer was commissioned to produce three woodcut illustrations that were published with the book, and thus was undoubtedly familiar with the following passage:

> *A sluggard is no use except to be a hibernating dormouse and to be allowed a full measure of sleep. To sit by the stove is his delight.... But the Evil One takes advantage of laziness and soon sows his seeds therein. Laziness is the root of all sin. It caused the children of Israel to grumble. David committed adultery and murder because he lolled in idleness.*[2]

In this composition Dürer vividly realized the images suggested by the text, focusing on a man dozing by a large tiled stove, his head supported by a pillow. In the man's unguarded state, a batlike demon places a bellows to his ear. A nude woman stands in the foreground beckoning to the man, presumably as a vision associated with the dreams of the sleeper. That this figure represents Venus, the Goddess of Love, is suggested by the small Cupid who maneuvers on stilts at her feet, next to a round sphere resting on the floor. The artist thus combined symbols of idleness (sleep) and lust (the nude), two concepts that, as is in the text quoted above, were often paired in literature of the period. One of the earliest genres of published books was this type of secular text: compendia of moralizing parables and stories that reinforced the virtues espoused by the Catholic Church and were central to social instruction.

In medieval art, the sleeper was commonly used to represent Sloth, his idleness making him easy prey for the Devil's mischief. The demon with the bellows, also a motif Dürer would have known from earlier examples, was associated with the concept of lust, since the bellows was used to stoke a fire and produce heat.[3] In this case, the presence of the Venus figure suggests that the demon employs the bellows to "literally inflame the sluggard's carnal desires."[4] Similarly, the stove reiterates the presence of heat and, with the pillow, implies excessive physical comfort.

As with other nudes featured in engravings of this era, the Venus figure was influenced by Italian examples and based on earlier Dürer study drawings. Her graceful curves and proportions and her *contrapposto* stance distinguish this figure from Northern examples.[5] Panofsky further elaborated on the interpretation of the figure as Venus, suggesting that the ring on her finger indicates that she represents the Venus of the legend of Astrolabius. Dating from at least the twelfth century, this story tells of a youth who was tricked by a statue of Venus that had been inhabited by a devil. By tricking the young man into placing his ring on the finger of the statue, he bewitches him. The youth is saved by a Christian priest who forces the devil to return the ring and leave the statue. Although this interpretation seems reasonable, particularly in light of its relationship to Christian rather than pagan legend, other prominent elements of the composition do not support the connection.[6] One further element that contributes to the multiple possible meanings of the work is Dürer's use of a sphere on the floor next to Venus, an attribute that is usually associated with the goddess Fortune.[7] The sphere, along with Cupid's awkward attempt to walk on stilts, imply the role of fate, and the fickleness of Fortune, in controlling man's destiny, as well as the precarious moral position of the man incited to lust who is made a fool by the futility of his desire.

Venus's prominent place in the foreground of the composition, and her rhetorical gesture, contrast markedly with the inactivity of the sleeper in the composition's recesses, identifying her as the controlling force and accentuating the sleeper's vulnerability to sin. In placing the event within a domestic setting (established by the stove and the wooden chest behind the nude), Dürer suggested the intersection of the natural and supernatural realms. The viewer is led to acknowledge that the Devil remains at work in everyday life, and that the fates (as indicated by Fortune's sphere) are similarly controlling factors. Using these symbols Dürer constructed a visual allegory of the moral dangers of indolence and luxury as suggested by Brant's text. **M.L.A.**

---

1 Other contemporaneous works featuring the female nude are *Fortune* (p. 26); *The Four Witches* (1497; M.69, B.75); *The Sea Monster* (1498; M.66, B.71) and *Hercules at the Crossroads* (p. 52). Dürer's interest in the nude figure is associated with his fascination with Italian classical and Renaissance art, particularly evident after his return from his first trip to Venice in 1495. See also cat. nos. 1 and 12.
2 Panofsky, pp. 71, 72.
3 See Stewart, p. 64, for a drawing by Niklaus Manuel, *Old Woman, Young Man and a Demon* (ca. 1515), with a similar depiction of a devil inciting the lust of an old woman for a younger man by blowing at her with a bellows. This activity was intended to signal foolish behavior, the word for fool deriving from the Latin *follis*, a term meaning windbag or bellows (p. 56).
4 Washington 1971, p. 124.
5 Two drawings, each dated 1498, are cited as sources for this nude figure in Washington 1971, pp. 36, 38. *The Nude Woman with the Herald's Wand* (W. 947, Sacramento, E. B. Crocker Art Gallery) and *Fortuna in a Niche* (W. 154, The Robert Lehman Foundation) are related in the positioning of the figures and their stances.
6 See Panofsky, p. 72, and Washington 1971, p. 124.
7 See the entry for *Fortune* (p. 26) for a discussion of the attributes of the goddess Fortune.

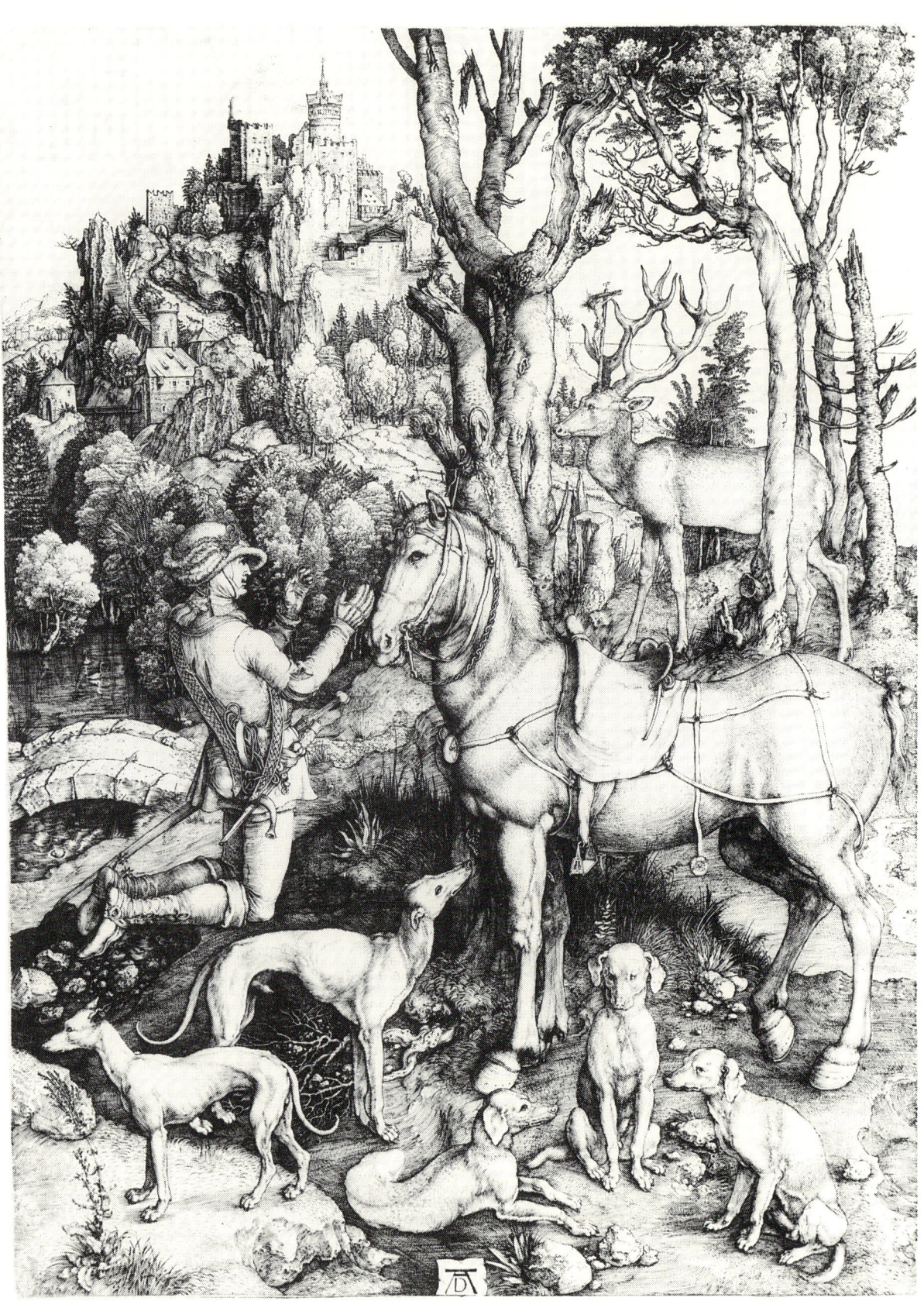

catalogue entry 15

St. Eustace, 1501

Engraving
Laid paper
Meder 60 b; Hollstein 60; Bartsch 57
Watermark: High Crown, Meder 20 (bottom center)
Sheet: 355 x 261 mm (sheet trimmed within plate mark)
Signed, recto: Monogram AD (bottom center)
1999.7.17
Catalogue number 15

St. Eustace, the largest of all Dürer's engravings, is the artist's first demonstration of his great mastery of the medium of printmaking. Whereas his engravings of just a few years earlier tend to be more linear with less modeling (for instance, *The Prodigal Son Amid the Swine*, p. 30), Dürer evidenced in *St. Eustace* a new skill in creating tonal values and textures. Using many closely spaced, deeply engraved lines, the artist delighted in depicting many varied surfaces, including animal fur, foliage, stone, and water. A new, silvery *chiaroscuro* bathes the scene. Dürer now was wielding the engraver's tool of the burin as if it were a painter's brush. His ease in using such tools undoubtedly stemmed from his early training under his father as a goldsmith. Perhaps it is not coincidental that in this first proclamation of his virtuosity in engraving, Dürer's famous monogram is also conspicuously presented for the first time. On a little tablet with a physical presence in the composition, it proudly announces the artist as the creator of the image.

Though the subject of the print has been mistakenly identified in the past as St. Hubert, who underwent a very similar conversion to Christianity, Dürer himself called it *Eustacium* in at least five different passages in his Netherlandish diary of 1520-21.[1] Originally named Placidas and a Roman general under the command of Trajan, the charitable future saint was on a hunt and chasing a large white stag, when he suddenly had a vision of Christ on the cross appearing between the animal's antlers. He then heard God speaking to him with the stag's voice: "O Placidus, why dost thou pursue Me? For thy sake I have appeared in this beast, for I am Christ, Whom thou unwitting adorest; thine alms-deeds have ascended before Me, and therefore am I come, that in this stag which thou didst hunt, I Myself might hunt thee."[2] The Lord then exhorted him to become a Christian and warned that he would endure many tribulations. He met his martyrdom by being enclosed within a bronze bull, which was then placed over a fire.

The patron saint of huntsmen, Eustace is usually depicted with the attribute of the stag, symbolizing piety and religious aspiration, with a crucifix between its antlers.[3] Ever aware of pictorial antecedents, Dürer has based his figure of the kneeling saint on a woodcut of the same subject published in Anton Koberger's 1488 *Lives of the Saints*.[4]

Along with demonstrating his skill as an engraver, this print also reveals Dürer's life-long interest in the wonders of the natural world. He left many carefully executed drawings and jewellike watercolors of plants, vegetation of all sorts, and animals ranging from the commonplace rabbit and elk to the more exotic lion, lynx, and even baboon.[5] In his nature studies the artist strived to depict the world around him with an almost scientific accuracy, often using them for details in his prints and paintings. The only extant study for *St. Eustace*, for the largest of the standing greyhounds (W. 241, Windsor, England, Windsor Castle, fig. 14, p. 63), is delicately rendered with brush and wash in shades of gray.[6] Dürer perfectly translated its tone and texture to the engraving.

With all of its detail and narrative, the main subject of this print is perhaps St. Eustace's horse. Presented in perfect profile, the horse displays an objective proportion. Shortly after this, Dürer might have seen Leonardo da Vinci's equine studies, which influenced Dürer's independent proportion drawing of a horse today in Cologne (W. 361).[7] About four years later, Dürer's interest in the idealized proportions of a horse was more fully realized in the engraving *The Small Horse* (fig. 13, p. 62), and culminated in the *Knight, Death, and Devil* of 1513 (fig. 4, p. 14). Although he never completed it, Dürer

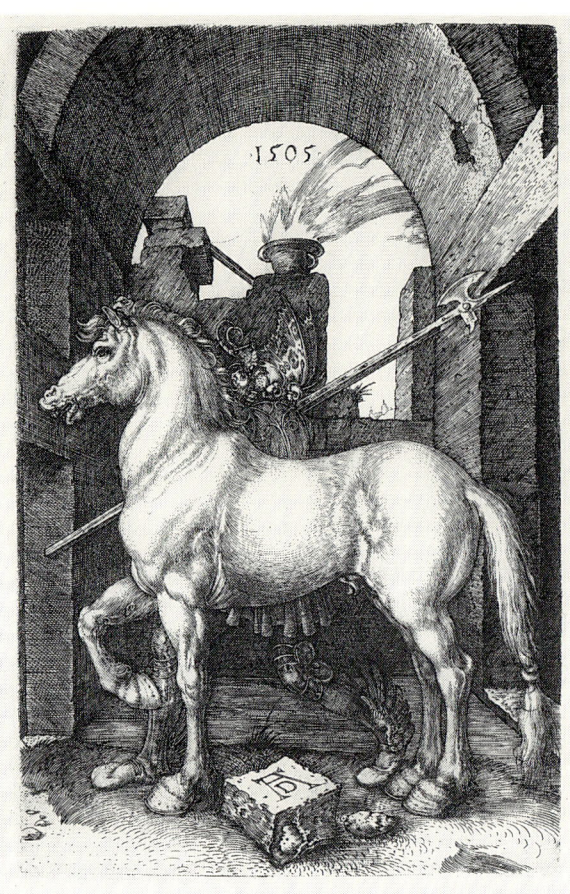

Figure 13 *The Small Horse*, 1505, Engraving on laid paper, Washington, National Gallery of Art, Rosenwald Collection, 1943.3.3558.

intended to write a general treatise on painting, *The Art of Measurement*, which included a section on the proportions of the horse.[8] With regard to the artist's special fondness for this animal, it is interesting to note that his father's family in Hungary made their living by breeding horses and cattle, traditional occupations of their native land.[9]

Since the sixteenth century, writers have commented on the facial resemblance between Eustace and the Holy Roman Emperor Maximilian I. At the end of the sixteenth century, Georg Danecker, an Ausburg Meistersinger, wrote a poem in which he not only called Dürer the "German Apelles," but stated that "He made a picture on one occasion of St. Eustace, the huntsman's occupation. He has given the saint, in any case, the Emperor Maximilian's face."[10] Colin Eisler believes the print *St. Eustace* was a vehicle for Dürer to flatter Maximilian in the hope of obtaining royal patronage.[11] Maximilian was a passionate hunter, even establishing game preserves, and could very well have identified with the hunter and soldier Eustace.[12] Walter Strauss has suggested that Dürer could even have been inspired to make the print when the emperor was visiting Nuremberg during Easter week in 1501.[13] However, Dürer's ambitions were not realized until some twelve to fourteen years later when he finally received Maximilian's official patronage in the form of a royal pension. His works in connection with Maximilian include a woodcut portrait of the emperor (1518-19; M. 255, B. 153) and two extremely large and impressive woodcuts, *The Triumphal Arch of Maximilian I* (1515; M. 251, B. 138) and *The Great Triumphal Chariot* (completed 1518 although dated 1522; M. 252, B. 139).[14]

Mentioned in Dürer's Netherlandish diary along with prints such as *Melencolia I* (fig. 5, p. 15), *St. Jerome in His Study* (fig. 6, p. 16), and *Knight, Death, and the Devil* (fig. 4, p. 14), *St. Eustace* impressions were sold or given away to people he met during his journey. Its fame also spread south of the Alps. Giorgio Vasari, writing in 1568, states that the print "is amazing, and particularly for the beauty of some dogs in various attitudes, which could not be more perfect."[15] At the end of the sixteenth century, the time of a "Dürer renaissance," the plate for the print came into the possession of the Holy Roman Emperor Rudolph II, who had additional impressions printed before having the plate gilded.[16] **G.D.J.**

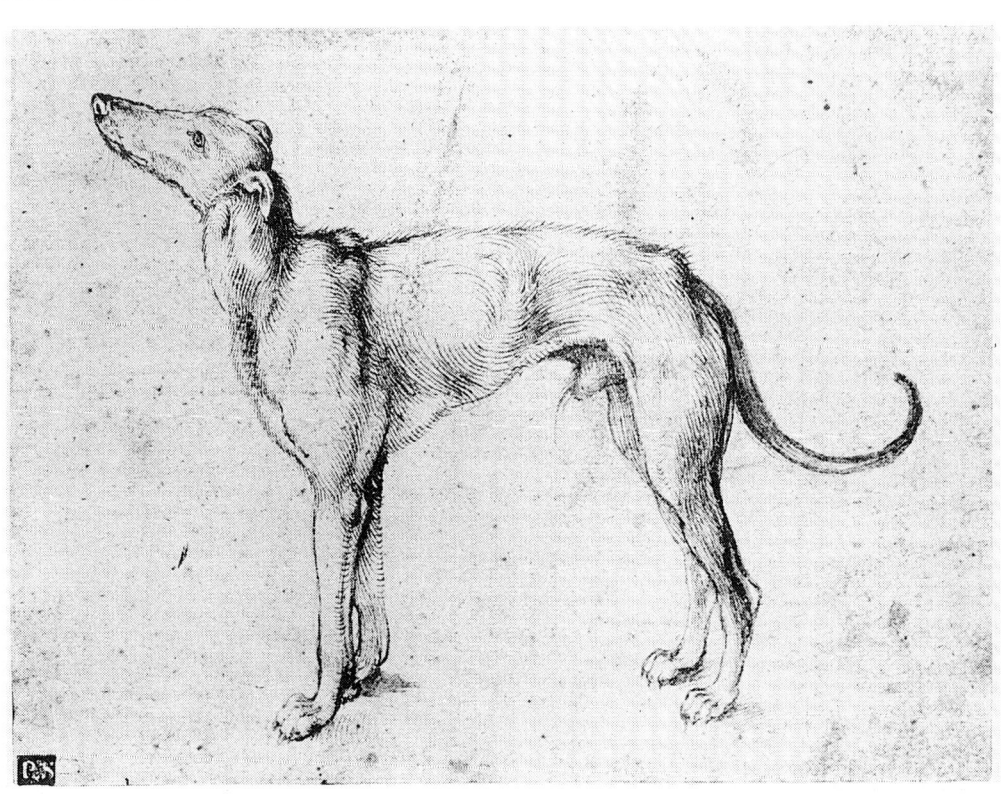

Figure 14 *A Greyhound*, c. 1500-1501
Brush drawing on paper, Windsor Castle, Collection of Her Majesty the Queen

1. Cited in Strauss 1975, p. 55. On the iconographic tradition of St. Eustace, see also Erwin Panofsky, "Dürer's 'St. Eustace,'" *Record of the Art Museum, Princeton University* 9, 1 (1950), pp. 2-10.
2. The Golden Legend, vol. 2, p. 555.
3. George Wells, Ferguson, *Signs and Symbols of Christian Art* (New York: Oxford University Press, 1954), pp. 26-27, 208.
4. Panofsky, pp. 9-10.
5. See *Young Hare* (Vienna, Albertina; see Strauss 1974, vol. 2, p. 594 [1502/2]); *Elk* (London, British Museum; see Strauss 1974, vol. 2, p. 568 [1501/1], and *Six Animals and Two Landscapes* (Williamstown, Massachusetts, Sterling and Francine Clark Museum; see Strauss 1974, vol. 4, p. 2072 [1521/40]). Dürer might have seen the more exotic animals in the Brussels zoological gardens in 1521. Studies on the subject of Dürer and nature include William A. Emboden, "Plants in the Works of Albrecht Dürer (1417-15218)," *Hortus aliquando 2* (1977), pp. 5-21; Vienna, Albertina, *Albrecht Dürer und die Tier- und Pflanzen Studien der Renaissance*, text by Fritz Koreny (Vienna, 1985); and Dagmar Eichberger, "*Naturalia und arte facta:* Dürer's nature drawings and early collecting," in *Dürer and His Culture* (Cambridge: Cambridge University Press, 1998), pp. 13-37.
6. Strauss 1974, vol. 2, p. 504 (1500/1).
7. Washington 1971, p. 134. Strauss 1974, vol. 2, p. 708 (1503/28).
8. Panofsky, p. 81. In 1528, shortly before Dürer's treatise was published, the Nuremberg publisher Hieronymus Andrae printed Sebald Beham's book on the proportion of the horse, which was partly derived from Dürer's work. See Lawrence, Kansas, Spencer Museum of Art, The University of Kansas, *The World in Miniature: Engravings by the German Little Masters, 1500-1550*, ed. Stephen H. Goddard (Lawrence, 1988), p. 223.
9. Hutchison, p. 5.
10. Cited in Strauss 1975, p. 55.
11. Colin Eisler, "Maximilian and Dürer's Major Engravings," in *Ars auro prior: Studia Ioanni Bialostocki sexagenario dicata* (Warsaw: Panstwowe Wydawn Nauk, 1981*)*, pp. 297-300.
12. On the character of Maximilian I, see Panofsky, p. 174.
13. Strauss 1974, vol. 2, p. 567.
14. For these and other projects for Maximilian, see Larry Silver, "Prints for a Prince: Maximilian, Nuremberg, and the Woodcut," in *New Perspectives on the Art of Renaissance Nuremberg*, ed. Jeffrey Chipps Smith (Austin, Texas: The Archer M. Huntington Art Gallery College of Fine Arts, 1985), pp. 7-21.
15. Vasari, vol. 6, p. 98
16. Detroit, The Detroit Institute of Arts, *From a Mighty Fortress: Prints, Drawings, and Books in the Age of Luther, 1483 – 1546*, text by Christiane Andersson and Charles Talbot (Detroit, 1983), p. 249. Bartsch was the first to report this information about the original plate. Later scholars say it might not be Dürer's plate, but rather a copy.

catalogue entry 16

Apollo and Diana, 1502

Engraving
Laid paper
Meder 64 b; Hollstein 64; Bartsch 68
Watermark: None
Sheet: 114 x 73 mm
Signed, recto: Monogram AD (lower right)
1999.7.19
Catalogue number 16

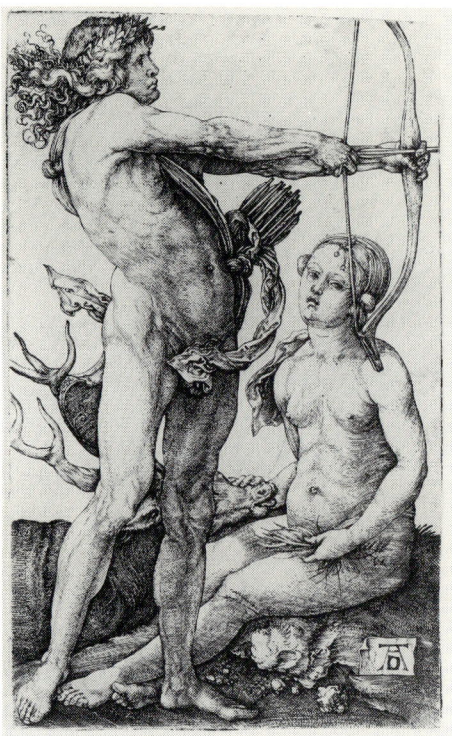

The engraving *Apollo and Diana* is an example of Dürer's interest in classical subject matter and classical form through the depiction of the nude figure. The mythological gods Apollo and Diana (Artemis to the Greeks) were twins, born on the island of Delos to the Titaness Leto, who conceived them with Zeus, the ruling deity of Mt. Olympus. Although Apollo is chiefly known as the god of the sun and Diana as the goddess of the moon, both are associated with the hunt, and the bow is a prominent element in this composition by Dürer.[1] Here, Diana, with her hand resting on the muzzle of a large stag, is also shown as the protector of game.[2] Apollo, in contrast, is portrayed as the hunter, with the attribute of a quiver of arrows. The laurel wreath encircling his brow is a symbol of his heroic exploits.

One of the best-known depictions of Apollo is the *Apollo Belvedere* (second century AD; Rome, Vatican Museum), a copy of a fourth-century BC original. As reproductions of this important example of the classical male nude spread throughout Europe, the attitude of the figure, with its naturalism and *contrapposto* stance, exerted considerable influence on the design of the nude male figure in art. In his own experimentation with the creation of nude figures according to classical concepts of ideal proportions as described by Vitruvius, Dürer created a drawing (*Poynter Apollo*, c. 1501-1503, New York, The Metropolitan Museum of Art, fig. 16, p. 67) that closely replicates the posture of the *Apollo Belvedere*. This drawing is considered to have served as the starting point for several other drawings and engravings by Dürer that include idealized male figures—the *Adam and Eve* (1504, M. 1, B. 1), for example, and this engraving of Apollo and Diana.

This composition was also substantially influenced by an engraving of the same title by the Italian painter Jacopo de' Barbari (died ca. 1515/16), who was instrumental in transmitting elements of the classical style to Northern Europe in the early sixteenth century. By most accounts a capable but not inspired artist, Barbari (or Jacob Wälsch—Jacob the Italian—as he was known in the North), was apparently familiar with the methods by which Italian painters constructed human figures according to ratios and proportions established in antiquity.[3] Anton Kolb, a Nuremberg merchant who served in Venice as an agent for Anton Koberger, Dürer's godfather, helped bring Barbari to the attention of Nuremberg's intellectual elite. Kolb commissioned Barbari to create a topographical map of Venice that was published in 1500, and probably facilitated his connection with the Holy Roman Emperor Maximilian I. Appointed court portraitist around 1500 by Maximilian, Barbari lived in Nuremberg until 1503. Subsequently he was employed by Frederick the Wise, Elector of Saxony, and then traveled to the Netherlands where he died while at the court of Margaret of Austria. Whether Dürer met Barbari on his first trip to Venice in 1495-1496, or later in Nuremberg, it is evident that Dürer and his circle of humanist friends were fascinated by this artist, who adventured beyond Italy to find greater fame and fortune in the North.[4]

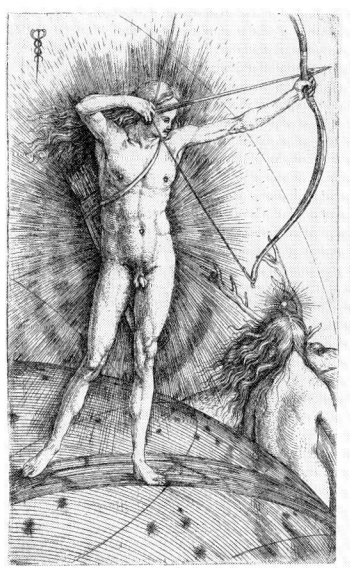

Figure 15 Jacopo de' Barbari, *Apollo and Diana*, c. 1503-1504, Engraving on laid paper, Washington, National Gallery of Art, Rosenwald Collection, 1943.3.940.

In the Barbari engraving (fig. 15, right), Apollo and Diana are shown as emblems of the sun and moon. The rays of the sun shine from behind Apollo, who prepares to unleash an arrow across the sky. Diana, who is also distinguished by the hunt attributes of the stag with antlers, is shown seated below Apollo and from the back. As with Dürer's composition, she is nestled beneath the bow of Apollo. Likewise, both figures of Apollo are shown at a large scale barely contained within the respective compositions, with emphasis placed on the robust musculature of the god in motion. Another Dürer drawing of Apollo (*Apollo and Diana*, 1501-1503, London, British Museum) shows that Dürer considered a treatment similar to Barbari's for his *Apollo and Diana* engraving, but developed his composition with the Diana figure facing forward rather than backward.

Panofsky theorizes that Dürer's *Apollo and Diana* is linked to the great *Adam and Eve* through the series of drawings (inscribed with lines to distinguish the idealized proportions) that he seemingly used in producing both these works. His observation that Dürer intended to create complementary prints—one a classical display piece and the other a showcase for his geometrically conceived figures—is not supported by other evidence, but seems a logical conclusion based upon Dürer's attention to classical nudes and their sources. Panofsky further elaborates that in the *Apollo and Diana*, Dürer wanted to contrast "masculine vigor in action and feminine loveliness in repose."[5] The juxtaposition of the standing, contorted Apollo with the seated, languid Diana would seem to support this observation.

At the turn of the sixteenth century, when Dürer produced this work, he was approaching his prime as an artist and establishing his reputation as an engraver of unparalleled ability. His subjects reflected his eclectic interests, with a special emphasis on classical themes in addition to the religious compositions that continued to dominate Northern art. By juxtaposing emblematic figures such as Adam and Eve and Apollo and Diana, Dürer was unifying concepts both spiritual and intellectual that were evolving as an elemental part of society in that age. **M.L.A.**

1 Mark P. O. Morford and Robert J. Lenardon, *Classical Mythology*, 5th ed. (New York: Longman Publishers, 1995), p. 169. The *Homeric Hymn to Apollo* states, "the lady Leto rejoices because she has borne a son who is a mighty archer."
2 In one of his best-known studies from nature, in 1504 Dürer produced a watercolor with a stag's head in a similar attitude (W.362, Paris, Bibliothèque Nationale).
3 Dürer reveals in an unpublished draft of his *Introduction to the Four Books of Human Proportion*, that Barbari once "showed me the figures of a man and a woman, which he had drawn according to a canon of proportions." It is assumed that the Italian artist provided an important stimulus for Dürer's own studies of the scientific measurement of the human body, despite the fact that Barbari, "did not want to show his principles to me clearly." "It was after this rebuff, when he was still quite young," says Dürer, that "I set out to work on my own and read Vitruvius, who writes somewhat about the human figure. . . and thereafter, from day to day, I have followed up my search according to my own design" (Hutchinson, pp. 71-72). For further information on Dürer's relationship with Barbari, see also Jay A. Levenson, "Jacopo de Barbari and Northern Art of the Early Sixteenth Century," PhD dissertation, New York University, 1978.
4 For an account of the Nurembergers' innovative business relationships with Barbari and Venice, see Landau and Parshall, p. 43.
5 Panofsky, p. 87. See further comments in Washington 1971, p. 131.

catalogue entry 17

The Standard Bearer, c. 1502

Engraving
Laid paper
Meder 92 a; Hollstein 92; Bartsch 87
Watermark: None
Sheet: 116 x 73 mm
Signed, recto: Monogram AD (center left)
1999.7.26
Catalogue number 17

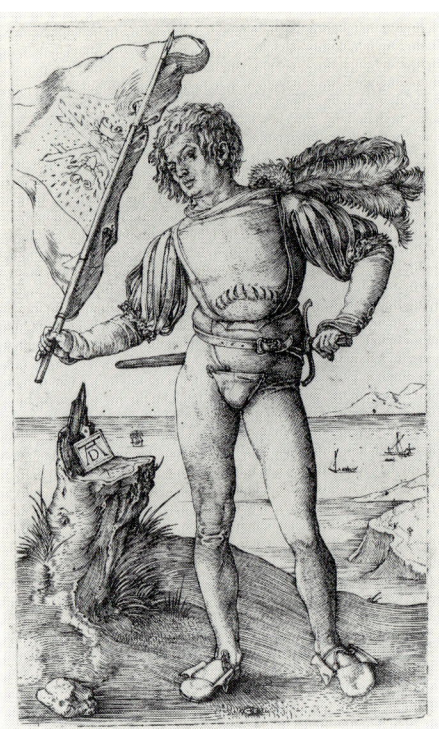

The subject of a single standard bearer, popular in art during the sixteenth century, was part of the increasing rise of secular imagery at the time. Dürer's print is one of the earliest examples of this theme.[1] Standard bearers were part of the basic infantry units of three to four hundred soldiers. With men fighting in dense packs, the flag served as a rallying point and, consequently, the standard bearer was an important element in a battle. He was paid five to six times more than a regular soldier and he adopted the most fashionable dress of the day. Depictions of standard bearers, and the related mercenaries (or *Landskneckte*), in sixteenth-century art are usually heroic, although negative connotations appear in contemporary satirical writings. A text accompanying a woodcut of a standard bearer by Sebald Beham states: "I want to let my flag fly / In a just and worthy war / And diligently serve a lord / who makes war for honor and renown."[2]

Such renderings of the standard bearer and the foot soldier recently have been viewed in the context of a rising German pride and nationalism, a new self-awareness that was encouraged under Maximilian I.[3] The banner in Dürer's engraving displays the insignia of the Order of the Golden Fleece, the cross of Saint Andrew with sparking flints. The order was founded by Duke Philip the Good of Burgundy in 1429, and Maximilian became its chief and sovereign after wedding Mary, duchess of Burgundy, in 1477.[4] The setting of Dürer's *Standard Bearer*, a coastline with mountains on the horizon, has been interpreted as referring to Germany's borders in the south, an area that was threatened by the Turks. The Turks were an ongoing rival factor in Northern Europe, and Maximilian called for several crusades to affect their expulsion.[5]

The Standard Bearer also demonstrates Dürer's early knowledge and exploration of classical human proportion. While his theories on the subject culminated in his treatise *Four Books on Human Proportion* (written in 1523 and published posthumously in 1528), his initial interest seems to have been inspired by the nude figures in the work of the Italian artist Jacopo de' Barbari (c.1460/70-1516 or before). The young Dürer was impressed by Barbari, who was appointed court painter by Emperor Maximilian on April 8, 1500, and came to reside in Nuremberg. Much later Dürer wrote of the importance of their meeting: "I have found no one who [knows or] has written about a system of human proportion, except Jacobus, a native of Venice and a lovely painter. He showed me how to construct man and woman based on measurement."[6] Dürer continued his early study of proportion by reading the works of Vitruvius, a Roman first-century BC architect and theorist.

The Standard Bearer can be viewed in relationship to Dürer's series of constructed male proportional studies known as the "Apollo group," and include the so-called *Poynter Apollo* in The Metropolitan Museum of Art (W. 262, fig.16, right).[7] The classical *contrapposto* of these figures was inspired by the famous antique sculpture *Apollo Belvedere*, unearthed at the end of the fifteenth century and bought in 1503 by Cardinal Della Rovere (later Pope Julius II), and placed in the Vatican garden.[8] Dürer might have had access to drawings after this sculpture. His culmination of these studies on classical proportion is the engraving *Adam and Eve* of 1504 (M.1, B. 1).

Done around the same time as this print is Dürer's pen-and-ink study *Lansquenet Seen from Behind* (W. 253).[9] Dürer's life-long predilection for costume studies is reflected in the soldiers' customary colorful and fashionable dress.[10] This love for costume studies, particularly of soldiers, was inspired by the works of the fifteenth-century printmakers known as Master E. S. (active 1450-1467) and the Housebook Master (active c. 1465-1500). **G.D.J.**

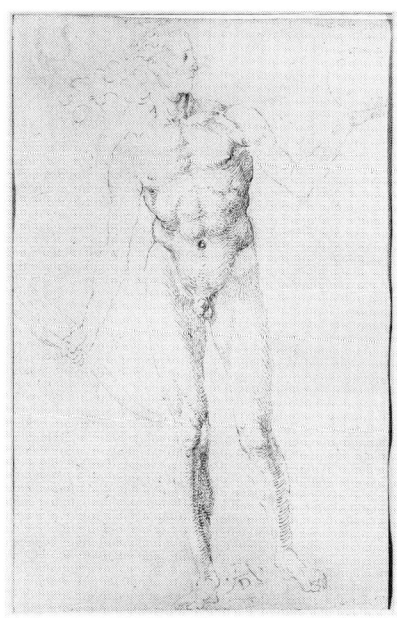

Figure 16 *Poynter Apollo*, c. 1501-1503, Pen and Brown inks on laid paper, New York, The Metropolitan Museum of Art, Gift of Mrs. William O. Osborn, 1963. 63.212.

---

1 Keith Moxey, "The Social Function of Secular Woodcuts in Sixteenth Century Nuremberg," in *New Perspectives on the Art of Renaissance Nuremberg*, ed. Jeffrey Chipps Smith (Austin, Texas: The Archer M. Huntington Art Gallery College of Fine Arts, 1985), pp. 63-81.
2 Cited in Ibid., p. 68. For the Beham print, see Hollstein, vol. 3, p. 262, no. 1256.
3 Larry Silver, "German Patriotism in the Age of Dürer," in *Dürer and his Culture* (Cambridge: Cambridge University Press, 1998), pp. 55-58.
4 For a succinct account of this history, Los Angeles, J. Paul Getty Museum, and Saint Louis Art Museum, *Painting on Light: Drawings and Stained Glass in the Age of Dürer*, text by Barbara Butts and Lee Hendrix (Los Angeles, 2000), p. 195.
5 Ibid., p. 55.
6 Cited in Strauss 1974, p. 532.
7 Ibid., vol. 2, p. 582 (1501/8). The others in this group are the *Apollo Medicus* in Berlin (Strauss 1974, vol. 6, p. 3008 [XW.263]); and the *Apollo* in the British Museum (Strauss 1974, vol. 2, p. 580 [1501/8]). This series was preceded by a group of construction drawings of the female nude (Strauss 1974, vol. 2, pp. 528-58). See Washington 1971, pp. 39-40, for the relationship between the Apollo drawings.
8 For a history of this important antique sculpture, see F. Haskell and N. Penny, *Taste and the Antique: The Lure of Classical Sculpture* (London and New Haven: Yale University Press, 1981), pp. 148ff.
9 Strauss 1974, vol. 2, p. 626 (1502/18).
10 Dürer's interest in dress dates to his first trip to Venice in 1494-95. For several of these works, see Strauss 1974, vol. 1, pp. 268-72. His trip to the Low Countries in 1520-21 inspired further costume studies. A particularly fine drawing from this period is the *Young Woman in Netherlandish Dress* in the National Gallery of Art, Washington, DC (Strauss 1974, vol. 4, p. 2040 [1521/23]).

Satyr Family, 1505

Engraving
Laid paper
Meder 65 a; Hollstein 65; Bartsch 69
Watermark: None
Sheet: 115 x 72 mm (trimmed along plate mark)
Signed, recto: Monogram AD 1505 (upper right)
1999.7.20
Catalogue number 19

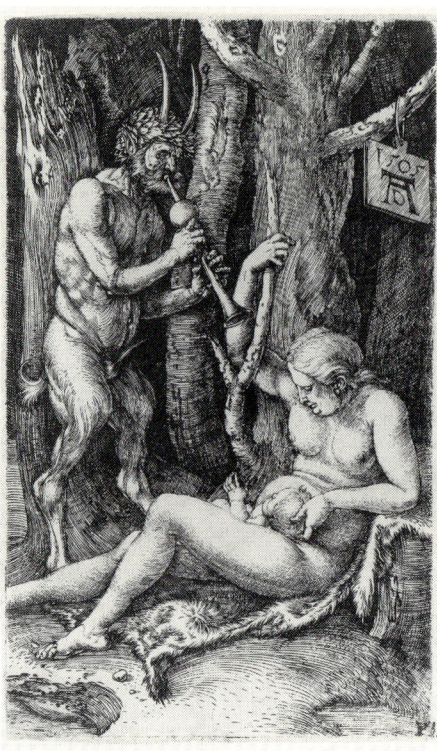

Dürer's interest in the art of the Italian Renaissance, including its classical subject matter, can be seen as early as 1494 when he copied in pen and ink several prints by Andrea Mantegna, including the famous *Battle of the Sea Gods* (Left Half).[1] Undoubtedly introduced to Italian art and culture even before his first trip south, Dürer would have been encouraged in this study by his close friend Willibald Pirckheimer (1470-1530), the leading humanist of Nuremberg, and by Konrad Celtis (1549-1508), professor of poetry at the University of Vienna and the first poet laureate of the empire. Wishing to elevate German culture based on Italianate Renaissance models, both men impressed upon Dürer the need for modern illustrations of mythological subjects and classical allegories. These humanists recognized that Dürer's great talents would help them achieve their goal of "bringing Apollo to Germany."[2]

The initial idea of the subject of this charming print, probably suggested to Dürer by Pirckheimer, is found in a rapid pen-and-ink sketch of a centaur mother nursing her young (W. 344, Coburg, Sammlung der Veste).[3] It may refer to a description by the classical author Lucian (whose work was partially translated by Pirckheimer), of a famous painting by the classical Greek artist Zeuxis.[4] Alternately, the print could have been based on a passage on centaurs in Philostratus's *Imagines*.[5] Closer to the final print is another pen-and-ink study, in reverse, of a centaur family (W. 345, fig. 17, right).[6] However, in the engraving the mother's horns have disappeared and the centaur father has become a satyr playing a rustic flute. The mother is now seen sitting on a fur rug. Finally, the single tree has become a dark primeval forest, even denser than the background in the engraving *Adam and Eve* (M. 1, B. 1,) done a year earlier.

Dürer might have changed the centaur family to that of a satyr after seeing a print of this subject (1503-1504) by the Venetian artist Jacopo de' Barbari (c. 1460/70 – 1516 or before).⁷ Dürer had met Barbari either when he was in Venice (1494-95), or when Barbari was working in Nuremberg (1500-1503). He later wrote how Barbari showed him the figures of a man and a woman constructed in geometrical proportion.⁸ Dürer's print shows a similarity in subject matter with Barbari's *Satyr Family*, but also in the technique of using long, tapering strokes that are characteristic of the Venetian's prints.

Suggesting that Dürer's *Satyr Family* is a companion piece to his *Apollo and Diana* (p. 64), Panofsky writes that "the two prints appeal indeed to two of the most potent impulses in the psychology of the Renaissance: to the nostalgias for the Olympian and for the idyllic."⁹ Though frequently found in Italian art, the subject matter of a satyr was introduced in the north only by Dürer, who was the first to emphasize the familial role of the mythological creature.¹⁰ Hutchison believes the print, with its esoteric content, was especially made for the community of scholars.¹¹ Not only was Dürer's *Satyr Family* copied six times during the sixteenth century, it, and Barbari's version of the same topic, inspired many Italian prints with the same theme.¹² **G.D.J.**

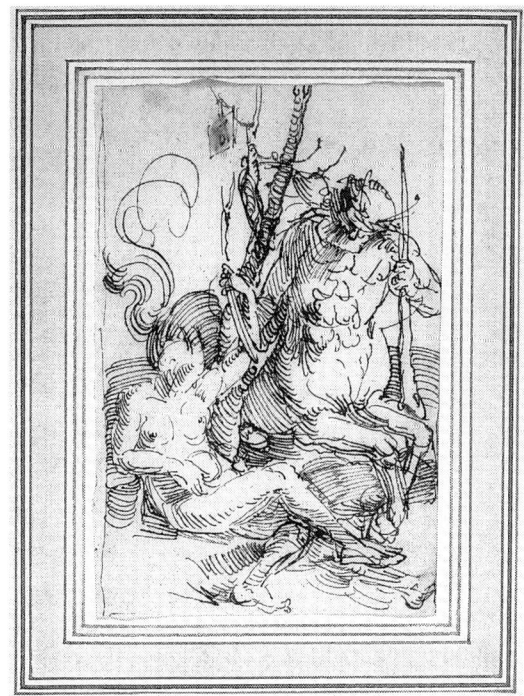

Figure 17 *The Centaur Family*, 1505, Pen and brown Ink on laid paper, Washington, National Gallery of Art, The Armand Hammer Collection, 1987.24.2

---

1. Strauss 1974, vol. 1, p. 224 (1494/13). Dürer later referred to this drawing for two prints of c. 1498: *The Sea Monster* (M. 66, B. 71), and *Hercules at the Crossroads* (cat. no. 12). He also made a drawn copy after Mantegna's print *Bacchanal with Silenus* (Strauss 1974, vol. 1, p. 222 [1494/12]). According to Hutchison 1990, p. 42, prints by Mantegna were being collected in Basel and probably in Nuremberg by the late fifteenth century.
2. Celtis, cited in Hutchison 1990, p. 69. On the subject of Pirckheimer and Celtis, see Hutchison 1990, especially pp. 48-56. Dürer made an engraved portrait of Pirckheimer in 1524 (M.103, B. 106). Pirckheimer composed Dürer's moving epitaph: "Whatever was mortal of Albrecht Durer is covered by this tomb" (cited in Panofsky 1971, p. 10).
3. Strauss 1974, vol. 2, p. 872 (1505/16).
4. Ibid., p. 872.
5. Panofsky 1971, p. 87.
6. Strauss 1974, vol. 2, p. 874 (1505/17)
7. Hind, vol. 5, p. 154, no. 19. See also Washington, DC, National Gallery of Art, *Early Italian Engravings from the National Gallery of Art*, text by Jay A. Levenson, Konrad Oberhuber, and Jacquelin L. Sheehan (Washington, 1973), p. 366, cat. no. 140.
8. Panofsky 1971, p. 35
9. Ibid., p. 87.
10. For a fascinating study on this subject in art, kindly brought to my attention by Barbara Butts, see Lynn Frier Kaufmann, *The Noble Savage: Satyrs and Satyr Families in Renaissance Art* (Ann Arbor, Michigan: UMI Press, 1984). The author devotes an entire chapter to Dürer's satyrs.
11. Hutchison 1990, p.55
12. Schoch et al. 2001, p. 124. For the Italian prints, see Washington 1973, Benedetto Montagna (cat. no. 130), Master of 1515 (cat. no. 164), and Master I.B. with a Bird (cat. no. 161).

catalogue entry 19

Crucifixion, 1508

Engraving
Laid paper
Meder 23 a; Hollstein 23; Bartsch 24
Watermark: None
Sheet: 132 x 97 mm (trimmed within plate mark)
Signed, recto: Monogram AD 1508 (bottom center)
1999.7.9
Catalogue number 20

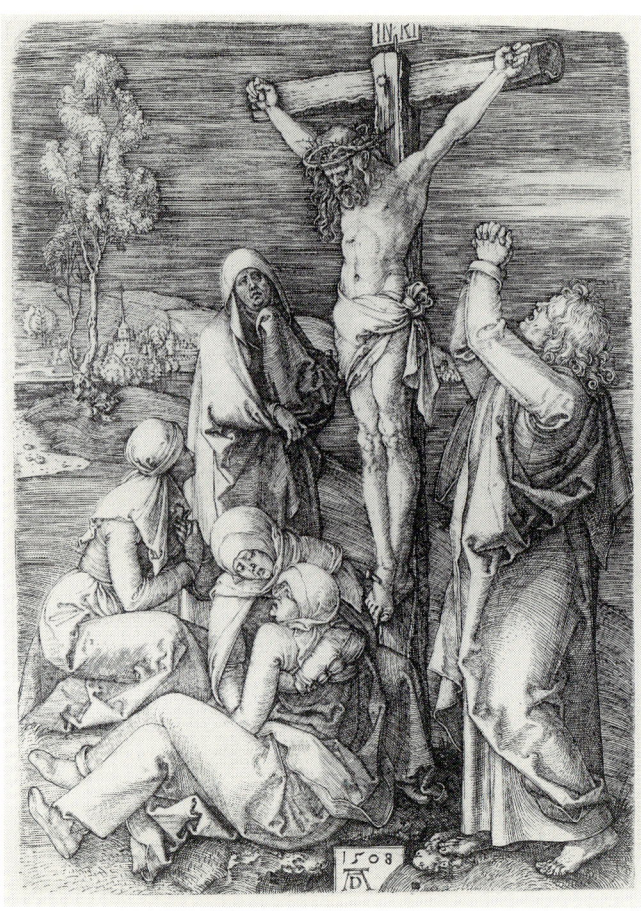

  Representations of the death of Christ dominated Christian art through the Middle Ages, and continued to be a major theme during the Renaissance and Baroque periods. Because the subject was so long-lived, its iconography was well established and scenes of Christ on the cross often had the dispassionate, formulaic quality of devotional objects. This small engraving by Dürer, however, demonstrates the artist's ability to breathe life and emotion into an important symbol of Christian piety. The very human spiritual intensity manifested in the figures is also reflected in the surrounding landscape and enveloping atmosphere.

  Here the cross, typically the centerpiece of the composition, is placed off center and shown at an oblique angle. Its position emphasizes in profile the suffering, broken body of Christ with his arms stretched taut and his head inclined over his chest. The extension of the cross back into space creates a sense of volume: an intimate area that is filled by the figures at its base. At the right, St. John the Evangelist extends his arms toward the heavens as he wails in profound grief. The Virgin swoons at the foot of the cross, comforted by Mary Magdalen, Mary Cleophas, and Mary Salome, who are shown to the left. These mournful figures and the crucified Christ form a triangle that fills the picture plane, and the position of Christ's body at its apex symbolizes his role as the intermediary between heaven and earth.

Of the fifteen prints Dürer created with the Crucifixion as the subject, the majority are woodcuts.¹ Several key representations are parts of the series in woodcut and engraving of the Passion of Christ that Dürer published later, (see fig. 18, right) but this small work is a singular edition, made in 1508. Of particular interest is the fact that by sensitive use of the burin, Dürer presented the event as a nocturne, which is visually signaled by the darkening sky. Although this approach was not typical in depictions of the Crucifixion, the gospels indicate that a solar eclipse occurred at the moment of Christ's death.² ("And it was about the sixth hour, and there was a darkness over all the earth until the ninth hour. And the sun was darkened, and the veil of the temple was rent in midst" Luke 23: 44-45). The darkness of the sky and land imply that the entire earth joins in the intense sorrow of the mourners at the foot of the cross.

This rich tonal character of the print is consistent with a change that occurs in Dürer's work after his return from his second trip to Venice (1505-1507). In his engraved works, he no longer emphasized the sharp contrast of light and dark that is typical of dark ink on light paper, as seen, for example, in *Madonna with the Monkey* (p. 55). Instead, using dense parallel lines, he created a middle range of tone referred to as *clair-obscur*.³ As is the case in this *Crucifixion*, the transitions from light to dark are subtle, and generate a more palpable atmosphere, as well as suggesting greater solidity in the figures and in their drapery.

Compared with other versions of the Crucifixion by Dürer, this composition appears focused on the humanity of the participants. The figures filling the picture plane are not the

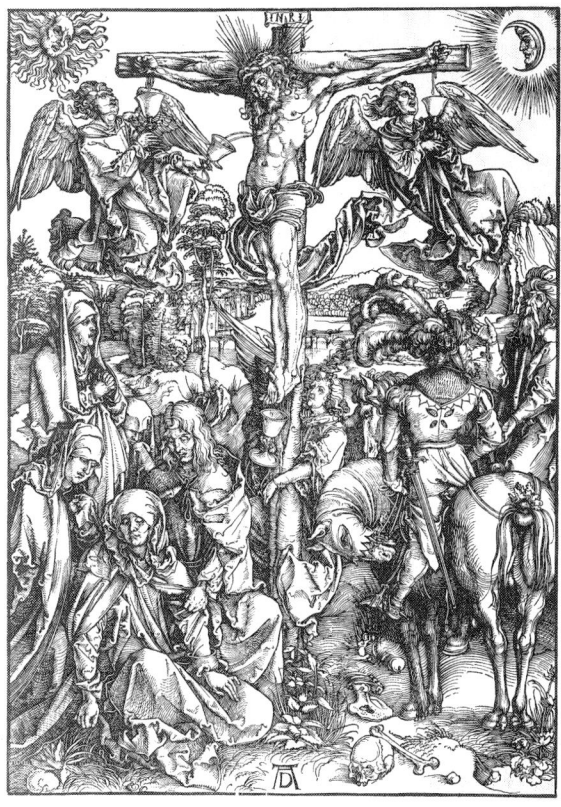

Figure 18 *Crucifixion* (from the *Large Passion*), c. 1497-1498, Woodcut on laid paper, Washington, National Gallery of Art, Rosenwald Collection, 1943.3.3621.

soldiers, angels, and attendants that illustrate narrative elements provided in the gospels, but are restricted to the people who were closest to the Savior during his life on earth. Many scenes of the Crucifixion focus attention on the figures of the Virgin and St. John because some of the final words spoken by Christ were addressed to them. ("When Jesus therefore saw his mother, and the disciple standing by whom he loved, he saith unto his mother, Woman, behold thy son!" Then saith he to the disciple, "Behold thy mother" John 19: 26-27). In this case, Dürer has the grief of these two figures mirror one another across the composition to enhance the sense of human loss rather than simply the symbolic character of the event.⁴

Panofsky suggests that the raw grief of the scene is related to the similar approach of artists such as Matthias Grünewald, who carried on the mysticism of a Gothic sensibility.⁵ Dürer's interest in the humanism of the Renaissance did stimulate him to go beyond the strictly symbolic depictions of previous versions of the Crucifixion in favor of presenting the deep feelings that identified these characters as authentic individuals affected by a human tragedy. **M.L.A.**

---

1 The engraved versions are M.13, M.23, M.24 and M.25; the eleven others are woodcuts.
2 Scholars note that the Betrayal of Christ in the Garden of Gethsemene was generally shown at night and usually by torchlight. See Panofsky, p. 145.
3 Ibid.
4 In the figure of St. John, who wrings his hands in despair and cries out with an open mouth, scholars have identified the influence of a figure from Mantegna's engraving of the *Deposition* (ibid., p. 146; Wölfflin, p. 733; Washington 1971, p. 136).
5 Any direct correlation between the compositions of Grünewald and Dürer is uncertain. See Washington 1971, p. 136, and Panofsky, p. 146.

Christ's Entry into Jerusalem, c. 1509-1510

From the edition of the *Small Woodcut Passion* after 1511
Woodcut
Laid paper
Meder 130; Hollstein 130; Bartsch 22
Watermark: None

Sheet: 133 x 103 mm
Signed, recto: Monogram AD (upper right)
2002.9
Catalogue number 21

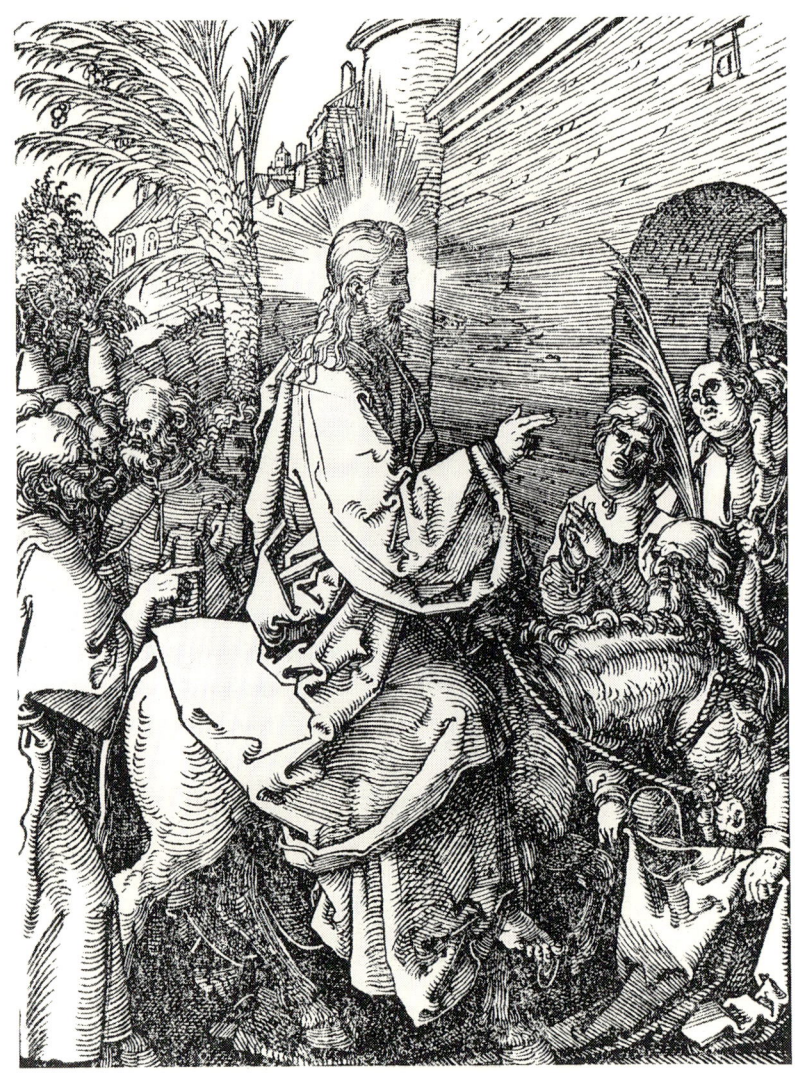

Dürer issued three important publications in book form in 1511: the *Large Passion*, the *Life of the Virgin*, and a collection of thirty-seven woodcuts that form the *Small Woodcut Passion*. The designs for the *Large Passion* and the *Life of the Virgin* were created over a number of years and were finally collected in the book format in 1511; however, the *Small Woodcut Passion* images were made within a few years prior to their publication, and consequently demonstrate a consistent stylistic approach.[1] In this publication Dürer included all the traditional images of Christ's Passion, but also added scenes at the beginning and end. *The Fall of Man, Expulsion from Paradise, Annunciation,* and *The Nativity* serve as an introduction; concluding the series are *Christ Appearing to His Mother, Noli Me Tangere, Christ in Emmaus, Doubting Thomas, Ascension, Pentecost,* and *The Last Judgment*. Benedictus Cheldonius composed the text in the form of twenty-line poems that are printed on the facing page for each plate.

Scholars have often noted that this publication (coming at the same time as the two noted above) seems to have been intended for a different audience. The artist is believed to have been inspired, at least in part, by Ulrich Pinder's book *Speculum Passionis (Mirror of the Passion)*, published in Nuremberg in 1507.[2] Dürer's compositions for this series as opposed to those for the *Large Passion* place a greater emphasis on conveying the narrative and the progression of events. The presence of scenes preceding and following the traditional Passion images reinforces the sense that Dürer wanted to tell the story of Christ's life in sequence, in a format accessible to an audience less sophisticated than the educated elite that formed a large part of the usual market for his works.

Christ's Entry into Jerusalem illustrates the opening of the Passion story with the triumphant procession of Christ and his disciples into the city of Jerusalem, celebrated in the Catholic Church on Palm Sunday. Early illustrated bibles such as the *Biblia Pauperum* established the iconography with Christ riding on the back of a donkey approaching an arched gateway, while a figure lays a cloak on the ground before him.[3] As with other images in the *Small Woodcut Passion*, the composition is crowded with figures as active participants, animatedly gesturing and engaging in conversation. This emphasis on physical activity establishes the overall tone of all the images in the series, which focuses on documenting the story of Christ's experience rather than conveying its spiritual significance. **M.L.A.**

1 For information on the *Large Passion*, see p. 48-51; for information on the *Life of the Virgin*, see p. 78-84.
2 See Washington 1971, p. 184.
3 For comparison with an earlier version, see *Christ's Entry into Jerusalem* by Master A.G., c. 1475-90 (Lehrs 409).

The Martyrdom of John the Baptist, 1510

Woodcut
Laid paper
Meder 231 a; Hollstein 231; Bartsch 125
Watermark: None
Sheet: 193 x 131 mm
Signed, recto: AD (lower left); 1510 (upper right)
1999.7.31
Catalogue number 22

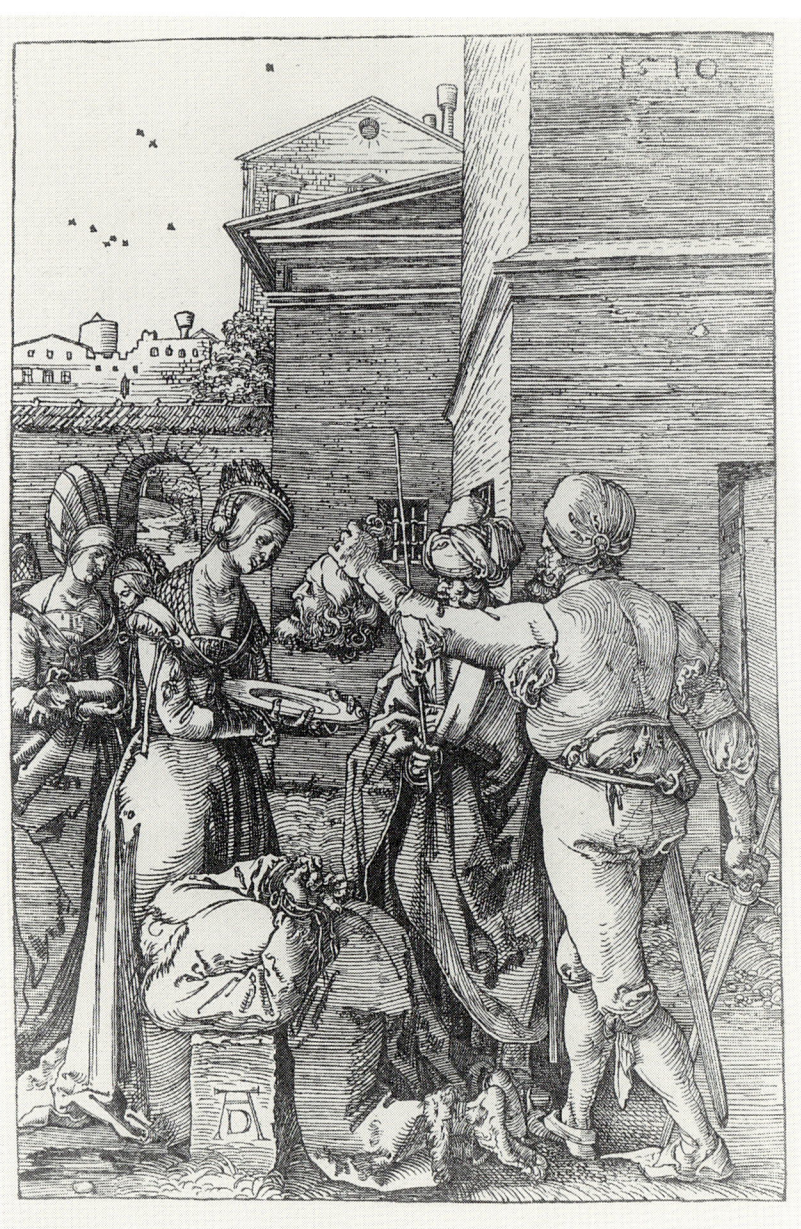

John the Baptist heralded the coming of Jesus Christ as the Redeemer of mankind, and thus was frequently a subject of religious art. In the first decade of the 1500s, Dürer created three woodblock prints depicting episodes from the life of St. John the Baptist. The first, *St. John the Baptist and St. Onuphrius* (M. 230, B. 112) was made in 1502. This scene of his execution was made in 1510, and a subsequent work of similar size was created the following year, *Salome Receiving the Head of St. John the*

Baptist (M. 232, B. 126, fig. 19, right). Because of the similarity in size and the fact that the two later works illustrate sequential episodes in the life of St. John, they are often considered as a pair.[1] The *Martyrdom of John the Baptist* shows John's execution by one of Herod's swordsmen, who places the saint's head on a charger that is held by a young, well-dressed woman of the court. In the companion print, *Salome Receiving the Head of St. John the Baptist*, it is apparent the young woman in the earlier print is Salome herself, since the clothing she wears in the second is identical. In the later woodcut, Salome presents the head to her mother, Herodias, in the presence of a bewildered King Herod of Judea.

John was the son of an Israelite priest, Zacharias, and his wife, Elizabeth, who was a cousin of Mary of Nazereth, Jesus's Mother. Jesus and John are often shown together playing as infants or small children, or as adults, when John baptizes Jesus in the Jordan River. Because of his preaching, and his public criticism of the king, John was imprisoned by Herod. Both Herod and Herodias were angered by John's condemnation of their marriage: contrary to religious law of the time, Herod had married his deceased brother's wife. Afraid of the consequences of condemning a holy man to death, Herod refused to execute John despite the urging of Herodias. His hand was forced at a feast when he promised to grant Salome, the daughter of Herodias, any favor if she would dance. Following her mother's instructions, she requested the head of John the Baptist.

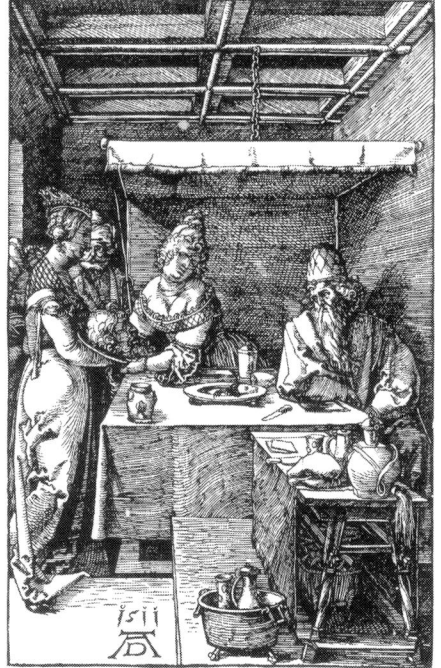

Figure 19 *Salome Receiving the Head St. John the Baptist*, (M.232, B.126)

The site of the execution is a courtyard surrounded by buildings, with an arched opening within a wall, surmounted by a view of distant hillside structures. Closely spaced parallel lines establish a variety of surface tones and patterns; the brightness of the sky and the reflected light on surfaces (which enters the scene from the left) are established by the white of the paper. As in the companion print, which by contrast is set in an interior space, the figures are arrayed across the middle ground. The headless body of John in the first print, and a table set for a meal in the second, establish the foreground planes. The sequence of the two prints follows the biblical narrative, but also visually prefigures the story of Christ's sacrifice and the symbolic meal that is the sacrament of Holy Communion.

Although not radical in his religious beliefs, Dürer was a pious man supportive of the goals of the Protestant Reformation. However, he was also a shrewd businessman who consistently provided prints for the popular market, largely in the medium of woodcut, and using conventional religious subject matter. Originally single sheet woodcuts such as this *Martyrdom of John the Baptist* might have been acquired and pasted into a folio or book to inspire devotion or to illustrate a biblical passage. More accessible to the lower classes because of the larger numbers that could be printed from a block (as opposed to engraving plates, which wore down more quickly), these less expensive alternatives were important to Dürer both as an outlet for creativity and as a significant source of income. Indeed, in a letter of 1509 to a patron, he confirmed that sales of his prints were critical to his survival as an artist: "So henceforth," he wrote, "I shall stick to my engraving, and had I done so before I should today have been a richer man by 1000 florins."[2] **M.L.A.**

---

1 Panofsky, p. 135.
2 Quoted in Washington 1971, Introduction.

David Penitent, 1510

Woodcut (with drawn additions)
Laid paper
Meder 108 unknown; Hollstein 108; Bartsch 119
Watermark: Coat of Arms with Crown, Meder 46, (center)
Sheet: 194 x 131 mm (borders added, paper augmented middle left)
Signed, recto: AD 1510 (upper right)
1999.7.28
Catalogue number 23

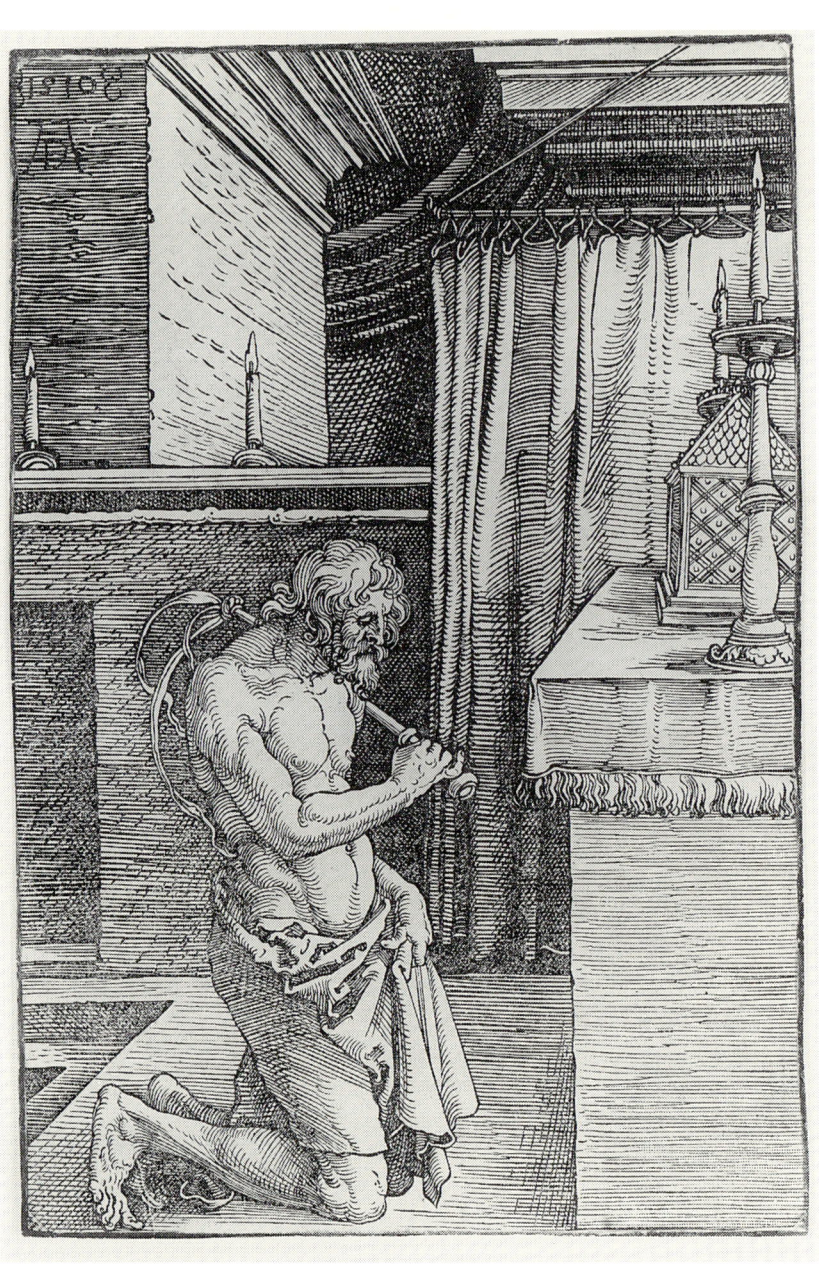

The rationally structured, geometric beauty of this architectural interior, as well as the horizontal emphasis of the lines created in the carving of the block, identify this woodcut as a work strongly influenced by Dürer's experiences in Venice from 1505 to 1507.[1] The form of the penitent, nude from the waist up, indicates Dürer's continuing commitment to the classical conception of the human figure. The refined technique necessary for the cutting of the block is one element that characterizes Dürer's contributions to woodcut as a medium, producing impressions in the early sixteenth century that far exceeded even his own earlier works in their enhanced tonal and pictorial qualities. This effect was achieved by having the lights and shadows set against a middle tone that is formulated in this print by the closely spaced horizontal lines that define the surfaces in the room.

This penitent figure has been associated with King David, and thus the title of the work alludes to David's repentance for the death of Uriah. In the biblical story from the Book of Samuel, David coveted Bathsheba, the wife of a Hittite, Uriah, and contrived to have her husband killed in battle so that he could marry her. As punishment for his action, God caused David and Bathsheba's first-born child to fall mortally ill. David repented his act, and in this woodcut is shown engaged in self-mortification.[2]

In the fifteenth century, woodcut was still "the poor cousin of the print family," primarily because more good impressions could be pulled from a woodblock than from an engraved plate, and thus they could be provided for a lower cost. Consequently, it was economic to use woodcuts for book illustration and for making the *Bilderbogen* (broadsheets) that were initially designed for a mass audience. Woodcuts were also traditionally associated with prints made in series, such as Dürer's *Apocalypse* or *Large Passion*.

Single-leaf woodcuts, such as this one, came to greater prominence in the early sixteenth century, largely through the influence of Dürer in Nuremberg and a few other artists located in key printing centers in Germany, such as Lucas Cranach in Wittenberg and Hans Burgkmaier in Augsburg, where great printing houses were located in conjunction with a population who valued humanist learning.[3] These artists were instrumental in refining the techniques and production of woodcuts as images independent of illustration for the masses, instead creating works with improved pictorial qualities for a more discriminating audience. **M.L.A.**

---

1 While in Italy, Dürer began drawing on papers that were colored, with the color creating a middle tone that contrasted with the darks and lights.
2 Panofsky, p. 135, notes that the penitent David has features that resemble those in Dürer's self-portraits.
3 See Landau and Parshall, pp. 169-74.

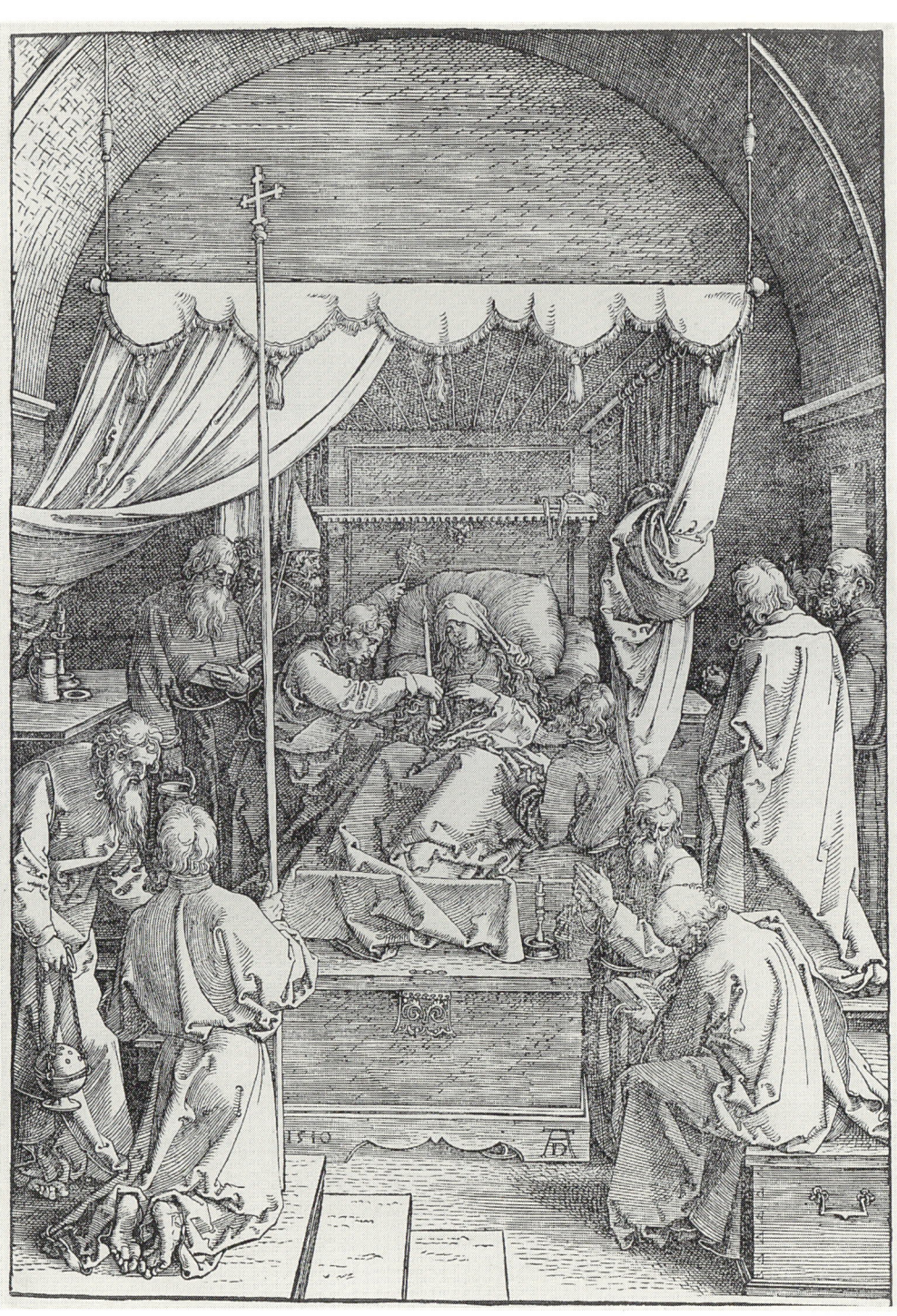

catalogue entry 23

Death of the Virgin, 1510

From the *Life of the Virgin* (without text)
Woodcut
Laid paper
Meder 205; Hollstein 205; Bartsch 98
Watermark: High Crown, Meder 20
Sheet: 290 x 207 mm
Signed, recto: Monogram AD (bottom center right); 1510 (bottom center left)
2001.4
Catalogue number 24

One of Dürer's greatest achievements during the first decade of the sixteenth century was his woodcut series *Life of the Virgin*, comprising nineteen full-page prints plus a frontispiece. He had completed seventeen woodcuts between 1502 and 1505 before leaving for his second trip to Italy. In 1510, three years after his return, Dürer finished the series with the *Death of the Virgin* and the *Assumption and Coronation of the Virgin* (p. 82) together with the title page. The completed series was published in book form in 1511, and was frequently bound together with the *Large Passion* and a reissue of the *Apocalypse*. The published woodcuts of *Life of the Virgin* are accompanied by Latin text, printed on the reverse side of the prints, written by Benedict Schwalbe. Also called Benedictus Chelidonius, the author was a monk in St. Aegidius's monastery in Nuremberg and a friend of the humanist Willibald Pirckheimer. Dürer's own faithful friendship with Pirckheimer is evident in the artist's dedication of the series to Pirckheimer's sister, Caritas. Not only the abbess of St. Clara's in 1503, she was also a gifted Latinist in her own right.[1]

The story of the death of the Virgin Mary does not appear in the Bible, but in apocryphal writings and then repeated in *The Golden Legend*.[2] While the subject was long favored in Byzantine art, it did not become popularly portrayed in Northern Europe until the end of the fifteenth century.[3] Mary is shown on her deathbed surrounded by the Twelve Apostles. St. John places a lighted candle in the Virgin's hand, said to prolong the life of the dying, while St. Peter kneels close to Mary's side as a priest sprinkles her with holy water. The remaining apostles are seen praying, meditating, and officiating in Mary's death.

Dürer's model for this print was Martin Schongauer's engraving of the same subject of c. 1470-75 (Lehrs, vol. 5, p. 106, no. 16, fig. 20, p. 80). The widely admired engravings of Schongauer (c. 1450-1491), the first major German painter-printmaker, had a profound influence on the young Dürer.[4] One of the purposes of his "bachelor's journey" was in fact to meet Schongauer in Colmar. Unfortunately, he arrived a full year after Schongauer's death, which occurred before May 1491.[5] While Dürer clearly borrowed certain details from Schongauer's print, such as the knotted bed curtain and the kneeling saint with bare soles at the bottom left, he also brought more spatial clarity to the scene.

This sense of rational space is a result of Dürer's initial mastering of the essential components of Italian Renaissance art theory, including linear perspective, which began in the period between 1500 and 1505. This interest was intensified during his second Italian trip and manifested itself in the prints he did after his return in 1507, such as the *Death of the Virgin*. In many of the prints from the *Life of the Virgin*, the perspective is partly defined by various architectural motifs; in *Death of the Virgin*, it is the barrel vault of the ceiling. In many of the prints, such as the *Annunciation* (M. 195, B. 83, fig. 21, p. 81), the scene is viewed through an archway. This construction recalls the fifteenth-century Italian art theorist Leon Battista Alberti's definition that a painting with correct perspective should be like looking through a window.[6] Also, this architecture is often of Italian Renaissance origin.[7]

The late prints from *Life of the Virgin*, such as the *Death...*, differ stylistically and technically from the earlier ones. Dürer has become more sophisticated in creating a subdued array of tonal values, ranging from dark black to various shades of gray. Unlike the rather unfocused compositions found in some of the earlier prints, that of *Death of the Virgin* now centers entirely on the main subject. All perspective lines converge to a point just above the Virgin's head.

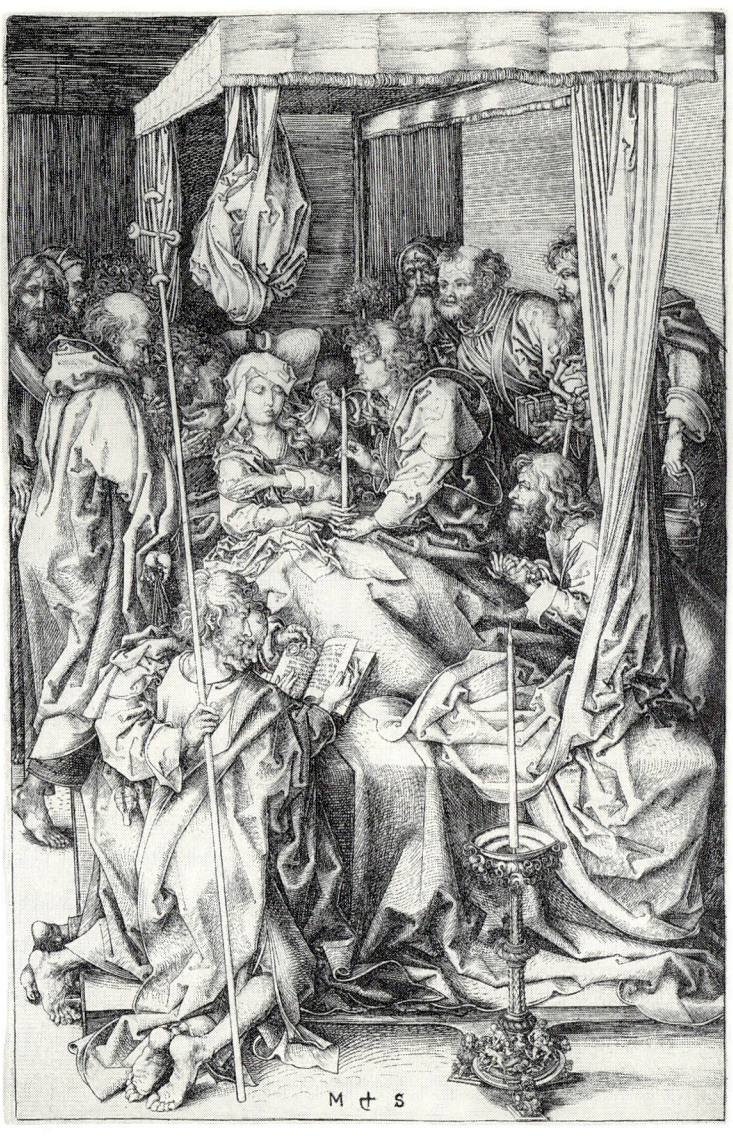

Figure 20 **Martin Schongauer**, *Death of the Virgin*, c. 1470-1475, (from the *Life of the Virgin*) Engraving on laid paper, Washington, National Gallery of Art, Rosenwald Collection, 1943.3.34

A preliminary drawing in pen and ink for the woodcut (W. 471, Vienna, Albertina) is rendered with minimal cross-hatching, characteristic of Dürer's drawings at this time.[8] The final print follows the drawing quite closely, the only major difference being that in the sketch the canopied bed is positioned slightly more in the center of the composition. **G.D.J.**

1 Hutchison, p. 54
2 The Golden Legend, vol. 2, pp. 449-51.
3 Paris, p. 87. See also Louis Réau, *Iconographie de l'art chrétien*, vol. 2 (Paris: Presses Universitaires de France, 1958), pp. 604ff.
4 Writing at length about Schongauer's prints, Giorgio Vasari reports that even Michelangelo as a young boy made a copy of the German artist's *Temptation of St. Anthony* (Vasari, p. 92).
5 Panofsky, p. 5.
6 Alberti, p. 56.
7 Washington 1971, p.179.
8 Strauss 1974, vol. 3, p. 1224 (1510/11).

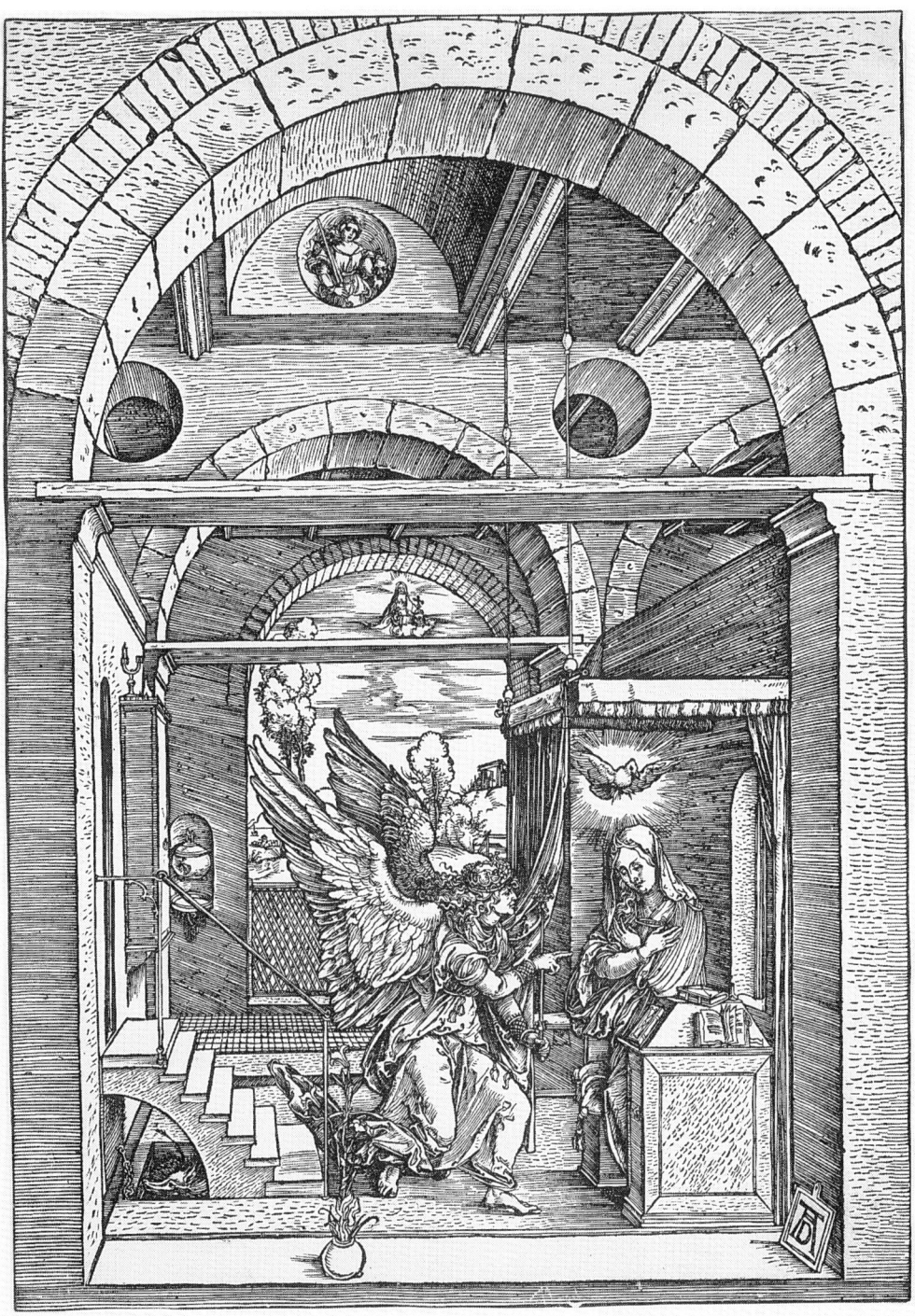

Figure 21 *Annunciation*, c. 1502-1504 (from the *Life of the Virgin*), Woodcut on laid paper, Washington, National Gallery of Art, Gift of Russell Allen, 1941.1.3

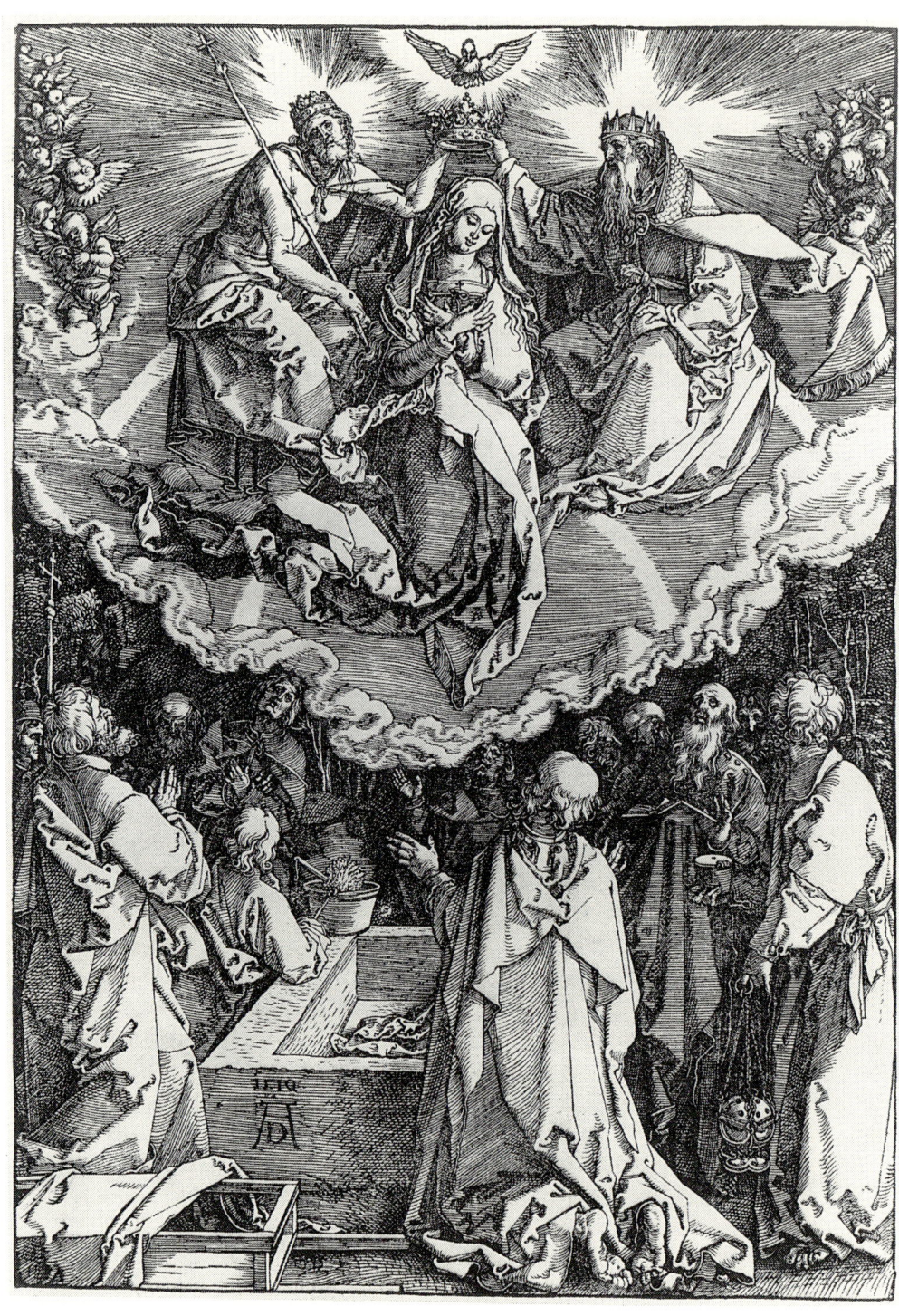

catalogue entry 24

Assumption and Coronation of the Virgin, 1510

From the *Life of the Virgin* (without text)
Woodcut
Laid paper
Meder 206 a; Hollstein 206; Bartsch 94
Watermark: High Crown, Meder 20
Sheet: 326 x 241 mm
Signed, recto: Monogram AD, 1510 (bottom center left)
2001.5
Catalogue number 25

As with the *Death of the Virgin* (p. 78), *Assumption and Coronation of the Virgin* was added to the *Life of the Virgin* in 1510, a year before the series was published. Dürer also added prior to publication the title page in which the Virgin sits on a crescent moon nursing the Christ Child (M. 188, B. 76; fig. 22, p. 84). The iconography of this image is derived from St. John's vision of the Virgin as described in the *Apocalypse*, or the *Book of Revelation* (12: 1): "And there appeared a great wonder in heaven, a woman clothed with the sun, and the moon under her feet, and upon her head a crown of twelve stars…." This image, known as the Apocalyptic Madonna, frequently appeared in fifteenth-century engravings.[1] Her sitting as she cradles Christ refers to her role as the Virgin of Humility.[2] The Montgomery *Assumption and Coronation of the Virgin* is a fine early impression, without text, printed before the 1511 publication.

The stories of the Assumption and Coronation of the Virgin do not appear in the Holy Scriptures, but instead are derived from apocryphal writings that were popularized in the thirteenth-century book *The Golden Legend* by Jacobus de Voragine. After the Virgin died, the apostles placed her body in a tomb and called after her:

> "O Virgin most prudent, whither goest thou? Be mindful of us O Lady!" Then the assemblage of those who stayed behind in Heaven, in admiration at the choiring of those who ascended, went swiftly forth to meet them; and seeing their King bearing in His own arms a soul of a woman, and her leaning upon Him, they began to exclaim, saying: "Who is this that cometh up from the desert, flowing with delights, leaning upon her beloved?" And those who accompanied her answered: "Fair is she among the daughters of Jerusalem, as ye have seen her filled with charity and love." And in this wise she was taken up into Heaven rejoicing, and placed upon a throne of glory at the right hand of her Son.[3]

Here Dürer combined into one single miraculous vision the Assumption and the Coronation, in which the Virgin is crowned Queen of Heaven by the Holy Trinity. He was most successful in blending the earthly apostles and the otherworldly revelation. The two registers are contrasted tonally, with the lower half darker and carrying densely crosshatched lines, while the upper half is lighter, with more widely spaced lines. Yet both halves harmoniously balance one another.

Dürer based the two-tiered composition of this woodcut on the central panel of his altarpiece commissioned by the merchant Jacob Heller for the Dominican church in Frankfurt (completed in 1509).[4] This painting in turn reflects various precedents for this arrangement of events in the Virgin's life, including a panel by the Master of the Imhof Altarpiece (1456), and the famous painting of the same subject by the Italian High Renaissance painter Raphael.[5] The major difference between the woodcut and the Heller altarpiece is that the print is much less hieratic. For a more integrated composition in the print, Dürer eliminated the carefully delineated horizon line in the painting, which clearly separates both halves of the composition. He retained in the woodcut the earthy detail of the kneeling apostle with bare feet—a depiction also included in the *Death of the Virgin*.

Figure 22 **Madonna on the Crescent**, 1501-1511, (from the *Life of the Virgin*), Woodcut on paper, Washington, National Gallery of Art, Gift of W.G. Russell Allen, 1941.1.27

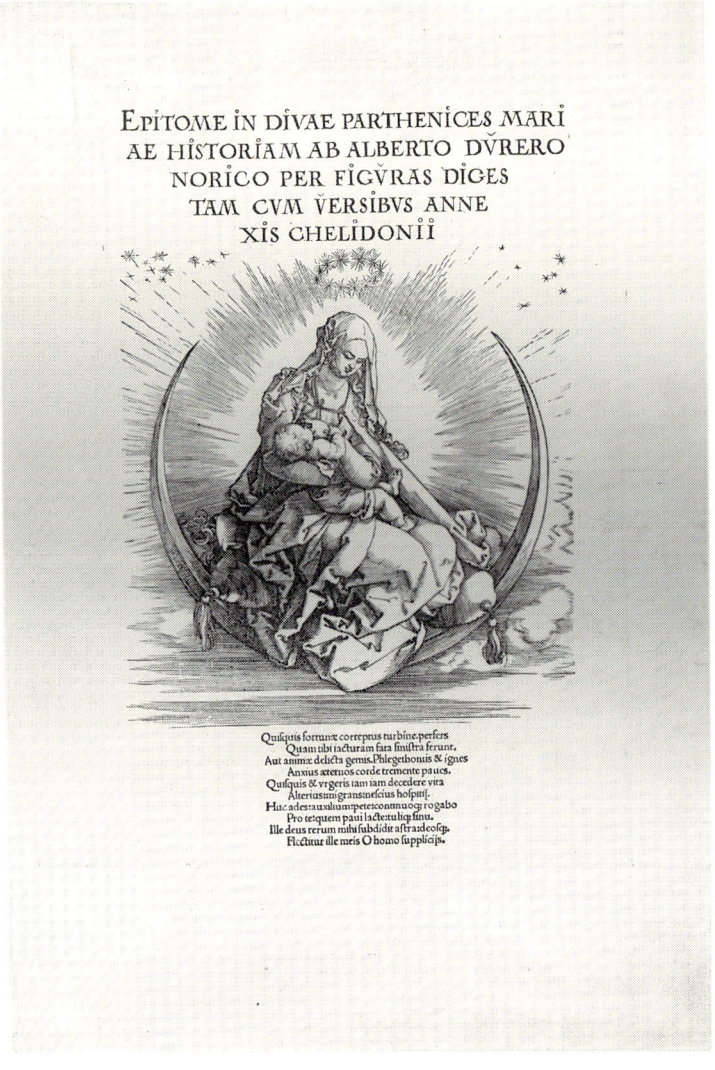

Though Dürer's original preparatory study for this woodcut does not exist, there are two sixteenth-century copies of it, one in the Berlin Kupferstichkabinett and the other in the Ambrosiania Library in Milan.[6] The popularity of the *Life of the Virgin* series prompted Marcantonio Raimondi to make pirated engraved copies after the earlier woodcuts in 1506.[7] This led to the copyright notice Dürer had published at the end of the 1511 edition, which colorfully states in part, "Secret begrudgers and thieves of the labor and invention of others: keep your audacious hands from this work."[8] **G.D.J.**

1 See Washington 1967, no. 35, for Schongauer's *Virgin on the Crescent Moon* (Lehrs, vol. 5, p. 199, no. 40).
2 Panofsky, pp. 137-38.
3 The Golden Legend, vol. 2, p. 452.
4 Panofsky, pp. 122-24; 136. The original painting was destroyed by fire in 1729. The central panel is known today through a copy by Jobst Harrich from the early seventeenth century. See also Anzelewsky, pp. 219-25.
5 Ibid., pp. 123-24.
6 Strauss 1974, vol. 3, pp. 1226 (1510/12 and 1510/13).
7 Panofsky, p. 101. Giorgio Vasari tells of this incident in the 1568 edition of the *Lives* (p. 96).
8 Cited in Strauss 1979, p. 450.

catalogue entry 25

Christ, Man of Sorrows, Mocked by a Soldier, 1511

Title page from the edition of the *Large Passion* after 1511
Woodcut
Heavy laid paper
Meder 113; Hollstein 113; Bartsch 4
Watermark: Flower with Triangle, Meder 127
Sheet: 338 x 206 mm (trimmed within block mark)
1981.20.1
Catalogue number 26

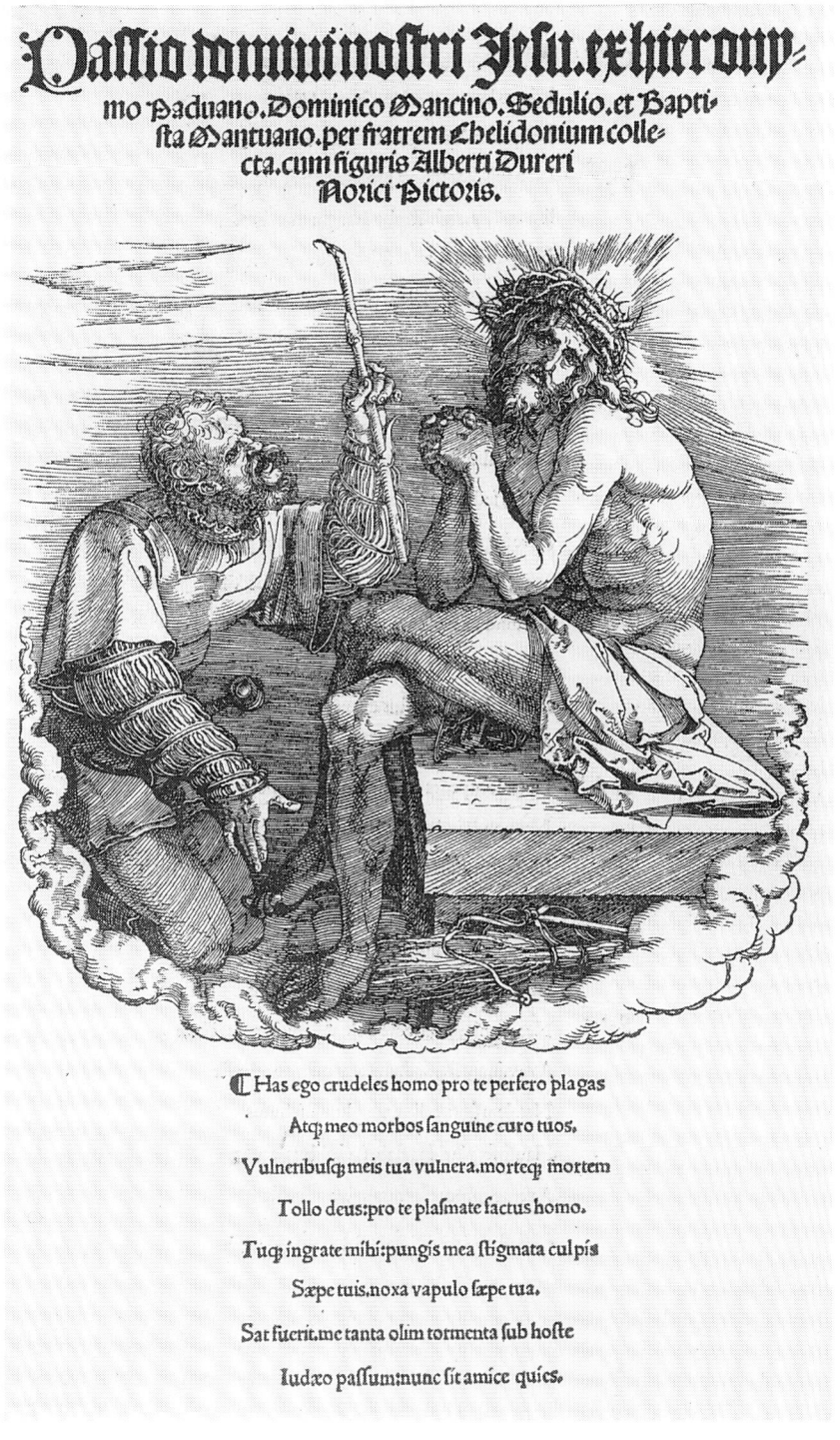

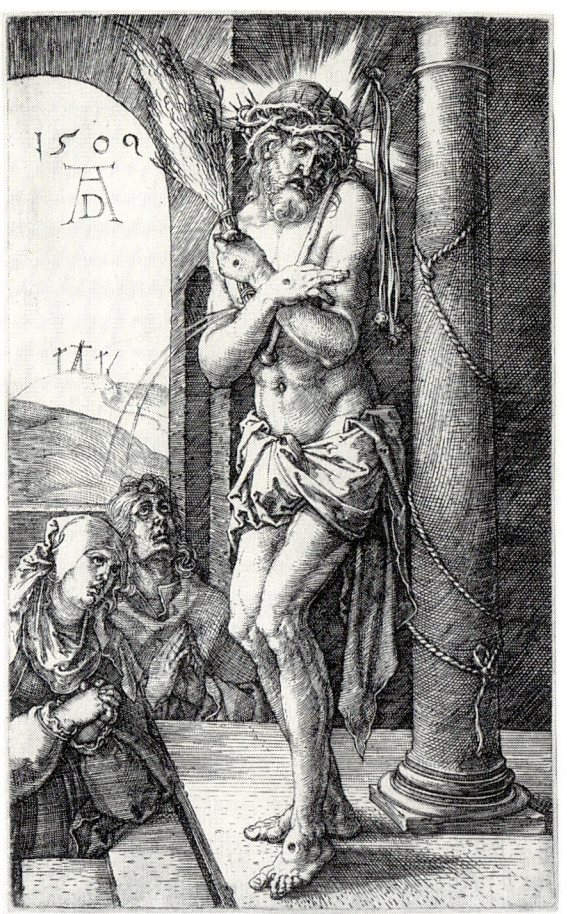

Figure 23 *The Man of Sorrows Standing by the Column*, 1509, (from *The Engraved Passion*), Engraving on laid paper, Washington, National Gallery of Art, Rosenwald Collection, 1943.3.3501

Christ as the Man of Sorrows is a subject that serves as the frontispiece for each of Dürer's printed versions of the Passion of Christ.[1] The earliest series, the *Engraved Passion*, begun in 1507, features a variant of the motif (M.3, B.3, fig. 23, left) showing the figure of Christ alongside the column on which his scourging took place. A second version, designed around 1510 (M.125, B.16), serves as the introductory print for the *Small Woodcut Passion* and shows a second variant: Christ seated on a stone, with his face buried in his hands. The following year Dürer used the print *Christ, Man of Sorrows, Mocked by a Soldier* as the title page for his woodcut series titled the *Large Passion*. This version shows Christ seated on a stone slab with his head turned toward the viewer; he is accompanied by instruments of the Passion, the scourge and the crown of thorns. A soldier kneels before him presenting a reed, mocking the concept of a scepter and thus alluding to the description of Christ as the King of the Jews.[2]

The Man of Sorrows is a traditional image related to the idea of the "Perpetual Passion," that is, the belief that the sins of mankind cause endless suffering to the Risen Christ, and thus until man ceases his sinfulness, Christ will suffer eternally. The image itself is variously interpreted as deriving from a vision of St. Bridget, or as a representation of Christ as prefigured in the Old Testament (Isaiah 53: 3): "He was despised and rejected of men. A Man of Sorrows, acquainted with grief, and we hid our face from him."[3] The image of Christ portrayed in eternal suffering had a long history as an object of devotion in Northern Europe, and in Dürer's time was also related to the spiritual practice called the Imitation of Christ. In this practice, which was inspired by the writings of Thomas à Kempis, the devotee was instructed to meditate on the sufferings of Christ in the Passion.[4] In some respects the image is also related to other Passion images such as the Mocking of Christ or the Flagellation, however, the presence of the marks of the stigmata, as well as the emphasis on the solitary suffering of the figure, distinguish the Man of Sorrows imagery.[5]

Christ, Man of Sorrows, Mocked by a Soldier was created some thirteen years after the initial woodcuts for the *Large Passion*. Dürer designed the first seven works between 1496 and 1499, and then created the final five about 1510. These later additions, which include the title page, were executed in his post-1505 woodcut style that utilizes the so-called middle tone, achieved by the use of closely spaced parallel hatchings (visible here in the background and on the front ledge of the stone slab).[6]

Dürer issued the twelve collected woodcuts as a volume in 1511 with a Latin text by Benedict Schwalbe (or Benedictus Chelidonius). His verses on the title page are appropriate to the consideration of the work as a reference to the "Perpetual Passion":

These cruel wounds I bear for thee, O man,
And cure thy mortal sickness with my blood.
I take away thy sores with mine, thy death
With mine—a God Who changed to man for thee.
But thou, ingrate, still stabb'st my wounds with sins;
I still take floggings for thy guilty acts.
It should have been enough to suffer once
From hostile Jews; now friend, let there be peace.[7]

In addition to the *Large Passion* and the *Life of the Virgin*, Dürer issued another edition of the *Apocalypse* with a Latin text in 1511. This event reiterated the importance of the woodcut both in Dürer's oeuvre and in the marketplace. It demonstrated woodcut's evolution from a medium designed primarily for book illustration and popular broadsides, into a sophisticated vehicle for images of devotion created for a literate audience. In each instance the text was clearly subordinate to the images, and the volumes spread throughout Europe as advertisements for the skill of Dürer as a master printmaker. Thus, "for at least two generations afterward the fine woodcut would be measured against Dürer's achievement."[8] **M.L.A.**

1 All the versions of the printed Passions series are ultimately related to drawings that Dürer did in 1504 on green prepared paper, which are known as the *Green Passion*. It is believed that these drawings were probably made in preparation for a painted work that was never executed. See London, p. 44.
2 Dürer also used the Man of Sorrows motif for a number works not associated with his Passion series. They include an oil panel painting, *Christ as Man of Sorrows* (Karlsruhe, Staatliche Kunsthalle) which probably dates from his travels as a journeyman (1490-94). Another engraving with Christ shown standing at the foot of the cross dates from about 1500 (M. 20, B. 20); a drypoint (M. 21, B. 21) dates from 1512, and the Man of Sorrows was probably the first subject he etched (M. 22, B.22) in 1515.
3 See Strauss 1975, pp. 90, 156.
4 Hutchinson, p. 187 and Butts's essay, p. 10.
5 Elements such as clouds and rays of light emanating from the head of Christ also suggest that the image portrays not an earthly event, but a visionary one.
6 Washington 1971, p. 175.
7 As translated in ibid. p. 176.
8 Landau and Parshall, p. 176.

St. Jerome in His Cell, 1511

Woodcut
Laid paper
Meder 228 a; Hollstein 228; Bartsch 114
Watermark: None
Sheet: 234 x 157 mm (trimmed to block mark)
Signed, recto: Monogram AD 1511 (bottom right)
1999.7.30
Catalogue number 27

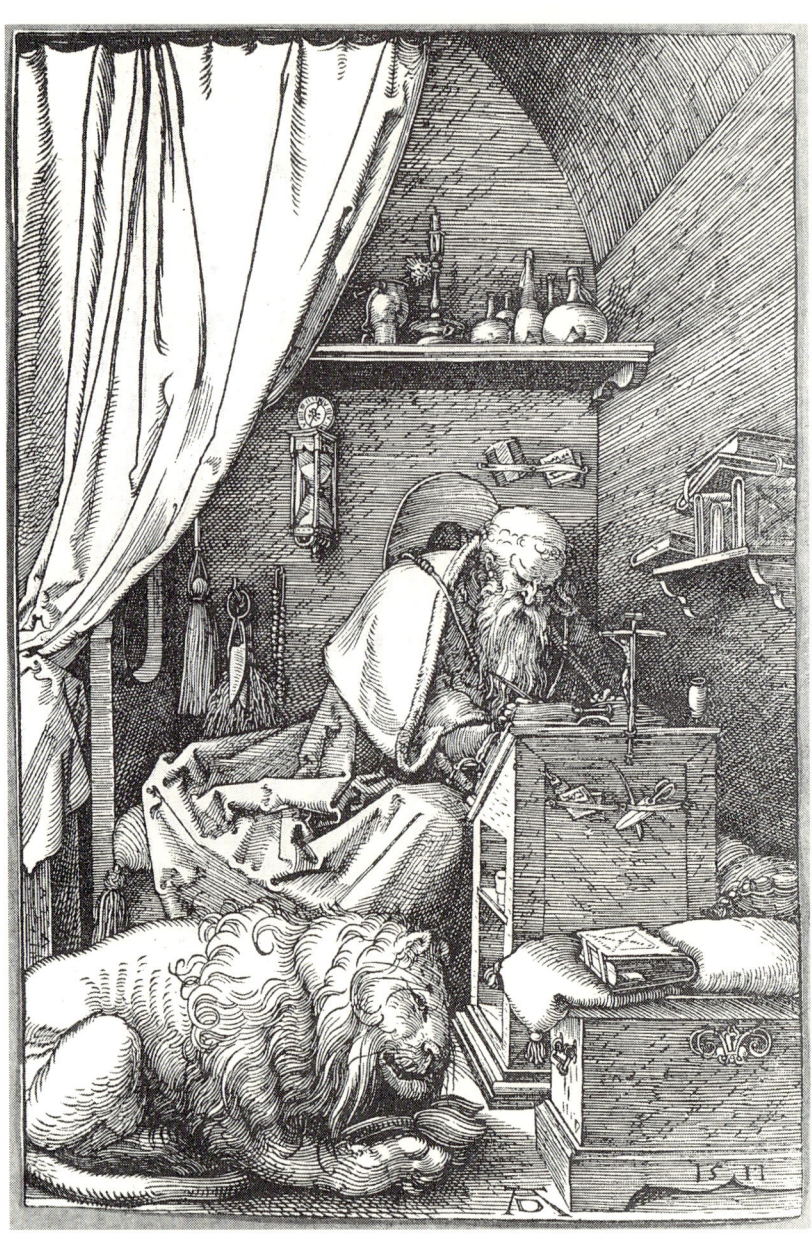

After spending three years as a hermit in the wilderness, St. Jerome was called to Rome by Pope Damasus to translate the Holy Scriptures into Latin, a work that became known as the Vulgate Bible. In this woodcut Dürer depicted the saint not as an ascetic, as in the c. 1496 engraving (p. 37), but rather as a scholar and critic. This role had special appeal to the humanists of Dürer's day. Martin Luther, however, did not hide his disregard for the saint. He wrote: "I know of no one among the teachers whom

I bear as much enmity as St. Jerome, for he speaks only of fasting, virginity, etc."¹ Here, Jerome wears the robe of a cardinal, although he never attained this rank.² This woodcut was completed in 1511, the year that also saw the important publication of Dürer's three major woodcut cycles, the *Apocalypse*, the *Large Passion*, and the *Life of the Virgin*.

Beginning in 1510, Dürer's woodcuts show a greater contrast between light and dark. To achieve these *chiaroscuro* effects, Dürer employed considerable crosshatching in the dark areas, such as in the deep folds of the saint's robes and in the shadowy corner behind him. He also found different graphic lines to portray the different surfaces and textures in the room. For the dark walls and furniture, he employed closely hatched parallel lines interspersed by short diagonals that help animate the forms. Long, tapered lines define the white expanse of various objects, such as the curtain, Jerome's robe, and the pillow resting on top of the chest. Squiggly, curly lines denote the shaggy coat of the lion.

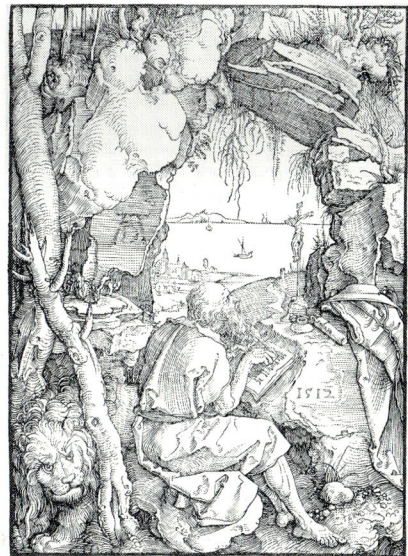

Figure 24 *St. Jerome in a Cave*, 1512, Woodcut on laid paper, Washington, National Gallery of Art, Robert A. McNeil Fund, 1992.43.1

The setting, an orderly chamber filled with everyday objects, is again an important feature in the composition. Delightful mini still-lifes abound: the candle and flasks on the shelf above Jerome's head, the hourglass (like the extinguished candle, a symbol of the transience of life) on the wall below; and another shelf holding a pile of leather-bound books at the right, to name a few. As in several of the interiors depicted in the *Life of the Virgin* woodcuts, Dürer constructed a rational perspective of the room. The preliminary ink drawing for this print (W. 590, Milan, Biblioteca Ambrosiana) shows a similarly conceived space, though it is noticeably deeper and more open and light-filled.³ Two years later, Dürer made an engraving of the same subject, which became one of his masterworks (fig. 6, p. 16). But while St. Jerome dominates the setting in the woodcut, in the engraving he is a small figure placed at the back of the room and almost overwhelmed by the furnishings of the homey interior.

Dürer introduced a novel illusionistic effect in this print by depicting a curtain suspended from the top of the composition and pulled to one side, emphasizing the idea that the viewer is looking through a window or doorway.⁴ In likening the picture plane to a window, Dürer was following a principle expounded by the fifteenth-century Italian humanist and art theorist Leon Battista Alberti (1404-1472). He writes in his *Della pittura* of 1436, a text that strongly influenced Dürer's own theories on art and inspired him to write his own treatises: "I inscribe a quadrangle of right angles, as large as I wish, which is considered to be an open window through which I see what I want to paint."⁵

The following year, in 1512, Dürer executed yet another woodcut of Jerome, again seen writing, though not in a comfortable study, but outdoors beneath a rocky cave or grotto (M. 229, B. 113; fig. 24, above). Here, the artist combined elements of the early engraving *St. Jerome Penitent in the Wilderness* (p. 37) with depictions of the saint at work. This woodcut served as the title page for H. Hölzel's *Beschreibung des heyligen Bischoffs Eusebij*, published in Nuremberg in 1514. **G.D.J.**

---

1 Cited in Strauss 1979, p. 458.
2 Washington 1971, p. 189.
3 Strauss 1974, vol. 3, p. 1282, (1511/15). A related pen drawing, *St. Jerome Contemplating a Skull* (Berlin Kupferstichkabinett), has been variously dated between 1511 and 1521 (Strauss 1974, vol. 4, p. 2006 [1521/5]). The skull is a symbol of transience.
4 Antonello da Messina's painting *St. Jerome in His Study*, c.1475-77, in the London National Gallery similarly shows a curtain pulled to the side (Paris, p. 186, no. 144).
5 Alberti, p. 56. This trompe l'oeil device of a depicted curtain separating the viewer from the work art became a common device in the seventeenth century. A famous example is Rembrandt van Rijn's painting *The Holy Family (with Painted Frame and Curtain)*, in Kassell, Germany; see A. Bredius, *The Complete Edition of the Paintings*, rev. by H. Gerson, 4th ed. (New York: Phaidon Publishers Inc, 1971), cat. no. 572.

St. Paul, 1514

Engraving
Laid paper
Meder 47 second state, a; Hollstein 47; Bartsch 50
Watermark: None
Sheet: 119 x 77 mm
Signed, recto: Monogram AD 1514 (bottom right)
1999.7.12
Catalogue number 31

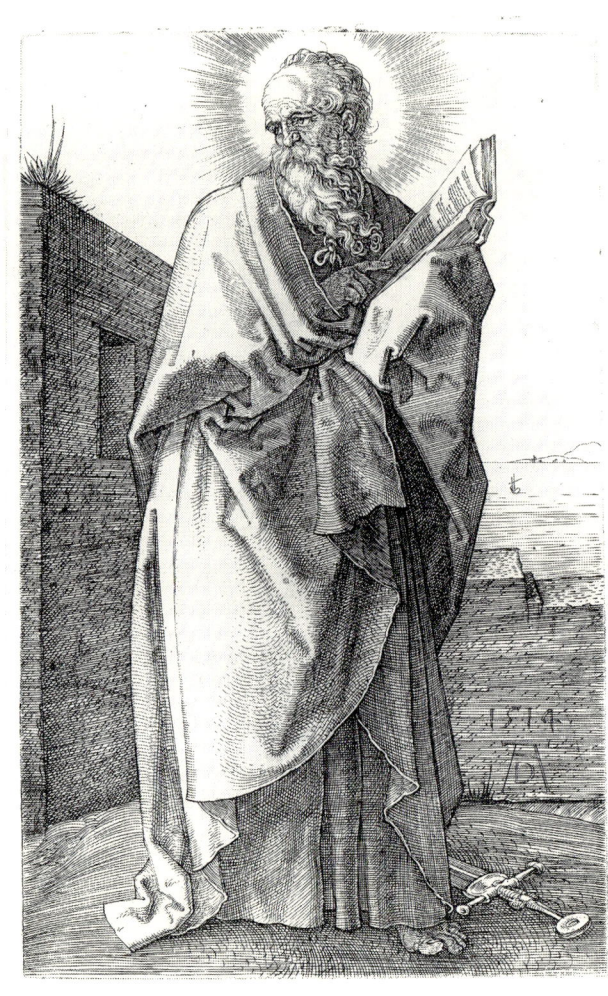

St. Paul is one of the earliest engravings in a projected series of prints that was left incomplete at the time of Dürer's death in 1528. The artist undoubtedly was inspired by earlier works created by Martin Schongauer and others that depicted the Twelve Apostles as single figures, accompanied by attributes that identified them according to their accomplishments or their form of martyrdom.[1] Like images of the Madonna and Child, these works were preserved as devotional objects, collected as sets, or pasted into prayer books to inspire contemplation of the martyr's death.

The conversion of Paul, an early believer in Jesus Christ as the Redeemer, provided a highly dramatic event frequently depicted in Western art.[2] Originally named Saul, Paul was born in Tarsus to Jewish parents who were Roman citizens. Commissioned by the Romans to persecute the early Christians, he was on his way to Damascus to do so when he was blinded by a great light from Heaven. Falling to the ground, he heard a voice asking, "Saul, Saul, why persecutest thou me?" He asked, "Who art thou, Lord?" and the voice responded, "I am Jesus whom thou persecutest" (Acts 9: 3-5). Led into Damascus by companions, Saul was visited by Ananias, who restored his sight. As a convert to Christianity, he was baptized with the name Paul.

After retiring to the desert for a period of contemplation, Paul became one of the great missionaries of the early Church, spreading the faith throughout Asia Minor and Greece. His epistles to the various Christian communities of his ministry (Romans, Corinthians, Galatians, etc.) are an important record of the early Church and central to the text of the New Testament. Eventually arrested by the Romans in Palestine, Paul was imprisoned in Rome and, legend says, beheaded. He is identified here by the sword of execution located at his feet, and by the book representing his epistles.

Dürer made two states of this print. The first more closely resembles antecedent works by artists such as Schongauer and shows the saint standing on a curved mound of earth against an empty background. In the second state, the artist inserted a wall and a landscape, presumably to provide a darker foil for the figure of the saint.[3] **M.L.A.**

---

1 See *St. Bartholomew* (p. 100) for further information on the projected series and its sources.
2 Perhaps the best known of these depictions is the *Conversion of St. Paul* (c. 1601) by Michaelangelo Merisi da Caravaggio (Rome, Cerasi Chapel, Santa Maria del Popolo).
3 Washington 1971, p. 147.

Agony in the Garden, 1515

Etching
Laid paper
Meder 19 first state, b-c; Hollstein 19; Bartsch 19
Watermark: Large City Gate, Meder 263
Sheet: 228 x 159 mm (trimmed yo plate mark)
Signed, recto: Monogram AD 1515 (bottom center)
1999.7.8
Catalogue number 32

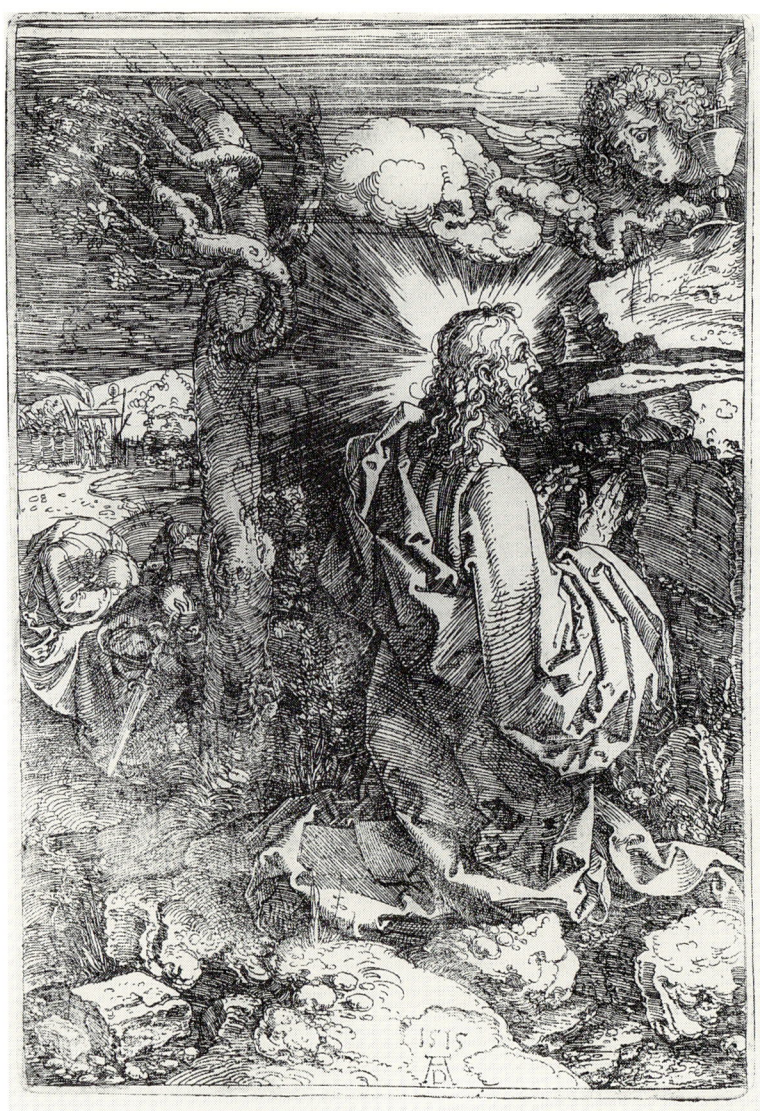

Dürer executed six etchings between c. 1514 and 1518. In addition to the *Agony in the Garden* are *The Man of Sorrows* (1515; M. 22, B. 22), *The Desperate Man* (c. 1515; M. 95, B. 70), *Sudarium Held by One Angel* (1516; M. 27, B. 26), *Abduction on a Unicorn* (1516; M. 67, B. 72), and *Landscape with Cannon* (1518; M. 96, B. 99, fig. 25, right). The etching process, which involves using acid to bite into exposed lines made by a needle on a wax-grounded plate, originated in the mid-fifteenth century with goldsmiths and armorers who etched designs into metal. Predating Dürer's etchings are those by the Augsburg printmaker Daniel Hopfer (c. 1470-1536).[1]

Unlike the medium of engraving, etching permits greater spontaneity and freedom of line—more like drawing with pen and ink on paper. Nevertheless, Dürer soon abandoned this medium because, probably for a combination of technical reasons, it ultimately proved inadequate for expressing the artist's graphic vocabulary at that time. The iron or steel plates that were used had the tendency to rust, and many later impressions of Dürer's etchings show spots of ink caused by rusting of the plate. In his later engravings Dürer moved toward using closer hatching and crosshatching to achieve greater tonal effects—a technique more difficult to employ in etching, since the acid could sometimes weaken the areas between the close lines.[2] In his last and largest etching,

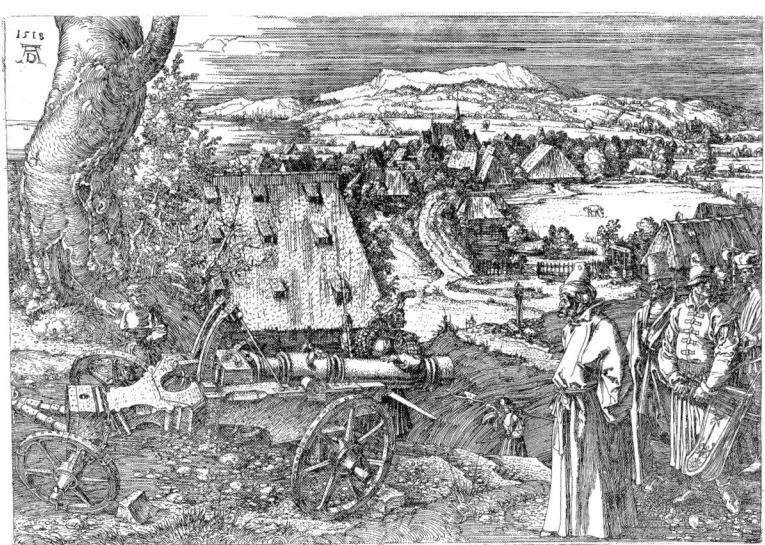

Figure 25 *Landscape with Cannon*, 1518, Etching on laid paper, Washington, National Gallery of Art, Gift of W.G. Russell Allen, 1941.1.21

Landscape with Cannon (fig. 25, above) Dürer avoided this problem by minimizing the crosshatching. The cannon, which bears the arms of Nuremberg, appears rather decrepit. Several Turks, who were a threatening presence in Northern Europe at this time, stand at the right. Even though the subject of the print is rather mysterious, it was a precursor for many panoramic landscape prints during the course of the sixteenth century, including those by Pieter Bruegel the Elder.[3]

Despite the problems with the medium, Dürer did realize that he was able to achieve different effects with etching than with engraving or woodcut. In the *Agony in the Garden,* thick, rough, and energetic lines emphasize the emotional intensity of the subject, filling the night scene with drama and tension.

The etching differs from the two extant preliminary drawings from 1515 (W. 584, Paris, Musée du Louvre; W. 585, Vienna, Albertina).[4] In working through the composition, Dürer focused more attention on Christ. In the Louvre sheet Dürer placed three sleeping apostles, Peter, John and James, in the foreground. They are rather large in proportion to Christ, who kneels in prayer before the cup of divine judgment, an allusion to the crucifixion[5] which is placed on top of a rocky ledge. The full figure of a robed angel hovers above the cup. The second preliminary study is closer to the final etching. Christ now has become the central figure with the apostles smaller in proportion and placed in the background. As in the final print, the angel has been reduced to head and wings. The weather-beaten tree behind Christ, done with an energetic and calligraphic line, has also been carried over into the print. In all three versions of the composition, the figures of Judas and soldiers can be seen entering through a gate in the distance.

As Panofsky aptly notes, Dürer used the medium of etching to combine the *chiaroscuro* effects of his prints after 1510 (for example, see p. 88) and the powerful linearity of the woodcuts of the *Large Passion* (p. 48-51).[6] The Montgomery impression is of the rarer first state, before the appearance of the rust spots. The original iron plate today is in the Bamberg Staatsbibliothek. **G.D.J.**

1 Hopfer's first etchings possibly date as early as 1500. See Landau and Parshall, pp. 323-32.
2 Washington 1971, pp. 151-52.
3 Ibid., p. 152. For a recent interpretation of this etching, see Larry Silver, "Germanic Patriotism in the Age of Dürer," in *Dürer and his Culture*, ed. Dagmar Eichberger and Charles Zika (Cambridge: Cambridge University Press, 1998), pp. 55-56.
4 Strauss 1974, vol. 3, pp. 1610-13 (1515/74, 1515/75).
5 Austin, Texas, Archer M. Huntington Art Gallery, *Nuremberg: A Renaissance City, 1500-1618,* text by Jeffrey Chipps Smith (Austin, 1983), p. 115.
6 Panofsky, p. 196.

catalogue entry 29

St. Anthony Reading, 1519

Engraving
Laid paper
Meder 51 b; Hollstein 51; Bartsch 58
Watermark: None
Sheet: 102 x 147 mm
Signed, recto: Monogram AD 1519 (bottom center)
1999.7.14
Catalogue number 33

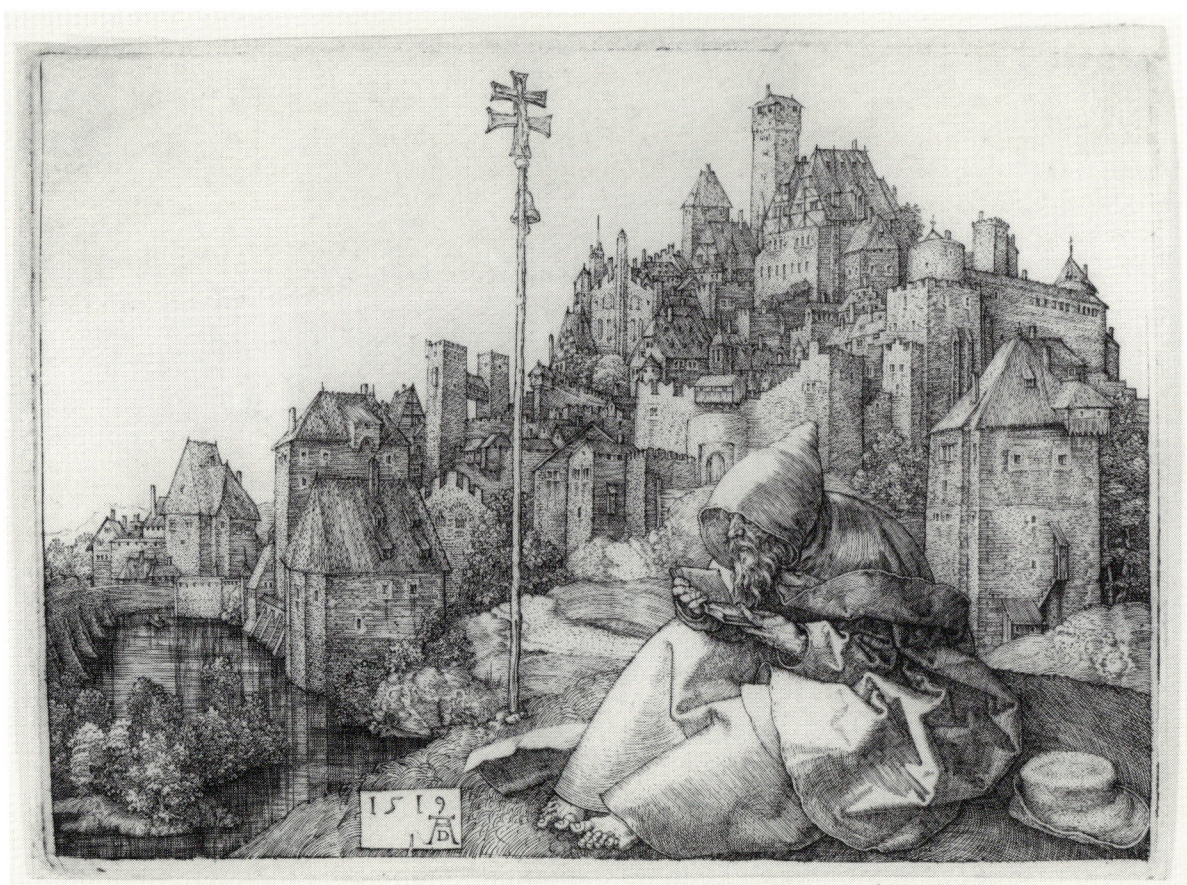

St. Anthony (c. 250-350), whose life is told by Jacobus de Voragine in his book *The Golden Legend*, lived as a hermit in the deserts of Egypt.[1] He is usually shown tormented by demons, as in Martin Schongauer's famous engraving of c. 1470-75.[2] His traditional attributes often include a pig, symbolizing his triumph over sensuality and gluttony, and a crutch, an allusion to his old age and failing faculties.[3] Dürer, however, in his unusual portrayal of the saint seated before a fictitious town and reading, created an image of the *vita contemplative* (contemplative life).[4] Next to the saint is a double-barred patriarchal cross bearing a bell to announce the arrival of an Antonite monk as he collected alms, and also believed to ward off evil spirits such as those that tormented the saint throughout his life. Considered the father of monasticism, St. Anthony is dressed in the Antonite habit with cowl; his traditional hat lies on the ground near him.[5]

As in many of Dürer's prints, the background setting plays an active role in the composition. Typically, it is carefully constructed from the artist's compendium of studies after nature. The town is taken from a much earlier drawing (W. 153, c. 1496; Windsor, England, Windsor Castle), which is inscribed in the artist's hand *Pupila Augusta*.[6] This drawing, which might be an allegory on the birth of Venus, is one of a group of works depicting classical subjects that were probably produced upon the advice of the artist's close friend and Nuremberg's leading humanist, Willibald Pirckheimer.[7] The cityscape includes characteristics of Trent and Innsbruck, both of which Dürer drew on his way to Italy in 1494-95, and also of his hometown of Nuremberg.[8]

There had been a tradition in Nuremberg of including views of the city in the backgrounds of altarpieces.[9] This trend had grown by the time two important publications appeared at the end of the fifteenth century: Bernhard von Breydenbach's *Peregrinatio in Terram Sanctum* (*Pilgrimage to the Holy Land*) of 1486 and Hartmann Schedel's *World Chronicle* (more commonly known as the *Nuremberg Chronicle*), published by Anton Koberger in 1493. Each publication included woodcut city views as subjects in their own right. Nuremberg humanists, such as the poet laureate Konrad Celtis, promoted this burgeoning interest in German geography. Erwin Panofsky notes the importance of the cityscape, stating: "Durer did not devise an architectural setting for a contemplated St. Anthony, but rather invented a St. Anthony for an architectural setting already on hand ...."[10] He goes on to note how the buildings and the figure of the saint have been defined in "stereometrical" terms, presenting a "'cubist' mode of vision."[11] It was precisely at this time that Dürer was working on his theories of human proportions, whereby he demonstrated that the body could be reduced to geometrical shapes.

This print shows a change in Dürer's engravings that occurred after 1519. Not only did they become smaller, but there was a reduction of the contrast between light and dark accompanied by diminished tonal values. The plate is more lightly worked than in earlier engravings and a silvery-gray light bathes the composition. Interestingly, a similar change can be detected in Dürer's late paintings in which he abandoned the vibrant colors of his early works and began to work in grisaille.

Mattias Mende writes that *St. Anthony Reading* might have been done as a New Year's greeting with wishes for a long life, since the saint is said to have lived to be over 100 years old.[12] Dürer held this print in high esteem, recording in his Netherlandish diary (1520–21) that along with impressions of *Melencolia I* (fig. 5, p. 15), *St. Jerome in His Study* (fig. 6, p. 16), and *St. Eustace* (p. 60) he had given it away to various people he met along the way.[13] **G.D.J.**

1 The Golden Legend, vol. 1, pp. 99-103.
2 Lehrs, vol. 5, p. 243, no. 54. See also Washington 1967, cat. no. 37.
3 These traditional attributes are seen in a later print of the saint by Schongauer (Lehrs, vol. 5, p. 240, no. 53). See also Washington 1967, cat. no. 66.
4 Schoch et al., p. 214
5 Washington 1971, p. 152.
6 Strauss 1974, vol. 1, p. 426 (1496/17).
7 London, p. 57. The drawing might have been for a print that was never executed.
8 Washington 1971, p. 153. This cityscape also appears in the background of his painting *Feast of the Rose Garlands* (Prague, National Gallery), done in Venice in 1506. See Panofsky, p. 202.
9 Hutchison, p. 45.
10 Panofsky, p. 202.
11 Ibid.
12 See Nuremberg, Germanisches Nationalmuseum, *Martin Luther und die Reformation in Deutschland* (Nuremberg, 1983), no. 83.
13 The particular passages are cited in Strauss 1975, pp. 148-49

The Peasant and His Wife at Market, 1519

Engraving
Laid paper
Meder 89 b; Hollstein 89; Bartsch 89
Watermark: None
Sheet: 116 x 73 mm
Signed, recto: Monogram AD (bottom center); 1519 (top center)
1999.7.25
Catalogue number 34

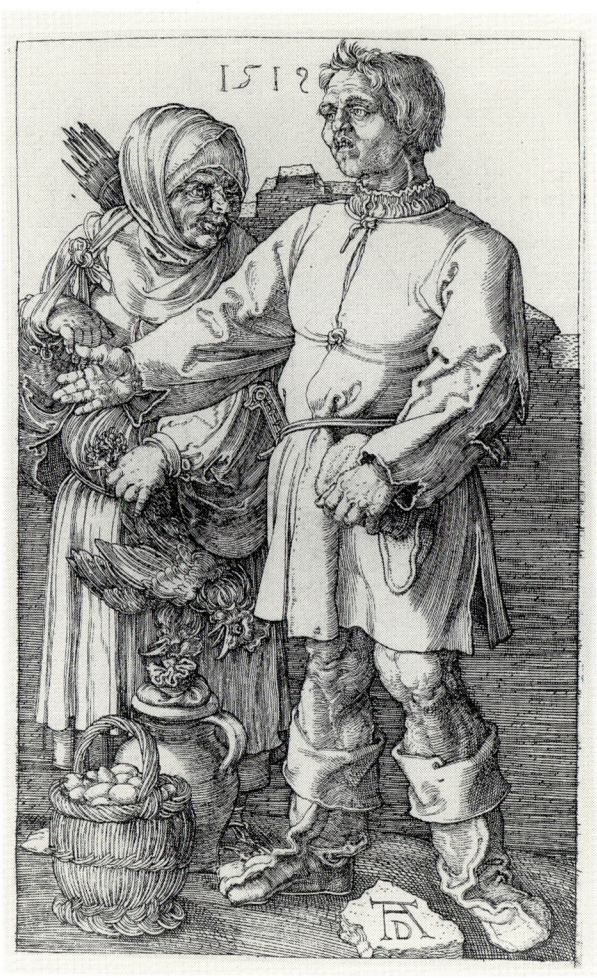

The peasant class was regularly depicted in prints of the sixteenth century, and usually not in a flattering light. Artists such as the Beham brothers, Barthel and Sebald (who succeeded Dürer as printmakers in Nuremberg), satirized the behavior, morals, and dress of peasants in prints that were obviously designed for an audience of city-dwellers who looked down upon the social practices of their country cousins. Imbued with a sense of the ridiculous, these subjects frequently were caricatures. The Peasants War of 1525, an uprising that further threatened the control of municipal councils such as the one in Nuremberg, led to an increase in the stereotyping of peasants as unruly and godless.[1]

Dürer, however, made only a few engravings of "rustics," as they were called: three in 1496-97, two in 1514, and *The Peasant and His Wife at Market*, which was the last of its type in 1519.[2] These few examples seem to suggest that Dürer saw peasants not as a threat to civil order, but as peculiarities. This print shows two country folk who have come into town to sell their produce. Attention is focused on the man, who stands slightly in front of his wife and gestures across her toward the left of the picture, opening his mouth as if speaking. This oratorical stance seems particularly incongruous under the circumstances, but imparts a strange sense of nobility. Dürer virtually filled the composition with the figures themselves, paying the utmost attention to the details of their clothing and the various bundles the woman is carrying. Although the figures are uncouth in form and dress, there is an element of the monumental about them as they stand together with their eggs and poultry.

The fact that Dürer created his peasant subjects as engravings is seen as significant to deciphering his intentions with regard to the works and their intended audience. Although depictions of the peasantry formed a significant part of secular subject matter in the Renaissance, these subjects were customarily treated in woodcuts, for a less affluent, broader market. Woodcut was also used to depict other subjects that were of popular interest, such as soldiers and their lifestyles.[3] Engravings, on the other hand, were the province of a wealthier and more sophisticated audience, such as the educated businessmen, scholars, and patrician classes that included Dürer's friends and sponsors. It has been suggested that prints such as *The Peasant and His Wife at Market* may be both celebrations of peasant life, as well as mocking reminders of the foibles of the lower classes. It is possible their ambiguity was intentional, and may have contributed to their success in the marketplace.[4] **M.L.A.**

1 See Keith P. F. Moxey, "The Social Function of Secular Woodcuts in Sixteenth Century Nuremberg," in Jeffrey Chipps Smith, ed., *New Perspectives on the Art of Renaissance Nuremberg* (Austin: Archer M. Huntington Gallery, The University of Texas at Austin, 1985), pp. 63-81.
2 One of these subjects is *The Cook and His Wife* (p. 33)
3 Moxey (note 3), p. 68. See also entry for *The Standard Bearer* (p. 66)
4 London, p. 112.

St. Christopher, Facing Right, 1521

Engraving
Laid paper
Meder 52 b; Hollstein 52; Bartsch 52
Watermark: None
Sheet: 116 x 73 mm (trimmed within plate mark)
Signed, recto: Monogram AD 1521 (lower left)
1999.7.15
Catalogue number 35

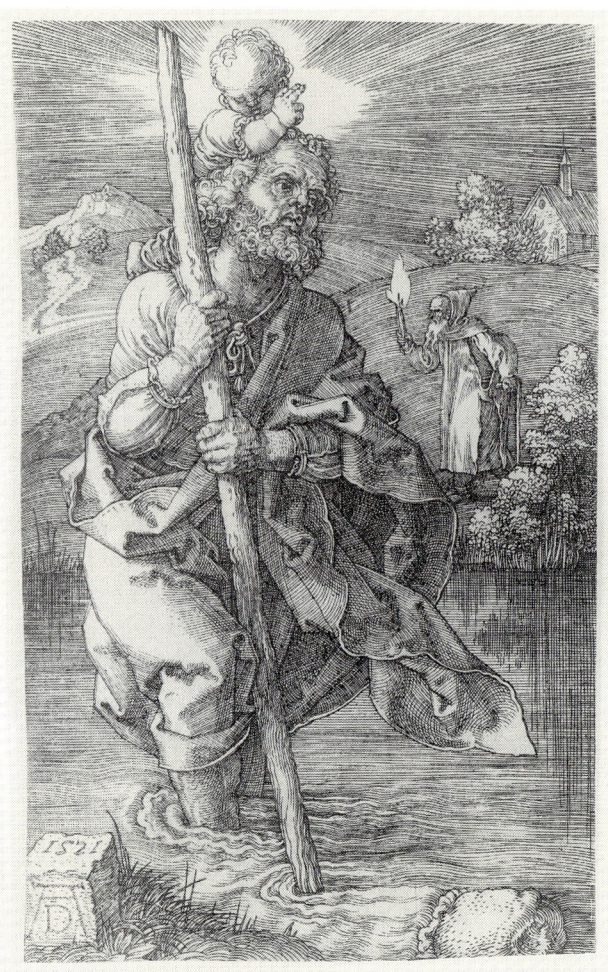

    This engraving was one of the first that Dürer made after his trip to the Netherlands in July 1521.[1] His return to Nuremberg was precipitated by his desire to confirm his annuity with the new Holy Roman emperor, Charles V. Unfortunately, the artist came home with what may have been malaria, contracted when he walked through a mosquito-infested swamp in order to view a beached whale.[2]

    Dürer's depiction of St. Christopher is drawn from the *The Golden Legend*, which had been translated into German as *Passional oder der Heiligen Leben* (*The Passion or Lives of the Saints*) and published in Nuremberg in 1488 by Anton Koberger, the artist's godfather. Christopher, a very large man who worked as a ferryman, was awakened one night by the voice of a child asking to be carried across the river. Christopher took the child, along with his staff, and began to cross. As the water rose higher, the child became heavier and heavier. When Christopher finally reached the opposite bank, he exclaimed, "'Child, thou has put me in dire peril, and hast weighed so heavy upon me that if I had borne the whole world upon my shoulders, it could not have burdened me so heavily!' And the child answered:

"Wonder not, Christopher, for not only hast thou borne the whole world upon thy shoulders, but Him Who created the world. For I am Christ thy King, Whom thou servest in this work!'"[3] The cult of St. Christopher (whose name literally means "Christ-bearer") flourished from the thirteenth to the sixteenth centuries. He is considered not only the patron saint of travelers, but also of sailors, porters, gardeners, athletes, and cloth dyers.[4] It is fitting that this was one of Dürer's first prints after returning from a long trip.

With many very fine parallel engraved lines, Dürer created a dramatic night print in which the landscape is punctuated by three different lights: that of the moon, Christ's halo, and the torch held by the desert hermit, standing on the opposite bank, who converted Christopher to Christianity. Typical of Dürer's late prints, it is small in scale and has a silvery-gray tone. This engraving and another done the same year of the same subject (M. 53, B. 51) are related to a sheet of nine studies of St. Christopher, also from 1521 (W. 800, Berlin, Kupferstichkabinett).[5] This drawing, executed when Dürer was in Antwerp, is probably connected to four other drawings of the saint executed on gray paper with highlights. The artist writes in his Netherlandish diary (May 19, 1521) that these were done for the Flemish painter Joachim Patiner.[6] Although not universally accepted as by Dürer, another drawing of St. Christopher done in pen and black ink on violet-grounded paper exists in the British Museum (W. 801).[7] Dürer made two earlier woodcuts of the saint, the first c. 1503-1504 (M. 222, B. 104) and the other in 1511 (M. 223, B. 103). His many renderings of this subject reflect its popularity as a devotional image. Larry Silver interestingly writes how the artist "recycled" traditional Catholic subjects into "a Luther-inspired reconception of the image to symbolize the role of each and every Christian to become a 'Christ-bearer' like the saintly model of Christopher."[8]

Six different copies were made after *St. Christopher Facing to the Right*, including one by Heinrich Aldegrever in reverse.[9] The two intaglio prints of St. Christopher elicited praise by Giorgio Vasari, who wrote: "And he engraved two different figures of St. Christopher carrying the Infant Christ, both very beautiful, and executed with much diligence in the close detail of the hair and in every other respect."[10] The massive figure of Christopher is very sculptural in its conception and Dürer could have been inspired by the 1422 sculpture *Schlüsselfelder Saint Christopher* which at that time was in the church of Saint Sebald in Nuremberg.[11] **G.D.J.**

1 Panofsky, p. 230.
2 Ibid., p. 10; Hutchison, p. 153
3 The Golden Legend, vol. 2, p. 379.
4 Schoch et al., p. 229.
5 Strauss 1974, vol. 4, p. 2024 (1521/15).
6 Washington 1971, p. 155
7 Strauss 1974, vol. 4, p. 2026 (1521/15).
8 Larry Silver, "The Influence of Anxiety: The Agony in the Garden as Artistic Theme in the Era of Dürer," *Umĕní. Bimonthly of the Institute for Art History of the Academy of Sciences of the Czech Republic* 45 (1997), p. 224; and Larry Silver, "Christ-Bearer: Dürer, Luther, and St. Christopher," in *Essays in Northern European Art Presented to Egbert Haverkamp-Begemann on his Sixtieth Birthday* (Dornspijk: Davco, 1983), pp. 238-44.
9 Hollstein, vol. 1, p.36
10 Vasari, vol. 6, p. 93
11 Schoch et al., p. 230.

catalogue entry 32

St. Bartholomew, 1523

Engraving
Laid paper
Meder 45 b; Hollstein 45; Bartsch 47
Watermark: None
Sheet: 122 x 177 mm (trimmed within plate mark)
Signed, recto: Monogram AD 1523 (center left)
1999.7.11
Catalogue number 37

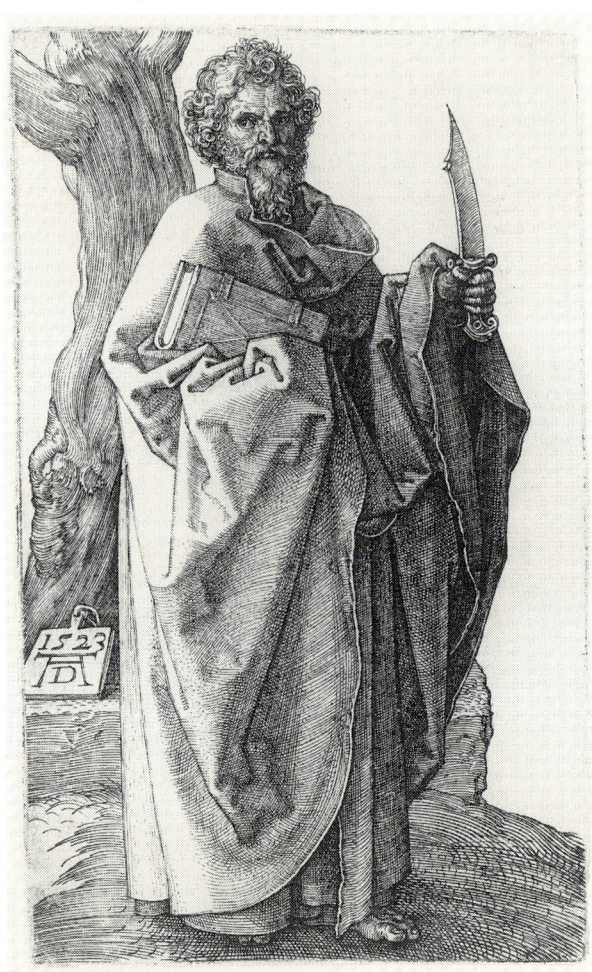

Dürer first conceived a series of the Twelve Apostles, to which this print belongs, in 1514. In that extremely fruitful year, which also saw the production of *Melencolia I* (fig. 5, p. 15), and *St. Jerome in His Study* (fig. 6, p. 16), Dürer executed the first two engravings of apostles, *St. Thomas* (M. 50, B. 48) and *St. Paul* (p. 90). *St. Bartholomew* and *St. Simon* (p. 102) were done in 1523 with *St. Philip* (M. 48, B. 46) finished in 1526. The series was left incomplete at the time of Dürer's death in 1528. Dürer likely based his cycle on fifteenth-century print series of the apostles, such as the one by Israhel van Meckenem from c. 1480 (fig. 26, right).[1] Like the earlier figures, Dürer's are shown full-length and standing, holding the various attributes of their life or martyrdom. By giving each apostle different physical traits, Dürer made them like portraits.

Though he was one of the twelve apostles, little is known about St. Bartholomew. He is possibly the same man named Nathaniel whose meeting with Christ is told in the gospel of St. John (1:45-51). Upon meeting Nathaniel (Bartholomew), Christ exclaimed, "Here is an Israelite worthy of the name; there is nothing false in him." Later writers associate him with spreading the teachings of Christ to India, Mesopotamia, Arabia, and Armenia.[2] In Armenia he was flayed by King Astrages for destroying the pagan gods and temples.

Dürer's portrayal of Bartholomew closely follows the description of the saint as recorded in *The Golden Legend*. According to one of the demons who tormented him: "His hair is black and crisped, his skin fair, his eyes wide, his nose even and straight, his beard thick and with few grey hairs; he is of medium stature; he is clothed in a white mantle bordered with purple, and wears over it a white cloak with purple gems at each corner."[3] St. Bartholomew holds a butcher knife, the instrument of his martyrdom, and a book of the *Roman Martyrology*.[4] In contrast to Dürer's earlier apostles of 1514, he does not wear a halo.

Compared to the earlier apostles of 1514 (p. 90), the late apostles appear subdued, unemotional, and less heroic. However, they are rendered in a much more sculptural manner, seen also in *St. Christopher Facing Right* (p. 98), and their bodies are covered with massive drapery. This monumental quality is characteristic of Dürer's late engravings. In describing a landscape background, Panofsky used the word "corrugated" to define this style: "Large simplified volumes are contrasted with complicated systems of prominences and indentations so that the whole gives the impression of a compact massif broken up into big tablelands, craggy rocks and deep ravines, though even these show a remarkable tendency toward geometrical schematization. . . ."[5]

A metalpoint drawing heightened in white, on a bluish-green prepared paper (W. 876, Vienna, Albertina) is very similar to the engraved *St. Bartholomew*. Even though it may not have been a direct preliminary study for the print, Dürer certainly referred to it when executing the engraving.[6] While the apostle in the drawing also cradles a book in his arm, he holds a staff rather than the knife seen in the print. Another reference could have been Dürer's much earlier pen-and-ink study of *St. Bartholomew* (c. 1510; Ottawa, National Gallery), which shows Frederick the Wise kneeling in prayer at the saint's side.[7] The way the saint holds the knife and the manner in which Bartholomew's sleeve falls over his arm are similar in both works.

There was a proliferation of printed apostle series in Germany during the first half of the sixteenth century.[8] Both Hans Baldung Grien (1484/85-1545) and Lucas Cranach the Elder (1472-1553) produced woodcut series of the saints in the years around 1519.[9] As late as 1545-46, the Nuremberg "Little Master," Sebald Beham (1500-1550), produced an engraved set of the apostles.[10] These engravings follow the same format—a single standing saint holding his attribute—of their fifteenth- and early sixteenth-century antecedents. G.D.J.

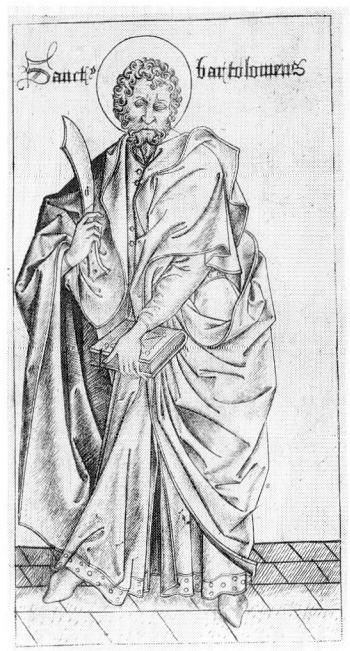

Figure 26 **Israhel van Meckenem,** *St. Bartholomew*, c. 1470-1480, **Engraving on laid paper, Washington, National Gallery of Art, Rosenwald Collection, 1943.3.125**

1 Washington 1967, cat. nos. 162-71. Meckenem's prints, in turn, are copies in reverse of an apostle series by Master E.S. from c. 1450-60. Martin Schongauer also executed a series of the Twelve Apostles (Lehrs, vol. 5, pp. 202-40, nos. 41-52). This series was copied by other printmakers thirteen times during the fifteenth and sixteenth centuries.
2 Paris, p. 294.
3 The Golden Legend, vol. 2, pp. 479-80.
4 Paris, p. 294.
5 Panofsky, p. 205.
6 Strauss 1974, vol. 4, p. 2228 (1523/12). Dürer also executed a similar drawing of St. Philip (Strauss 1974, vol. 4, p. 2226 (1523/11) which he then used for the print of the saint issued in 1526 (M. 48, B. 46).
7 Strauss 1974, vol. 3, p. 1250 (1510/29). See also Washington 1971, cat. no. 76.
8 Schoch et al. 2001, p.189.
9 See Hans Baldung Grien (Hollstein, vol. 2, p. 101, nos. 67-78; and vol. 2, pp. 102-103, nos. 79-91); Lucas Cranach the Elder (Hollstein, vol. 6, pp. 30-33, nos. 31-44).
10 Lawrence, Kansas, The University of Kansas, *The World in Miniature: Engravings by the German Little Masters, 1500-1550*, ed. Stephen H. Goddard (Lawrence, 1988), cat. no. 39; and Hollstein, vol. 3, pp. 34-35, nos. 45-56.

catalogue entry 33

St. Simon, 1523

Engraving
Laid paper
Meder 49 b; Hollstein 49; Bartsch 49
Watermark: None
Sheet: 118 x 73 mm (trimmed along plate mark)
Signed, recto: Monogram AD 1523 (lower right)
1999.7.13
Catalogue number 38

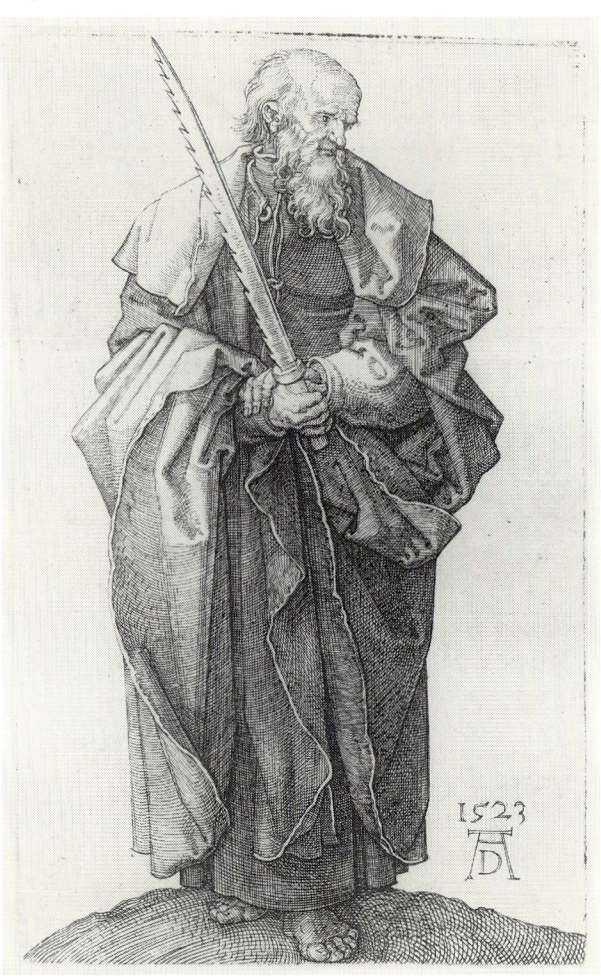

    This engraving depicting the Apostle Simon was intended to be a part of a series that was never completed by Dürer. He created the first two works, *St. Paul* (p. 90) and *St. Thomas* (M. 50, B. 48), in 1514. Nine years later he made two others, *St. Bartholomew* (p. 100) and this *St. Simon*. In 1526 he added *St. Thomas* (M. 48, B. 46), which was the final subject he created for the series before his death in 1528.[1]

    Like the first state of its predecessor *St. Paul*, this composition shows Simon standing on a curved mound of earth, silhouetted against a vacant background. This presentation closely resembles the works of earlier printmakers such as Martin Schongauer, who produced a similar series depicting the apostles. (See fig 27, right)[2]

    According to legend, Simon Zelotes was one of the shepherds to whom angels announced the birth of Christ. After Christ's death, Simon and Jude traveled as evangelists, preaching the gospel throughout Mesopotamia and Syria. They were martyred in Persia. Although the method of his martyrdom is disputed, Simon is traditionally shown with the attribute of a saw, reputedly the instrument of his death.

Dürer created a number of works of art in the mid-1520s associated with the fathers of the early church.[3] In a diptych for the City Council of Nuremberg, he presented standing figures of saints John and Peter on one panel and saints Paul and Mark on the second one (*The Four Apostles*, 1526; Munich, Alte Pinakothek). As in the engravings, these full-length figures are shown with their identifying attributes. The panels were painted at a time when the City of Nuremberg, which had officially accepted the Reformation in 1525, was in the process of converting social structures from religious to secular control. Dürer intended these panels to be housed in an upper chamber of the City Hall; the inscriptions they bear suggest that they were designed as reminders to the city fathers of their role as civic leaders.[4]

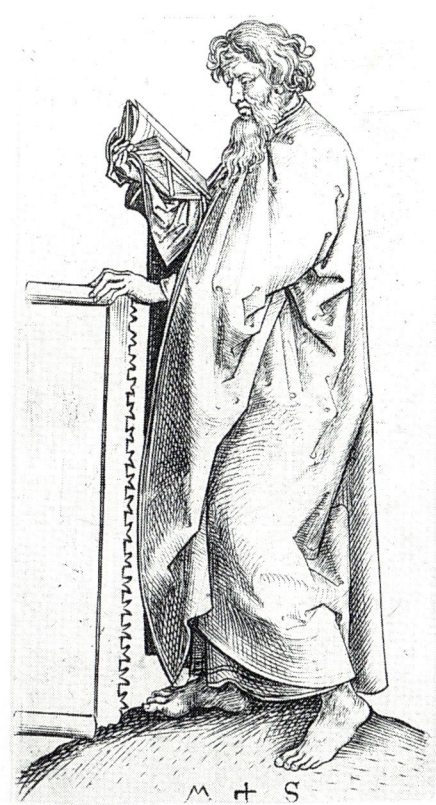

While there is no apparent direct correlation between the paintings and prints other than preparatory drawings that were used for one or the other, the subject of the apostles was apparently foremost in Dürer's mind in the last years of his life. One reason for this may have been his disillusionment with some of the political consequences of the Reformation.[5] In focusing on the apostles, Dürer may have hoped to reiterate the importance of both God's word and responsible government in an age of transition. **M.L.A.**

Figure 27 **Martin Schongauer,** *The Apostles: St. Simon*, c. 1480, Engraving on laid paper, Washington, National Gallery of Art, Rosenwald Collection, 1943.3.55

---

1 See *St. Bartholomew* (p. 100), for further information about this series and its sources.
2 Alan Shestack, *The Complete Engravings of Martin Schongauer* (New York: Dover Publications, 1969), nos. 45-56.
3 A metal point drawing of St. John that was intended as a study for an anticipated painting of the Crucifixion was instead adapted and used for this engraving of St. Simon. See Panofsky, p. 230. There are also drawings featuring the saints at the Musée Bonnat in Bayonne and at the Kupferstichkabinett in Berlin (Streider, p. 324).
4 The inscription is taken from the Book of Revelation (22: 18-19), "All worldly rulers in this threatening time, beware not to take human delusion for the Word of God. For God wishes nothing added to his Word nor taken from it…." Although Dürer intended that the works be housed in Nuremberg, in 1627 there was political pressure to send them to Munich, where they came to reside in the Alte Pinakothek.
5 Streider, pp. 322-24.

catalogue entry 34

Philip Melanchthon, 1526

Engraving
Laid paper
Meder 104 c; Hollstein 104; Bartsch 105
Watermark: Small Jug, Meder 158 (center left)
Sheet: 173 x 127 mm
Signed, recto: AD 1526 (bottom center)
1999.7.27
Catalogue number 40

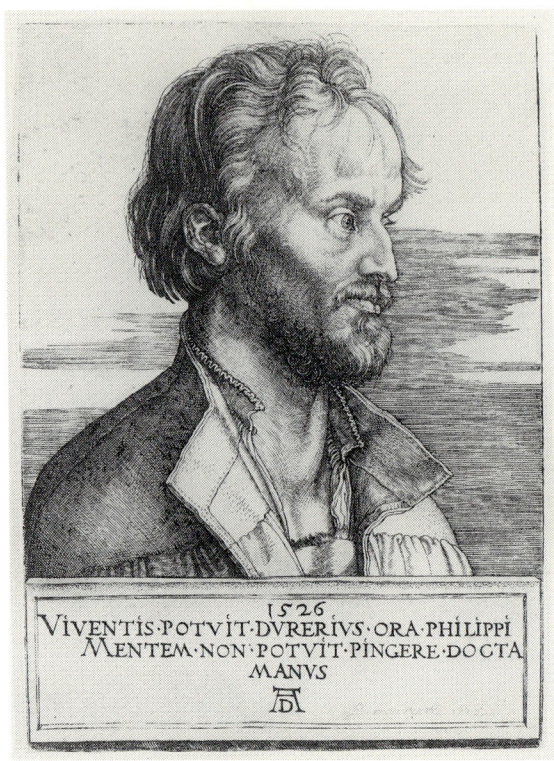

I recall that the painter Albrecht Dürer, a man of the highest talent and skill, once said that in his youth he loved paintings with lively and sparkling colors, and he enchanted an admirer of his works with the marvelous variety of his palette. Later, as an old man, he began to look closely at nature, and attempted to convey its actual appearance; in the process he realized that it was precisely this same simplicity which was the greatest achievement of art. Since he could not reach it he had, as he said, ceased to admire his own work but often sighed, when he looked at his paintings, and thought of his own weaknesses.

Philip Melanchthon, December 17, 1546[1]

The humanist thinkers and educators who formed Dürer's circle in Nuremberg included the subject of this portrait, Philip Melanchthon (1497-1560). A renowned educator and a prominent follower of Martin Luther, Melanchthon probably knew Dürer through their mutual association with the artist's close friend, Willibald Pirckheimer. The engraving was made during Melanchthon's stay in Nuremberg between November 1525 and May 1526. Melanchthon came to the city at the request of the Nuremberg Council to reorganize the school curriculum in light of the city's official acceptance of the Reformation in 1525. This image is one of seven bust-length print portraits that Dürer made beginning about 1519. Integrated into these compositions are inscriptions in Latin characterizing the subjects of the portraits and commemorating their various accomplishments and their social or political positions.[2]

Melanchthon was appointed professor of Greek at the university in Wittenberg in 1518 when he was only twenty-one years old. His acceptance of the Reformation and support for Luther's teachings inspired him to write several important texts. His scholarly dissertation, *Loci Communes Rerum Theologicorum* (1521), summarized the theology of Luther; *Antithesis Figurate Vitae Christi et Antichristi* (commonly called *Passional Christi und Antichristi*) spread the doctrine to a wider audience. The latter work, also published in 1521, is a variation on the traditional *Passional*, a prayer book incorporating narratives from the life of Christ or the Virgin Mary that was published in numerous editions in both Latin and German.[3] Because of his influential writings and his support for the establishment of secular schools in Germany, Melanchthon was given the honorific title *Praeceptor Germaniae* or "Germany's Schoolmaster."

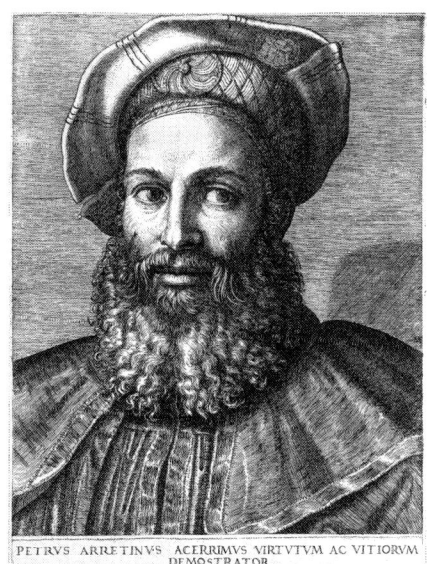

Figure 28 **Marcantonio Raimondi,** *Pietro Aretino*, **c. 1517-20, Engraving on laid paper**

Dürer was a practiced portraitist in both oil and the print media. The engraved portraits, though falling within an established and restrictive format, reflect both his significant experience and his sensitivity to individual character. Engraved portraits served an important purpose in preserving and disseminating the image of respected and influential figures. The specific format, with the inclusion of a laudatory text in Latin, reflects a general trend in the practice of reinforcing the status of secular and spiritual leaders, philosophers, writers, and even artists. Marcantonio Raimondi's engraved *Portrait of Pietro Aretino*, c. 1517-20 (fig. 28, right) demonstrates the international nature of this trend, and confirms that images of the same type were also being produced in the South. The practice of mimicking an inscription chiseled in stone is believed to have derived from the influence of ancient Roman tomb relief carvings that were being unearthed across the former empire, linking the image of the individual depicted with the world of humanism and classicism.

In *Philip Melanchthon*, Dürer was depicting both a prominent educator and a close acquaintance.[4] Here the inscription reads: "Dürer was able to depict Philip's features as if living, but the practiced hand could not portray his soul." The subject is shown in three-quarter profile dressed in a loose fitting, open-collared shirt, silhouetted against a cloud-streaked sky. The composition focuses the viewer's attention on the scholar's large, domed forehead, prominent hooked nose, and penetrating gaze. Interestingly, reflected in his eyes is a window—a seeming anomaly since he is depicted out-of-doors. It has been suggested that this motif, which was used by Dürer in other engraved portraits, signifies a "mystical window," or perhaps it may be a reference to the idea that the eyes are a window to the soul.[5]

As the inscription implies, Melanchthon was an admirer of Dürer's prodigious artistic talent and intellectual accomplishments. In a rhetoric textbook written after the artist's death, he compared Dürer's art to the highest level of rhetoric as defined by the ancient Greeks.[6] He is believed to have owned prints by Dürer (perhaps even a complete set) and a German copy of Dürer's book on proportion.[7] He also owned the plate from which this engraving was made, which now is preserved in the museum in Gotha.[8] Dürer's portrait captures the image of a man who is both intellectually and spiritually free—a description that might have applied to the artist as well. **M.L.A.**

1 Quoted in Streider, p. 367.
2 One of Dürer's most impressive early portrait prints is a woodcut made for the Emperor Maximilian I around 1518 (M. 225, B.154). The engraved portraits follow a similar format, and include *Cardinal Albrecht of Brandenberg (The Small Cardinal)* (M. 100, B. 102); *Cardinal Albrecht of Brandenburg (The Large Cardinal)* (M. 101, B. 103); *Frederick the Wise Elector of Saxony* (M. 102, B. 104); *Willibald Pirckheimer* (M. 103, B. 106); and the larger plate, *Erasmus of Rotterdam* (M. 105, B. 107).
3 London, p. 178.
4 Washington 1971, p. 157. Dürer made a pen-and-ink drawing (W.901, Florence, Casa Horne) that is believed to be a working drawing for this engraving.
5 Ibid., p. 158. See also Butts' Essay, p. 10.
6 Hutchison, p. 183.
7 London, p. 61, and Hutchison, p. 183.
8 Meder noted that modern impressions were taken from this plate (Strauss 1975, p. 288).

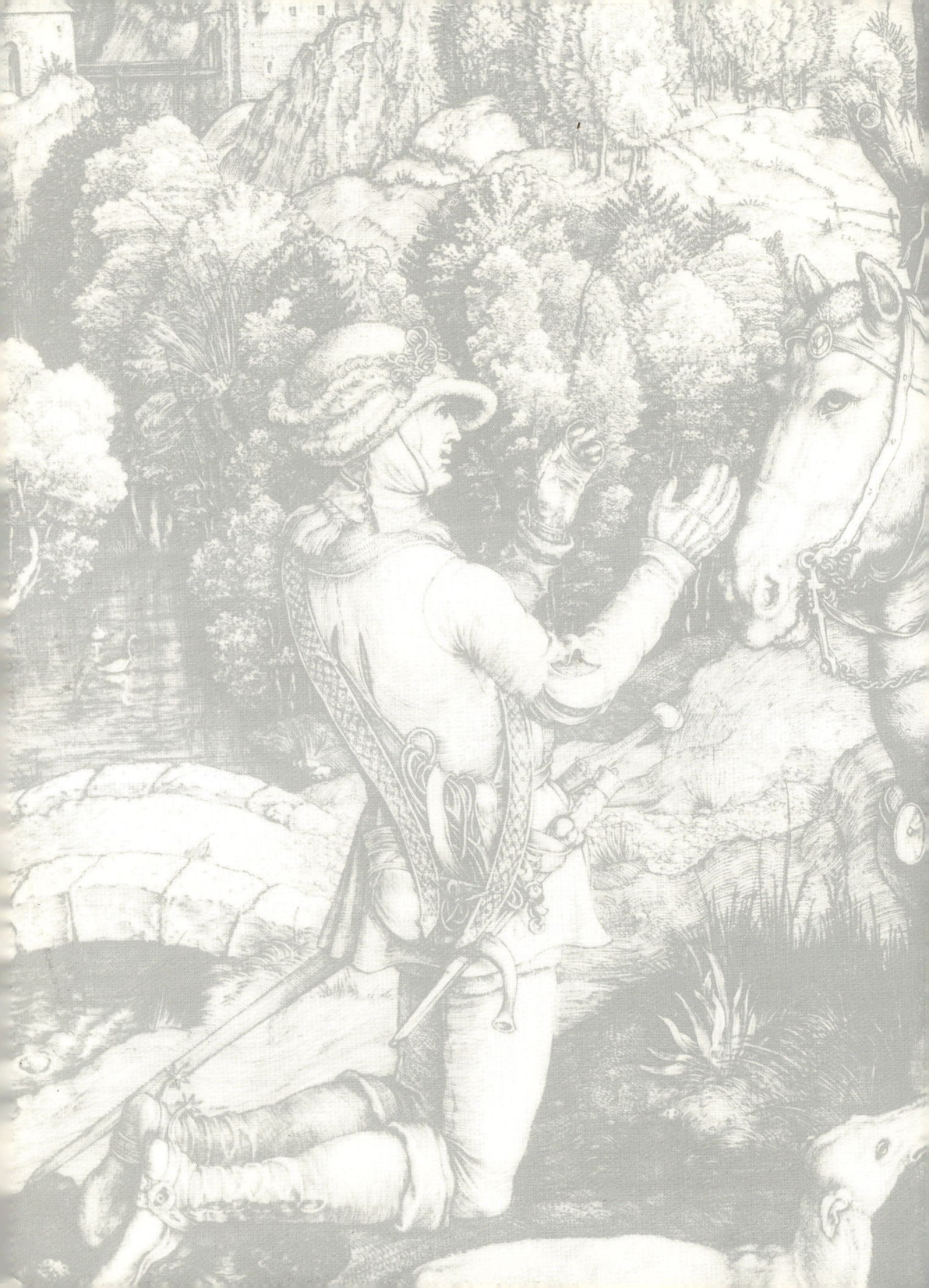

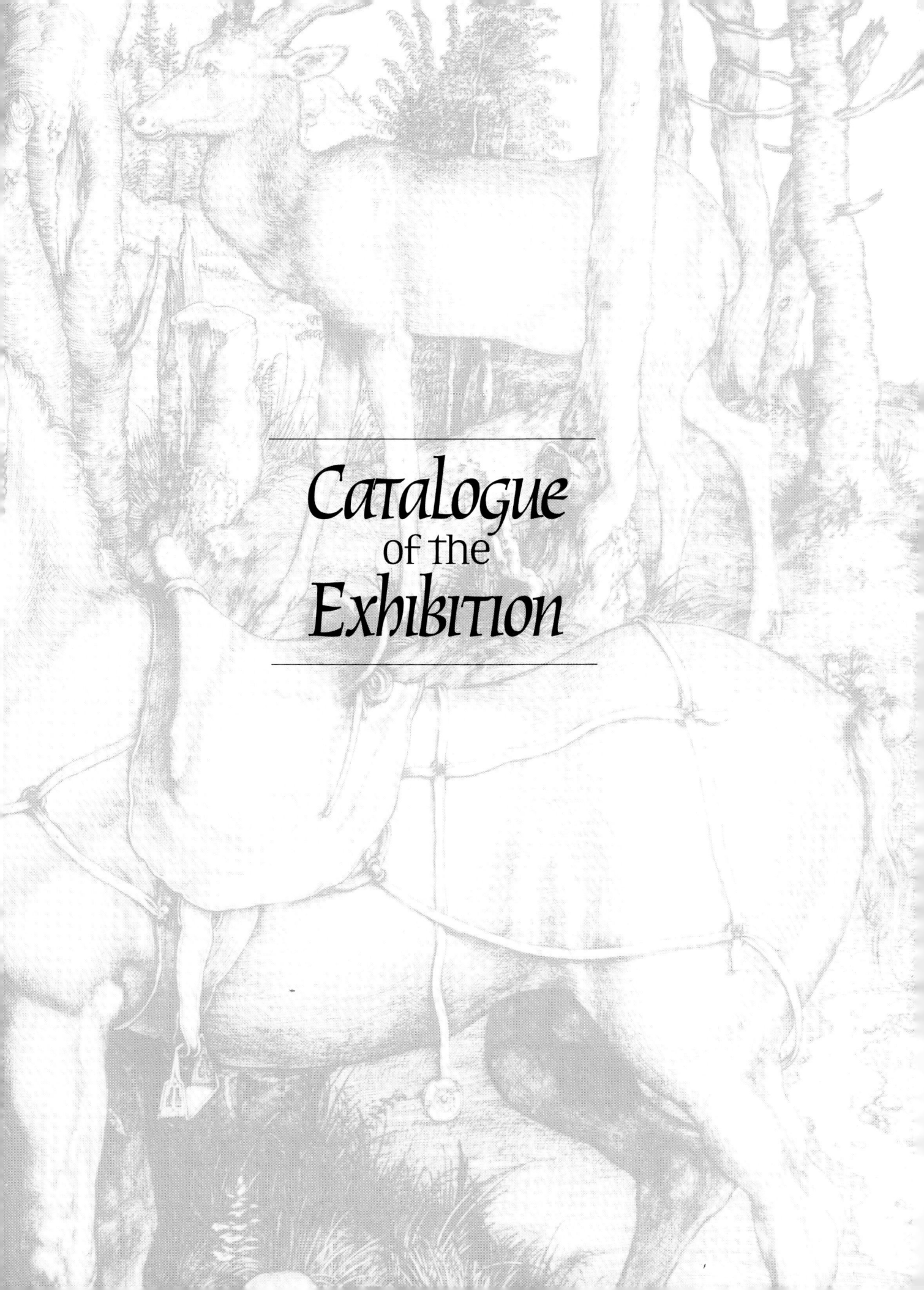

Catalogue of the Exhibition

catalogue of the exhibition

1 *Fortune (Das Kleine Gluck)*, 1495

Engraving
Laid paper
Meder 71 c; Hollstein 71; Bartsch 78
Sheet: 4 1/4 x 2 9/16 in. (108 x 64 mm)
Watermark: Bull's Head (not described by Meder)
Signed, recto: Monogram AD (bottom center)
Marks, verso: C (in brown ink): " P. Mariette, 1664" (Lugt 1788); BC (in brown ink): "no." (illegible); BC (in graphite): "1952"

Provenance: Pierre Mariette, Paris (Lugt 1788); Adolph Weil, Jr., Montgomery, Alabama

Montgomery Museum of Fine Arts, Gift of Jean K. Weil in memory of Adolph "Bucks" Weil, Jr.
1999.7.22

2 *The Ill-Assorted Couple*, 1495

Engraving
Laid paper
Meder 77 c; Hollstein 77; Bartsch 93
Watermark: None
Sheet: 6 x 5 1/2 in. (150 x 140 mm)
Signed, recto: Monogram AD (bottom center)
Marks, verso: BC (in blue ink): "RHS" (in a box; not in Lugt); BL (in graphite): "B93"

Provenance: Adolph Weil, Jr., Montgomery, Alabama

Montgomery Museum of Fine Arts, Gift of Jean K. Weil in memory of Adolph "Bucks" Weil, Jr.
1999.7.23

3 *The Prodigal Son Amid the Swine*, c. 1496

Engraving
Laid paper
Meder 28 c; Hollstein 28; Bartsch 28
Watermark: Gothic P with Flower, Meder 321
Sheet: 9 3/4 x 7 9/16 in. (250 x 192 mm), trimmed along the plate mark
Signed, recto: Monogram AD (bottom center)
Marks, recto: BC, in brown ink, P. Mariette, 1666 (Lugt 1788); BC; embossed oval with inscription initials R D (Lugt 2200)
Marks, verso: C (in graphite): "1896.3.8"; (stamped in brown ink): "Cooper Union Museum, New York" (in a box; Lugt 457e); C (in graphite): "B.28c"; BL (in graphite), "Vente Beckford, L oxoxo"; BL (stamped in black ink): "J.G." (in a box; John Griffith, Oxford; Lugt 1464)

Provenance: Pierre Mariette, Paris (Lugt 1788);) A.P. F. Robert-Dumesnil (Lugt 2200); Rev. John Griffith, Oxford (Lugt 1464); Cooper Union Museum, New York (in a box; Lugt 457e); Adolph Weil, Jr., Montgomery, Alabama

Montgomery Museum of Fine Arts, Gift of Jean K. Weil in memory of Adolph "Bucks" Weil, Jr.
1999.7.10

4 *The Cook and His Wife*, 1496

Engraving
Laid paper
Meder 85 a; Hollstein 85; Bartsch 84
Watermark: None
Sheet: 4 1/4 x 3 1/16 in. (108 x 77 mm)
Signed, recto: Monogram AD (bottom center)
Marks, verso: C (in brown ink): "P. Mariette, 1684" (Lugt 1788); BR (in brown ink): " no. 229" (?)

Provenance: Pierre Mariette, Paris (Lugt 1788); Adolph Weil, Jr., Montgomery, Alabama

Montgomery Museum of Fine Arts, Gift of Jean K. Weil in memory of Adolph "Bucks" Weil, Jr.
1999.7.24

5 *The Martyrdom of the Ten Thousand*, c. 1496

Woodcut
Laid paper
Meder 218 b; Hollstein 218; Bartsch 117
Watermark: None
Sheet: 15 5/16 x 11 5/16 in. (389 x 287 mm), trimmed at the block mark
Signed, recto: Monogram AD (bottom center)
Marks, verso: BL (in graphite): "B.117. Dodg. 3"; (in graphite): "Bll, 87.4758"; BR (in graphite): "348"

Provenance: Adolph Weil, Jr., Montgomery, Alabama

Montgomery Museum of Fine Arts, Gift of Jean K. Weil in memory of Adolph "Bucks" Weil, Jr.
1999.7.29

6 *St. Jerome Penitent in the Wilderness*, c. 1496

Engraving
Laid paper
Meder 57 c; Hollstein 57; Bartsch 61
Watermark: City Crest with Three Towers, Meder 46 (top center)
Sheet: 12 7/16 x 8 3/4 in. (315 x 222 mm), trimmed within the plate mark
Signed, recto: Monogram AD (bottom center)
Marks, verso: BR (in graphite): "30033"

Provenance: Adolph Weil, Jr., Montgomery, Alabama

Montgomery Museum of Fine Arts, Gift of Jean K. Weil in memory of Adolph "Bucks" Weil, Jr.
1999.7.16

catalogue of the exhibition

7 *The Four Horsemen of the Apocalypse,* 1498
From the Latin edition (1511) of the *Apocalypse*

Woodcut
Heavy laid paper
Meder 167; Hollstein 167; Bartsch 64
Watermark: Castle, Meder 259 (center)
Sheet: 15 5/8 x 11 1/16 in. (397 x 280 mm), trimmed at the block mark
Signed, recto: Monogram AD (bottom center)
Marks, recto: BC (stamped in black ink): "M" (with cross top; Lugt 1845); "Joseph Maberly, London"
Marks, verso: BL (in graphite): "AW" (Adolph Weil, Jr.); BL (in graphite): "B.67, P128, No 64"; BR (in graphite): "B64 R 42 148"; BR (in brown ink): "Alb Durer"; (in brown ink): "no./" (number indecipherable)

Provenance: Joseph Maberly, London; Adolph Weil, Jr., Montgomery, Alabama

Montgomery Museum of Fine Arts, Gift of Mr. and Mrs. Adolph Weil, Jr., in memory of Mr. and Mrs. Adolph Weil, Sr.
1991.3.1

8 *Beast with Two Horns Like a Lamb,* 1496-97
From the Latin edition (1511) of the *Apocalypse*

Woodcut
Heavy laid paper
Meder 175; Hollstein 175; Bartsch 74
Watermark: Flower with Triangle, Meder 127 (center right)
Sheet: 15 5/16 x 10 7/8 in. (389 x 277 mm), trimmed to the block mark
Signed, recto: Monogram AD (bottom center)
Marks, verso: BR (in graphite): "B74, M.175, C.26088" (Colnaghi)

Provenance: Purchased Colnaghi, London, December 9, 1970

Montgomery Museum of Fine Arts, Montgomery Museum of Fine Arts Association Purchase
1970.15

9 *Angel with the Key to the Bottomless Pit,* 1496-97
From the German edition (1498) of the *Apocalypse*

Woodcut
Heavy laid paper
Meder 178; Hollstein 178; Bartsch 75
Watermark: None
Sheet: 15 1/2 x 11 1/8 in. (394 x 283 mm), trimmed at the block mark
Signed, recto: Monogram AD (bottom center)
Marks, verso: BL (in brown ink): "16.e La Viscation da blaue en Soaftze Eouge" (17th-century hand); (in graphite): "TR 15761/54.2"; (in graphite): "Engel mit dem Schlüssel zum Abgrund. B. 75"; "M.178. Einzeldruck vor dem Text Selten!"

Provenance: Willam H. Schab Gallery, New York, April 18, 1972

Montgomery Museum of Fine Arts, Montgomery Museum of Fine Arts Association Purchase
1972.81

10 *The Agony in the Garden,* 1496-97
From the edition of the *Large Passion* after 1511 (without text)

Woodcut
Heavy laid paper
Meder 115; Hollstein 115; Bartsch 6
Watermark: None
Sheet: 15 3/8 x 11 1/8 in. (389 x 283 mm), trimmed at the block mark
Signed, recto: Monogram AD (bottom center)
Marks, verso: None

Provenance: Robert Dance, Inc., March 3, 1986

Montgomery Museum of Fine Arts, Montgomery Museum of Fine Arts Association Purchase and Gift of Mr. and Mrs. Adolph Weil, Jr., in memory of Mr. and Mrs. Adolph Weil, Sr.
1986.1

11 *The Flagellation,* 1496-97
From the edition of the *Large Passion* after 1511

Woodcut
Heavy laid paper
Meder 117; Hollstein 117; Bartsch 8
Watermark: None
Sheet: 15 7/8 x 11 3/8 in. (403 x 292 mm), trimmed at the block mark
Signed, recto: Monogram AD (bottom center)
Marks, recto: BR (in brown ink): "257.6"
Marks, verso: BL (in graphite): "151" (in a box); (in graphite): "AW"; (printed in black ink): "F" (with a crown in a circle; Ferdinand of Portugal; Lugt 968); BR (stamped in black ink): "JC" (in a circle) (Thomas Jefferson Coolidge, Jr., Boston; Lugt 1429); BR (in graphite): "64736"

Provenance: Ferdinand of Portugal (Lugt 968); Thomas Jefferson Coolidge, Jr., Boston (Lugt 1429); Sotheby Parke-Bernet, November 13, 1975, auction 3807, lot 46. Adolph Weil, Jr., Montgomery, Alabama

Montgomery Museum of Fine Arts, Gift of Mr. and Mrs. Adolph Weil, Jr., in memory of Mr. and Mrs. Adolph Weil, Sr.
1981.20.2

12 *Hercules at the Crossroads (Jealousy),* 1498

Engraving
Laid paper
Meder 63 second state, a-b; Hollstein 63; Bartsch 73
Watermark: Small Jug, Meder 158 (top center)
Sheet: 12 3/4 x 8 7/8 in. (323 x 225 mm), trimmed at the plate mark
Signed, recto: Monogram AD (bottom center)
Marks, verso: UR (in graphite): illegible; UC (in brown ink): "G. Storck a Milano 1799" above "IN # 10713" (Lugt 2319); BC (in graphite): "B.73, H.63" (illegible and erased)

Provenance: Giuseppe Storck, Milan (Lugt 2319); Adolph Weil, Jr., Montgomery, Alabama

Montgomery Museum of Fine Arts, Gift of Jean K. Weil in memory of Adolph "Bucks" Weil, Jr.
1999.7.18

catalogue of the exhibition

13 Madonna with the Monkey, 1498

Engraving
Laid paper
Meder 30 a; Hollstein 30; Bartsch 42
Watermark: High Crown, Meder 20
Sheet: 7 5/8 x 4 15/16 in. (193 x 125 mm), sheet restored at edges
Signed, recto: Monogram AD (bottom center)
Marks, verso: BR (in graphite): "FYX o"; BL (in graphite): "B.42 D.41341"; C (in graphite): "9670" (in a circle); (in graphite): "Extremely fine on paper with the watermark of the high crown"

Provenance: C.J. Goodfriend Drawings and Prints, November 16, 2001

Montgomery Museum of Fine Arts, Gift of the Weil Print Endowment in memory of Mr. and Mrs. Adolph Weil, Sr.
2001.10

14 The Temptation of the Idler (The Dream of the Doctor), 1498

Engraving
Laid paper
Meder 70 b; Hollstein 70; Bartsch 76
Watermark: None
Sheet: 7 1/2 x 4 7/8 in. (190 x 123 mm)
Signed, recto: Monogram AD (bottom center)
Marks, verso: UC (in graphite): (illegible); BL (in graphite): "11067"; BC (in graphite): "B.76 A915"

Provenance: Adolph Weil, Jr., Montgomery, Alabama

Montgomery Museum of Fine Arts, Gift of Jean K. Weil in memory of Adolph "Bucks" Weil, Jr.
1999.7.21

15 St. Eustace, 1501

Engraving
Laid paper
Meder 60 b; Hollstein 60; Bartsch 57
Watermark: High Crown, Meder 20 (bottom center)
Sheet: 13 15/16 x 10 1/8 in. (355 x 261 mm), trimmed within the plate mark
Signed, recto: Monogram AD (bottom center)
Marks, verso: UC (in graphite): "9691" (in a circle); LC (in graphite): "Beautiful impression on High Crown paper from the famous Liphart collection"; BC (printed in black ink): "Liphart" (Lugt 1687)"; BL (in graphite): "A. 61.5 (?)"; BC (in graphite): "B.57"; LR (in graphite): "C.28936 (Colnaghi)"

Provenance: K.E. Von Liphart, Bonn and Florence (Lugt 1687); Frederick Keppel, New York; Colnaghi, London; Adolph Weil, Jr., Montgomery, Alabama

Montgomery Museum of Fine Arts, Gift of Jean K. Weil in memory of Adolph "Bucks" Weil, Jr.
1999.7.17

16 Apollo and Diana, 1502

Engraving
Laid paper
Meder 64 b; Hollstein 64; Bartsch 68
Watermark: None
Sheet: 4 1/2 x 2 7/8 in. (114 x 73 mm)
Signed, recto: Monogram AD (lower right)
Marks, verso: BL (printed in black ink): "BH" (in circle); "B. Hausmann" (David Bernard Hausmann, Hanover; Lugt 377); BC (in graphite): "B68"

Provenance: B. Hausmann, Hanover (Lugt 377); Adolph Weil, Jr., Montgomery, Alabama

Montgomery Museum of Fine Arts, Gift of Jean K. Weil in memory of Adolph "Bucks" Weil, Jr.
1999.7.19

17 The Standard Bearer, c. 1502

Engraving
Laid paper
Meder 92 a; Hollstein 92; Bartsch 87
Watermark: None
Sheet: 4 5/8 x 2 7/8 in. (116 x 73 mm)
Signed, recto: Monogram AD (center left)
Marks, verso: BL (in graphite): "55477"; (in graphite): "AW"; (in brown ink): "Boerner, NY"; BR (in graphite): "V+"

Provenance: C. G. Boerner, Inc., New York; Adolph Weil, Jr., Montgomery, Alabama

Montgomery Museum of Fine Arts, Gift of Jean K. Weil in memory of Adolph "Bucks" Weil, Jr.
1999.7.26

18 The Nativity, 1504

Engraving
Laid paper
Meder 2 b or c; Bartsch 2; Hollstein 2
Sheet: 7 3/8 x 4 3/4 in. (186 x 121 mm), trimmed to the plate mark
Watermark: Bull's Head (Meder 62)
Signed, recto: Monogram AD (upper center)

Provenance: J.D. Passavant (Lugt 1449; sale, C.J. Boerner's, Leipzig, May, 1929); Lessing J. Rosenwald

National Gallery of Art, Washington, Rosenwald Collection, 1943
1943.3.3557

catalogue of the exhibition

19 *Satyr Family*, 1505

Engraving
Laid paper
Meder 65 a; Hollstein 65; Bartsch 69
Watermark: None
Sheet: 4 9/16 x 2 13/16 in. (115 x 72 mm), trimmed along the plate mark
Signed, recto: Monogram AD 1505 (upper right)
Marks, verso: BL (in graphite): "5072 a 36470"

Provenance: Adolph Weil, Jr., Montgomery, Alabama

Montgomery Museum of Fine Arts, Gift of Jean K. Weil in memory of Adolph "Bucks" Weil, Jr.
1999.7.20

20 *Crucifixion*, 1508

Engraving
Laid paper
Meder 23 a; Hollstein 23; Bartsch 24
Watermark: None
Sheet: 5 1/4 x 3 7/8 in. (132 x 97 mm), trimmed within the plate mark
Signed, recto: Monogram AD (bottom center)
Marks, verso: BL (stamped in purple ink): "Felix Somary"; (stamped in black ink): "P. Davidsohn" (Lugt 654); C (stamped in purple ink): "Dubbel R.P.K." (Lugt 699)

Provenance: Felix Somary ; P. Davidsohn, Berlin (Lugt 654); Rijksprentenkabinet, Amsterdam (Lugt 699); Adolph Weil, Jr., Montgomery, Alabama

Montgomery Museum of Fine Arts, Gift of Jean K. Weil in memory of Adolph "Bucks" Weil, Jr.
1999.7.9

21 *Christ's Entry into Jerusalem*, c. 1509-1510
From the edition of the *Small Woodcut Passion* after 1511

Woodcut
Laid paper
Meder 130; Hollstein 130; Bartsch 22
Watermark: None
Sheet: 5 1/4 x 4 1/16 in. (133 x 103 mm)
Signed, recto: Monogram AD (upper right)
Marks, verso: BL (in graphite): K.11027; BL (in graphite): 22; BL (in graphite): a24057; UR (in graphite): 5

Provenance: C. J. Goodfriend Drawings and Prints, New York July 15, 2002

Montgomery Museum of Fine Arts, Gift of the Weil Print Endowment in memory of Mr. and Mrs. Adolph Weil, Sr.
2002.9

22 *The Martyrdom of John the Baptist*, 1510

Woodcut
Laid paper
Meder 231 a; Hollstein 231; Bartsch 125
Watermark: None
Sheet: 7 5/8 x 5 in. (193 x 131mm)
Signed, recto: Monogram AD (lower left); 1510 (upper right)
Marks, verso: BL (in graphite): "K.2117"; BC (in graphite): 31 (with 9 beneath); BR (in graphite): "400"

Provenance: Adolph Weil, Jr., Montgomery, Alabama

Montgomery Museum of Fine Arts, Gift of Jean K. Weil in memory of Adolph "Bucks" Weil, Jr.
1999.7.31

23 *David Penitent*, 1510

Woodcut with drawn additions
Laid paper
Meder 108 unknown; Hollstein 108; Bartsch 119
Watermark: Coat of Arms with Crown, Meder 46 (center)
Sheet: 7 11/16 x 5 in. (194 x 131 mm), borders added, paper augmented middle left
Signed, recto: Monogram AD 1510 (upper left)
Marks, verso: BL (in graphite): "AW"

Provenance: Adolph Weil, Jr., Montgomery, Alabama

Montgomery Museum of Fine Arts, Gift of Jean K. Weil in memory of Adolph "Bucks" Weil, Jr.
1999.7.28

24 *Death of the Virgin*, 1510
From the *Life of the Virgin* (without text)

Woodcut
Laid paper
Meder 205; Hollstein 205; Bartsch 98
Watermark: High Crown, Meder 20
Sheet: 11 7/16 x 8 3/16 in. (290 x 207 mm)
Signed, recto: Monogram AD (bottom center right); 1510 (bottom center left)
Marks, verso: BL (in graphite): "B90 (/)"; (in graphite): "7322A" (or 4); BR (in graphite): "ss" (with dash above)

Provenance: C. J. Goodfriend Drawings and Prints, New York, July 24, 2001

Montgomery Museum of Fine Arts, Gift of the Weil Print Endowment in memory of Mr. and Mrs. Adolph Weil, Sr.
2001.4

catalogue of the exhibition

25 *Assumption and Coronation of the Virgin*, 1510
From the *Life of the Virgin* (without text)

Woodcut
Laid paper
Meder 206 a; Hollstein 206; Bartsch 94
Watermark: High Crown, Meder 20
Sheet: 12 13/16 x 9 1/2 in. (326 x 241 mm)
Signed, recto: Monogram AD, 1510 (bottom center left)
Marks, verso: BL (stamped in brown ink): "GOTTFRIED EISSLER" (in a box; Lugt 805b); BC (in graphite): "DTIKAKMK"; BL (in graphite): "15628"; BC (in graphite): "C.13705 (8?)"; BC (in graphite): "B94 I"

Provenance: Dr. Gottfried Eissler, Vienna (Lugt 805b); David Tunick, Inc. Prints and Drawings, New York, July 13, 2001

Montgomery Museum of Fine Arts, Gift of the Weil Print Endowment in memory of Mr. and Mrs. Adolph Weil, Sr.
2001.5

26 *Christ, Man of Sorrows, Mocked by a Soldier*, 1511
Title Page from the edition of the *Large Passion* after 1511

Woodcut
Heavy laid paper
Meder 113; Hollstein 113; Bartsch 4
Watermark: Flower with Triangle, Meder 127
Sheet: 13 1/4 x 8 1/8 in. (338 x 206 mm), trimmed within the block mark
Marks, verso: BL (in graphite): "AW"; BL (in graphite): "1721"; CR (in graphite): "27"

Provenance: Karl und Faber Auction, Bern (?), sale November 13, 1975, auction 144, lot 157; Adolph Weil, Jr., Montgomery, Alabama

Montgomery Museum of Fine Arts, Gift of Mr. and Mrs. Adolph Weil, Jr., in memory of Mr. and Mrs. Adolph Weil, Sr.
1981.20.1

27 *St. Jerome in His Cell*, 1511

Woodcut
Laid paper
Meder 228 a; Hollstein 228; Bartsch 114
Watermark: None
Sheet: 9 1/4 x 6 1/4 in. (234 x 157 mm), trimmed to block mark
Signed, recto: Monogram AD 1511 (bottom right)
Marks, verso: C (in graphite): "M228"; (in graphite): "L.?"; (in graphite): "a19998" above "GL"; BL (in graphite): "AW"

Provenance: Adolph Weil, Jr., Montgomery, Alabama

Montgomery Museum of Fine Arts, Gift of Jean K. Weil in memory of Adolph "Bucks" Weil, Jr.
1999.7.30

28 *Knight, Death and the Devil*, 1513

Engraving
Laid paper
Meder 74; Hollstein 74; Bartsch 98
Watermark: None
Sheet: 9 7/8 x 7 9/16 in. (228 x 178 mm)
Signed, recto: Monogram AD 1513 (lower left)
Provenance: Kennedy Galleries, June 12, 1970; Adolph Weil, Jr., Montgomery, Alabama

Hood Museum of Art, Dartmouth College, Hanover, New Hampshire; Gift of Jean K. Weil in memory of Adolph Weil, Jr., Class of 1935
PR.997.5.53

29 *Melencolia I*, 1514

Engraving
Laid paper
Meder 75 second state; Hollstein 75; Bartsch 74
Watermark: None
Sheet: 9 3/8 x 7 6/16 in (240 x 188 mm)
Signed, recto: Monogram AD 1514 (lower right)

Provenance: J.F. Gigoux (Lugt 1164); Lessing J. Rosenwald

National Gallery of Art, Washington, Rosenwald Collection, 1943
1943.3.3523

30 *St. Jerome in His Study*, 1514

Engraving
Laid paper
Meder 59; Hollstein 59; Bartsch 60
Watermark: None
Sheet: 9 7/8 x 7 1/4 in (250 x 192 mm)
Signed, recto: Monogram AD (bottom right)
Marks, verso: UC (in brown ink): "P. Mariette, 1668" (Lugt 1788); BC (in graphite): "100"; BR (in graphite): H (?) enry D (?) avis, Jr.; BL (in graphite) "Mariette Coll" above "a70209", (stamped in black ink) "R" over "S" "H" in a triangle (Lugt 2243), (stamped in grey ink): "V." W." in a circle (Lugt 2539b).

Provenance: Pierre Mariette, Paris (Lugt 1788); R.S. Holford, London (Lugt 2243); Valentin Weisbach, Berlin (Lugt 2539b); Adolph Weil, Jr., Montgomery, Alabama

Collection of Mrs. Adolph Weil, Jr., Montgomery, Alabama

catalogue of the exhibition

31 St. Paul, 1514

Engraving
Laid paper
Meder 47 second state, a; Hollstein 47; Bartsch 50
Watermark: None
Sheet: 4 3/4 x 3 1/16 in. (119 x 77 mm)
Signed, recto: Monogram AD 1514 (bottom right)
Marks, verso: UC (in brown ink): "P. Mariette, 1661" (Lugt 1788); C (in brown ink): "WY" (?); BC (in graphite): "B 50"; "C 10633"; BR (in graphite): "6"

Provenance: Pierre Mariette, Paris (Lugt 1788); Adolph Weil, Jr., Montgomery, Alabama

Montgomery Museum of Fine Arts, Gift of Jean K. Weil in memory of Adolph "Bucks" Weil, Jr.
1999.7.12

32 Agony in the Garden, 1515

Etching
Laid paper
Meder 19 first state, b-c; Hollstein 19; Bartsch 19
Watermark: Large City Gate (Meder 263)
Sheet: 9 x 6 1/4 in. (228 x 159 mm), trimmed to plate mark
Signed, recto: Monogram AD 1515 (bottom center)
Marks, verso: BL (in graphite): "12351.1"; UR (in graphite): "4" (in a circle)

Provenance: Adolph Weil, Jr., Montgomery, Alabama

Montgomery Museum of Fine Arts, Gift of Jean K. Weil in memory of Adolph "Bucks" Weil, Jr.
1999.7.8

33 St. Anthony Reading, 1519

Engraving
Laid paper
Meder 51 b; Hollstein 51; Bartsch 58
Watermark: None
Sheet: 4 1/16 x 5 13/16 in. (102 x 147 mm)
Signed, recto: Monogram AD 1519 (bottom center)
Marks, verso: UL (in graphite): "90"; BL (in graphite): "C.11343" (with line through); BC (in graphite): "B.58"; BC (in brown ink): "G. Storck a Milano 1798. In #5222" (Giuseppe Storck, Milan; Lugt 2318); BR (in graphite): "192"(in a circle); "C.36670 (Colnaghi)"; BR (in graphite): "H6"

Provenance: Giuseppe Storck, Milan (Lugt 2318); Adolph Weil, Jr., Montgomery, Alabama

Montgomery Museum of Fine Arts, Gift of Jean K. Weil in memory of Adolph "Bucks" Weil, Jr.
1999.7.14

34 The Peasant and His Wife at Market, 1519

Engraving
Laid paper
Meder 89 b; Hollstein 89; Bartsch 89
Watermark: None
Sheet: 4 9/16 x 2 7/8 in. (116 x 73 mm)
Signed, recto: Monogram AD (bottom center); 1519 (top center)
Marks, verso: CL (in red ink): " M-J" (in an oval; not in Lugt); BC (in graphite): (illegible marks) "13 M"

Provenance: Adolph Weil, Jr., Montgomery, Alabama

Montgomery Museum of Fine Arts, Gift of Jean K. Weil in memory of Adolph "Bucks" Weil, Jr.
1999.7.25

35 St. Christopher, Facing Right, 1521

Engraving
Laid paper
Meder 52 b; Hollstein 52; Bartsch 52
Watermark: None
Sheet: 4 9/16 x 2 7/8 in. (116 x 73 mm), trimmed within the plate mark
Signed, recto: Monogram AD 1521 (lower left)
Marks, verso: BL (in graphite): "12351" above "DZ"); BC (in graphite): "W DZZ" (beneath); BR (in graphite): "M52 a-b"

Provenance: Adolph Weil, Jr., Montgomery, Alabama

Montgomery Museum of Fine Arts, Gift of Jean K. Weil in memory of Adolph "Bucks" Weil, Jr.
1999.7.15

36 The Last Supper, 1523

Woodcut
Laid paper
Meder 184; Hollstein 184; Bartsch 53
Sheet: 9 1/16 x 12 7/16 in. (229 x 316 mm)
Watermark: Bull's Head with caducus (Meder 67)
Signed, recto: Monogram AD (lower right)

Provenance: Vincent Mayer; W.G. Russell Allen

National Gallery of Art, Washington, Gift of W.G. Russell Allen, 1941
1941.1.25

catalogue of the exhibition

37 St. Bartholomew, 1523

Engraving
Laid paper
Meder 45 b; Hollstein 45; Bartsch, 47
Watermark: None
Sheet: 4 13/16 x 3 in. (122 x 177 mm), trimmed within the plate mark
Signed, recto: Monogram AD 1523 (center left)
Marks, verso: BL (in graphite): "12174613"; BC (in graphite): "S.43778"; "B 47"; BR (in graphite): "MSXX"

Provenance: Adolph Weil, Jr., Montgomery, Alabama

Montgomery Museum of Fine Arts, Gift of Jean K. Weil in memory of Adolph "Bucks" Weil, Jr.
1999.7.11

38 St. Simon, 1523

Engraving
Laid paper
Meder 49 b; Hollstein 49; Bartsch 49
Watermark: None
Sheet: 4 5/8 x 2 7/8 in. (118 x 73 mm) trimmed along the plate mark
Signed, recto: Monogram AD 1523 (bottom right)
Marks, verso: UR (in graphite): "35"; BL (in graphite): "a 61406" above "E 1530" (crossed out); BC (in graphite): "B49" above "a 36507"; BL (in graphite): "5340 Co," above "7308"; BR (in graphite): "H 1"; (stamped in blue ink): "Collection d'Arenberg" (Lugt 567)

Provenance: Ducs d'Arenberg, Brussels (Lugt 567); Adolph Weil, Jr., Montgomery, Alabama

Montgomery Museum of Fine Arts, Gift of Jean K. Weil in memory of Adolph "Bucks" Weil, Jr.
1999.7.13

39 Erasmus of Rotterdam, 1526

Engraving
Meder 105; Hollstein 105; Bartsch 107
Watermark: Fleur de Lis, two, in Crowned Shield with pendant b (Br. 8288)
Sheet: 10 3/8 x 8 in. (264 x 203 mm)
Marks, recto: Monogram AD MDXXVI (center left)
"Imago Erasmi roteroda Mi ab Alberto Durero ad vivam effigiem deliniata"
Marks, verso: BC (in graphite): B 479; BL (in graphite): B.107; BL (in graphite) illegible inscription; CL (in graphite) 107/7.114; CL (in graphite) 125:15; UC (in graphite) illegible inscription

Provenance: Albert Roullier, 1915

The Saint Louis Art Museum, Purchase
125:1915

40 Philip Melanchthon, 1526

Engraving
Laid paper
Meder 104 c; Hollstein 104; Bartsch 105
Watermark: Small Jug, Meder 158 (center left)
Sheet: 6 13/16 x 5 in. (173 x 127 mm)
Signed, recto: Monogram AD 1526 (bottom center)
Marks, recto: BR, in brown ink, P. Mariette 1662 (Pierre Mariette, Paris; Lugt 1788)
Marks, verso: UC (in brown ink): "P. Mariette, 1662" (Lugt 1788); C (in brown ink): "fB1602" (Paul Beham, Nuremburg (?); Lugt 365); BC (in graphite): "eef"; BC (in graphite): "C.6785"; BC (in graphite): "7"

Provenance: Pierre Mariette, Paris (Lugt 1788); Paul Beham, Nuremberg (Lugt 365); Adolph Weil, Jr., Montgomery, Alabama

Montgomery Museum of Fine Arts, Gift of Jean K. Weil in memory of Adolph "Bucks" Weil, Jr.
1999.7.27

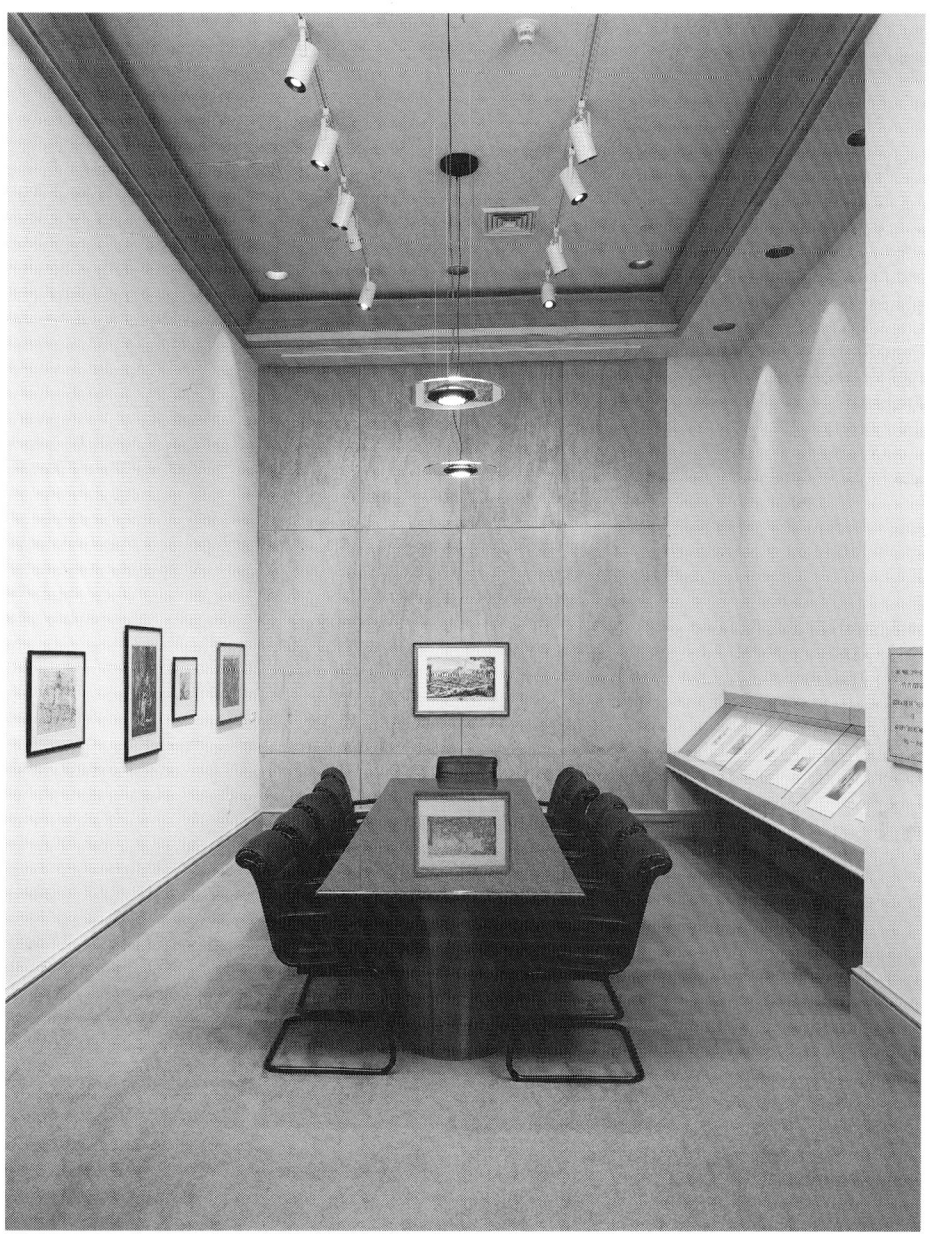

**The Weil Graphic Arts Study Center at the Montgomery Museum of Fine Arts
Dedicated May 20, 1998 in Memory of Adolph "Bucks" Weil, Jr.**

selected Bibliography

With Abbreviations for Frequently Cited Sources

Alberti
Alberti, Leon Battista. *On Painting*. 1436. Intro. and trans. John R. Spencer. 2nd ed. New Haven and London: Yale University Press, 1966.

Anzelewsky
Anzelewsky, Fedja. *Albrecht Dürer, das malerische Werk*. Berlin: Verlag für Kunstwissenschaft, 1971.

Bartsch
Spike, John T., ed. *The Illustrated Bartsch*. Vol. 7. New York: Abaris Books, 1993.

Boston
Boston, Museum of Fine Arts. *Dürer: Master Printmaker*. Boston, 1971.

Cambridge
Cambridge, MA, Harvard University Art Museums. *Dürer's Passions*. Text by Jordan Kantor. Cambridge, 2000.

The Golden Legend
The Golden Legend of Jacobus de Voragine. Trans. Granger Ryan and Helmut Ripperger. 2 vols. London: Longmans, Green and Co., 1941.

Hind
Hind, Arthur M. *Early Italian Engravings: A Critical Catalogue with Complete Reproductions of All the Prints Described*. 7 vols. Washington, DC: National Gallery of Art, 1938-48.

Hollstein
Hollstein's German Engravings, Etchings, and Woodcuts, 1400-1700. 59 vols. to date. Blaricarum: A.L. Van Gendt B.V., 1954-present.

Hutchison
Hutchison, Jane Campbell. *Albrecht Dürer: A Biography*. Princeton, NJ: Princeton University Press, 1990.

Landau and Parshall
Landau, David and Peter Parshall. *The Renaissance Print, 1470-1550*. New Haven and London: Yale University Press, 1994.

Lehrs
Lehrs, Max. *Geschichte und Kritischer Katalog des Deutschen, Niederlandischen und Französischen Kupferstichs im XV. Jahrhundert*. Vol. 5. Vienna: Gesellschaft für Vervielfältigende Kunst, 1925.

London
London, British Museum. *German Renaissance Prints, 1490-1550*. Text by Giulia Bartrum. London, 1995.

Lugt
Lugt, Frits. *Marques de Collections (Dessins-Estampes)*. San Francisco: Alan Wofsy Fine Arts, 1975; supplement, 1988.

Meder
Meder, Joseph. *Dürer-Katalog*. Vienna: Verlag Gilhofer & Ranschburg, 1932.

Panofsky
Panofsky, Erwin. *The Life and Art of Albrecht Dürer*. Princeton, NJ: Princeton University Press, 1955; reprint, 1971.

Paris
Paris, Musée du Petit Palais. *Albrecht Dürer, Oeuvre gravé*. Text by Sophie Renouard de Bussierre. Paris, 1996.

Rupprich
Rupprich, Hans, ed. *Dürer: Schriftlicher Nachlass*. 3 vols. Berlin: Deutscher Verein für Kunstwissenschaft, 1956, 1966, 1969.

selected bibliography

Russell
Russell, H. Diane. *Eva/Ave: Women in Renaissance and Baroque Prints*. Washington, D.C.: National Gallery of Art and The Feminist Press at The City University of New York, 1990.

Schoch et al.
Schoch, Rainer, Matthias Mende, and Anna Scherbaum. *Albrecht Dürer: Das druckgraphische Werk*. Vol. 1. Munich: Prestel Verlag, 2001.

Schuster
Schuster, Peter-Klaus. *Melencolia I: Dürers Denkbild*. 2 vols. Berlin: Gebr. Mann Verlag, 1991.

Stewart
Stewart, Alison G. *Unequal Lovers: A Study of Unequal Couples in Northern Art*. New York: Abaris Books, 1977.

Strauss 1974
Strauss, Walter L. *The Complete Drawings of Albrecht Dürer*. 4 vols. New York: Abaris Books, 1974.

Strauss 1975
Strauss, Walter L. *Intaglio Prints of Albrecht Dürer: Engravings, Etchings and Drypoints*. New York: Kennedy Galleries, 1975.

Strauss 1979
Strauss, Walter L. *Albrecht Dürer: Woodcuts and Woodblocks*. New York: Abaris Books, 1979.

Streider
Streider, Peter. *Albrecht Dürer: Paintings, Prints and Drawings*. Trans. Nancy M. Gordon and Walter L. Strauss. New York: Abaris Books, 1982.

White
White, Christopher. *Durer, The Artist and His Drawings*. New York: Watson Guptill Publications, 1971.

Vasari
Vasari, Giorgio. *The Lives of the Most Excellent Painters, Sculptors, and Architects*. 1568. Trans. Gaston Du C. de Vere. 6 vols. London: Philip Warner, Publisher, 1912.

Washington 1967
Washington, DC, National Gallery of Art. *Fifteenth Century Engravings of Northern Europe*. Text by Alan Shestack. Washington, 1967.

Washington 1971
Washington, DC, National Gallery of Art *Dürer in America: His Graphic Work*. Ed. Charles W. Talbot. Washington, 1971.

Winkler
Winkler, Friedrich. *Die Zeichnungen Albrecht Dürers*. 4 vols. Berlin: Dutscher Verein für Kunstwissenshaft, 1936-1939.

Wölfflin
Wölfflin, Heinrich. *The Art of Albrecht Dürer*. Trans. Alastair and Heide Grieve. New York: Phaidon Publishers, Inc., 1971.

Glossary

Block A specially prepared wooden slab from which the image is carved for a woodcut.

Burin A tool used for engraving; its sharp tip is diamond-shaped, allowing the engraver to control the width of the line by varying the pressure on the instrument. The burin generally produces a sharp, clean-edged line.

Burnishing A method of removing marks from a metal plate; the printmaker uses a smooth tool to rub out unwanted lines.

Collector's Mark A stamp or inscription left on a print by an owner to identify it as a work from his collection; generally found on the back of the printed sheet or on the front margin.

Engraving An intaglio method in which the printmaker cuts lines into a copper plate with a burin.

Etching An intaglio technique; the etcher coats the plate with a ground and draws on the ground with a needle to reveal the metal beneath and immerses the plate in acid, which bits into the exposed metal lines.

Ground The waxy or resinous substance with which an etcher coats a plate to protect it in an acid bath.

Impression Each time a plate or block is printed, the resulting image is an impression; impressions of the same print can vary.

Intaglio A printmaking technique in which lines are cut into a plate; when the plate is inked, the ink sinks into the channels and print as black lines.

Laid paper A handmade paper cast from a mold with vertical wire marks and horizontal "chains."

Plate A flat piece of metal used for techniques such as engraving or etching.

Plate mark The impression made by the beveled edge of the plate as the paper and plate pass through the printing press. The plate mark is generally seen as an embossed line which surrounds the composition.

Relief Printmaking techniques in which areas that should print as white voids are scooped out, leaving raised lines to print as black.

State Used to note both major and minor changes made to a plate; different states of the same print feature adjustments like the addition of an inscription or the burnishing away of part of the composition.

Suite Prints related in theme or image and sometimes in technique. A suite of prints, such as Dürer's *Life of the Virgin,* is sometimes published in a portfolio with a title page.

Watermark Hallmarks identifying the manufacturer of paper stock which are visible when light is transmitted through paper. Marks are created by wires attached in a pattern to the mold in which paper is formed. Such marks are helpful in documenting the date and origin of a particular impression of a print.

Woodcut Relief technique using a wood block; the cutter removes much of the block with knives, gouges and chisels so that the resulting image prints as a white sheet with black lines.

Wove paper A hand made paper made from a mold in which the wires are so tightly woven that no wire lines are visible in transmitted light.

photographic credits

Unless otherwise noted, photography is courtesy of Robert Fouts, Fouts Commercial Photography

Figure 1: © Scala, provided by Art Resource, New York.

Figure 2: © 2002 Board of Trustees, National Gallery of Art, Washington

Figure 3: © 2002 Board of Trustees, National Gallery of Art, Washington

Figure 4: © 2002 Board of Trustees, National Gallery of Art, Washington

Figure 5: © 2002 Board of Trustees, National Gallery of Art, Washington

Figure 6: Photography by Robert Fouts, Fouts Commercial Photography, Montgomery, Alabama

Figure 7: © 2002 Board of Trustees, National Gallery of Art, Washington

Figure 8: Courtesy of the Saint Louis Art Museum

Figure 9: © 2002 Board of Trustees, National Gallery of Art, Washington

Figure 10: Photography by J. G. Berizzi, © Réunion des Musées Nationaux/Art Resource, New York.

Figure 11: © 2002 Museum of Fine Arts, Boston, all rights reserved

Figure 12: Photography by Robert Fouts, Fouts Commercial Photography, Montgomery, Alabama

Figure 13: © 2002 Board of Trustees, National Gallery of Art, Washington

Figure 14: © Foto Marburg/Art Resource, NY, Windsor Castle, Windsor, Great Britain

Figure 15: © 2002 Board of Trustees, National Gallery of Art, Washington

Figure 16: The Metropolitan Museum of Art, New York, all rights reserved

Figure 17: © 2002 Board of Trustees, National Gallery of Art, Washington

Figure 18: © 2002 Board of Trustees, National Gallery of Art, Washington

Figure 19: © 2002 Board of Trustees, National Gallery of Art, Washington

Figure 20: © 2002 Board of Trustees, National Gallery of Art, Washington

Figure 21: © 2002 Board of Trustees, National Gallery of Art, Washington

Figure 22 © 2002 Board of Trustees, National Gallery of Art, Washington

Figure 23: © 2002 Board of Trustees, National Gallery of Art, Washington

Figure 24: © 2002 Board of Trustees, National Gallery of Art, Washington

Figure 25: © 2002 Board of Trustees, National Gallery of Art, Washington

Figure 26: © 2002 Board of Trustees, National Gallery of Art, Washington

Figure 27: © 2002 Board of Trustees, National Gallery of Art, Washington

Figure 28: The Metropolitan Museum of Art, New York, all rights reserved

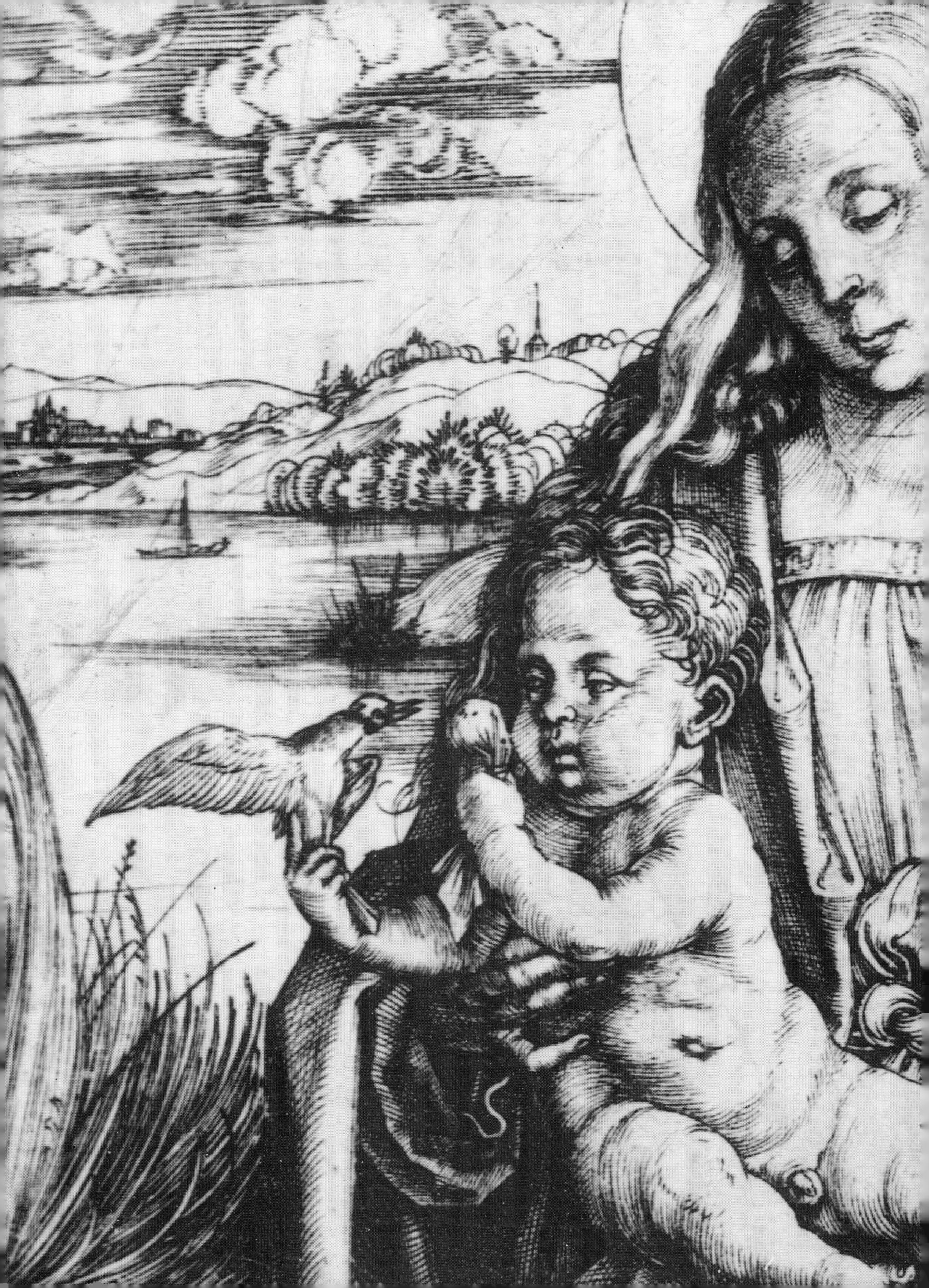